Flaming Dene

Flaming Dene

A Victorian stunner, actress and nude model

by

Eilat Negev and Yehuda Koren

Psychology News Press

First published in Great Britain in 2019
Psychology News Press
9a Artillery Passage
London E1 7LJ
dcpsychologynews@gmail.com

Typeset by Keyboard Services, Luton, Beds.

Printed by Spauda in Lithuania.

ISBN 978-0-90-763364-8

Contents

Our deepest thanks to Dr. Daniel Robbins, Professor Leonée Ormond, Philippa Martin, Katherine Tozer, Angela Bolger, Colin Craven, Jeremy Robson, and Dr. David Cohen.

Prologue

Today top models like Cara Delavigne are rich and glitzy – celebrities who get more than Warhol's 15 minutes of fame. Contrast the fate of those who grace the front covers with that of the models who pose for an artist. The artist's model today is not paid thousands per session, nor splashed all over the press. Fashions in fame, and in fashion, change.

The Industrial Revolution of the 19th century was not just industrial; it was also a media revolution. The so-called penny dreadfuls were packed with juicy tales of railway accidents, randy vicars, husbands who poisoned their wives and shipwrecks. More people than ever before could read, and they had more leisure than before. This more literate population wanted information, entertainment and, best of all, titillation.

In Britain W.H. Smith became a national business with kiosks selling books and magazines on every railway station. Smith did so well he became a Cabinet minister.

Dorothy Dene became the most famous model in the 1880s and 1890s. She was being painted by Frederic Leighton, one of the most famous painters of the day and the President of the Royal Academy. The Academy still lords it over Piccadilly facing the oldest bookshop in London, Hatchards, and Fortnum and Masons, one of London's grandest shops which has a warrant to supply the Queen with caviar. Leighton used to order food for his famous parties there.

Today's Vogue-ish models would be happy if two of the great writers of the day discussed them. Dorothy Dene had that accolade as George Bernard Shaw and Oscar Wilde both knew her. Shaw reviewed her, and she played a leading role in Wilde's *A Woman of No Importance.*

Dorothy would never have become famous if she had not knocked on the door of Frederic Leighton. To make sense of her story, and their story, one also must examine the Victorian theatre. The stage was a risqué profession; actresses were seen as no better than prostitutes who could learn their lines; yet some catapulted not just into fame but made it into society. Vesta Tilley, the wonderful male impersonator who sang Piccadilly Johnny and married a Tory MP, was one of those. She never set foot on the stage again after she married. Dorothy Dene was not so lucky because Sir Frederic Leighton clearly had what we would now call intimacy and sexual issues. Nicknamed "a modern Adonis," he kept many secrets.

Freud was interested in the motivations of artists. He was inspired by Michaelangelo's sculpture of Moses in Rome, read Vasari and suggested that Leonardo da Vinci's homosexuality was linked to the artist's childhood memory of a vulture. Leighton would have been an intriguing subject for Freud. Freud's grandson, Lucien, is seen as one of the great artists of the late 20th century. He did not sublimate much, it seems, as he had many lovers. You could argue one of his secret motivations was not to be a proof of grandpa's theory. Art is perplexing. If Freud had ever analysed Leighton, he might well have told him that he sublimated his sexual drive which allowed him to paint like a dervish and produce hundreds of canvasses.

When I did history at school we were taught the Victorians were so prudish they even covered piano legs. Dorothy Dene was one of a number of Victorian women who did not conform to convention because they did not marry or have a family. Did she, like Leighton, fear intimacy?

There is also an interesting comparison to be made between Dorothy and the pioneer nurse, Florence Nightingale. They were both frank about the body – in Nightingale's case mainly that of soldiers, in Dorothy's her own. Psychologists tend to underestimate the role of chance in determining our lives. Dorothy was ambitious and driven by the need to support herself and her family. That led her to Leighton who cocooned her enough for her to enjoy the demands he made.

It took a hundred years from their deaths for Dorothy Dene to be crowned his "great muse" by the guardians of his legacy, the Leighton House Museum.

To begin their story, it is best to begin with Leighton's most famous painting of her.

David Cohen, Psychology News Press

Chapter One

The discovery

24 Battersea Rise, London, 1962.

One late spring afternoon, unlikely clients walked into the Ingo Fincke Gallery and Framers. The men were covered in dust and struggling with a bulky, large square painting in an imposing golden frame. Mr Fincke quickly made room for it, leaned forward and then stepped back, scrutinizing the image.

With lazy grace and voluptuous curves, the sleeping beauty was coiling on a white marble bench by the sea. The contours of her naked

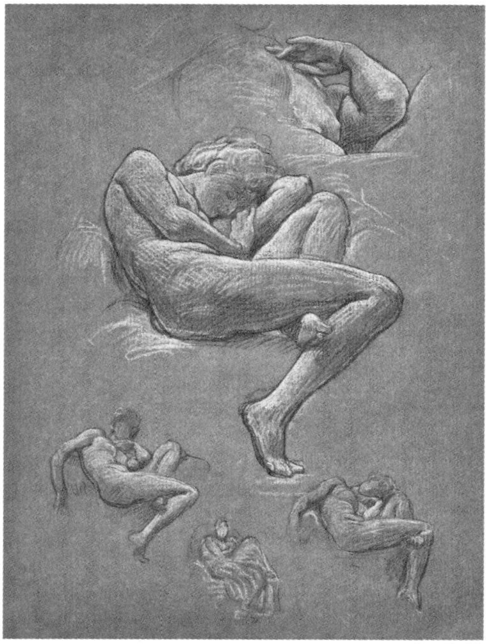

Study for Flaming June, c.1894

body projected through the transparent wrap of pale blood orange. Her glorious auburn hair was flowing free, her limbs loose, her arms bare and the right toes touched the floor while her left knee was raised as a cushion for her head. A nipple peeped out. The sideways posture, on a rough platform, with bent knees, elbows and neck, seemed awkward for a woman in repose, and certainly agonizing for the model. Still, it did not look like the sleep of the weary, but of the pampered, enjoying the stone as if propped up with cushions. Her off-guard posture was inviting and provocative.

When first shown it caused a sensation: "The breath of the sleeping girl comes hot from her gently parted lips ... Her cheeks are flushed with the impulse of youthful love. Her bosom is pulsating: her arms and her feet are bathed in gracious sensibility," gushed writer Edgcumbe Staley. "Involuntarily you hold your step lest a creak on the floor should disturb the slumbering girl." She induced a soothing tranquillity, but voyeurs – and the double entendre is apt – were even more intrigued by her mysterious dreams.

However, Mr Fincke was not thrilled by the exposed young woman, and he especially disliked her disproportionately heavy thigh which dominated the canvas. He asked the strangers how they got hold of the painting. The builders said that they were renovating a large house nearby and found it while ripping out a wooden panel which covered a chimney piece. The sheer size of the painting, 175 cm by 177 cm, made the story implausible. How could this enormous and heavy object be concealed in a wall? Was it stashed-away during WW2 to protect it from German bombs? But if so, how could the owners forget its existence afterwards? Or, for some reason, did they find the image disturbing, and hid it? But why bother to build a partition to hide it when you could shove it into the attic, or better still, sell it? Or was the story of the chance discovery simply a sham, to cover up a theft?

Fincke kept his doubts to himself. It was clearly a Victorian painting, and the label on the back read "Flaming June, by Lord Leighton." At that time, Victorian art was at its lowest ebb, and Christie's managed to get only £21 for Leighton's *The Bracelet.* The model for both paintings was the same young woman, draped in a fine primrose tissue, open at the side to show her massive thigh and shapely leg. The frame was similar, also designed by Lord Leighton, and the columns within the picture echoed the tabernacle frame's Ionic pilasters. Mr Fincke trusted that the splendid, ornately carved frame would at least ensure his profit. Little did he know that it was a bargain even at the price he paid – a mere few dozen pounds.

For a few months, the work was displayed in the window, nearly blocking it, but no one was interested, so Mr Fincke moved it to the back of his shop. Bernard Nevill, a young lecturer at the St Martin's School of Art, and a bargain-hunter of Victorian artefacts, was struck by the painting, but, as he had that same day received a very nasty letter from his bank manager, the asking price of £60 was way above his means. In his frustration, Mr Fincke decided to separate the artwork, and asked £65 for the frame and £50 for the painting. It was an insulting price for Lord Leighton, the ninth president of the Royal Academy. Mr Fincke was offering the masterpiece for a pittance.

Some weeks later, 14-year-old Andrew Lloyd Webber chanced upon the painting in Fincke's shop. He was a budding collector and his hobby was financed by his grandmother, who had just shelled out £50 for beautifully-illustrated three huge volumes of Dugdale's *History of Ancient Abbies and Monasteries.* The boy described in detail the painting he had fallen in love with, but his grandmother was adamant: "I will not have Victorian junk in my flat."

At last a buyer was found in Mr Demaine, a hair stylist from Mayfair who also traded in antiques. Soon, he got rid of the reclining beauty, selling it to one of his clients, a retired colonel Frederick Beddington. A game of "pass the parcel" began: when it was delivered to his Kensington home, Beddington found it too large and offered it to his daughter, who politely declined. He showed the frameless painting to Jeremy Maas, who had left Bonham's to open his own art gallery. By then, within a few months, the price tag had soared to a staggering £1000. "I thought that if I bought it, I would never be able to sell it, but it was too marvellous to turn down," recalled Maas. Hoping to revive the market for Victorian art, he had it cleaned, framed and did some research, but his worst fears were confirmed; no client was in sight.

Seven decades earlier, however, the future of *Flaming June* looked promising. "Probably the most wonderful painting in existence," the collector Samuel Courtauld waxed lyrically, while Edgcumbe Staley praised the features of the life-like beauty, as so "British in type." Leighton gave credit to his model: "the design was not a deliberate one, but was suggested by the chance attitude of a weary model that had a peculiarly supple figure." After a long session for another painting, the young woman seemed hazy and clearly needed a break. Too exhausted to go to her corner at the edge of the studio, and comfortable enough in the company of the distinguished artist, she slumped into the armchair and dozed off. Leighton was suddenly struck by the unconscious pose, and quickly sketched it on brown paper in white chalk. When she woke up, he showed her his sketch, and during the next three years they developed the sleeping pose in many variations. When the painting was complete, he spent a fortune on the exceptional frame. *Flaming June* was such a catching title, that it became an entity of its own ever since.

In the summer of 1895, thousands flocked around her at the Royal Academy summer exhibition. A "picture impossible to pass over," wrote the *Country Gentleman.* Grasping its commercial potential, William Luson Thomas bought the painting for his *Graphic* magazine, and to boost sales, added a meticulously-produced colour poster to its Christmas edition. The sum he paid Leighton – £1154 – was money well-spent, since he sold his one-shilling print to over half a million homes in Britain and the USA.

After Luson Thomas died the work was sold to Mrs Blanche Watney of the famous London brewing family. At her death in 1915, it was passed on to her son Vernon. He loaned it to the Ashmolean Museum in Oxford, and when he died in 1928, the work returned to his family. No museum found *Flaming June* worth the expense, and it was sold to a private collector and disappeared for three decades.

History did not bring in cash and Jeremy Maas was getting impatient. After all these failures, he approached every curator in every major museum and art gallery in England, some of which already owned works by Leighton. To no avail. On June 10th Mass found a sign of good omen in the *Evening Standard*'s weather report: "Flaming June, which has given us temperatures well up in the late 70's over the last 10 days, looks like living up to its name for some time to come."

A few days later, Don Luis Ferré, a Puerto-Rican politician and cement magnate and the founder of the Museo de Arte de Ponce, and his curator the art historian Rene Taylor, walked into his gallery. Both men travelled through Europe and hunted works of old masters of the Flemish, Dutch and Italian Baroque. In London, Ferré looked for beautiful women in romantic scenes. *Flaming June* was just perfect. The tycoon was besotted by the work but still, he judged £2000 to be too pricey. Failing to haggle Maas down, Ferré shook hands on the deal and spent a sleepless night until the money was wired from Puerto Rico. "Everyone thought I was crazy," recalled Ferré, "the scholars and critics all called it kitsch." He could not anticipate that it would become the jewel of his collection. *Flaming June* found its home in the small sleepy town of Ponce, 120 kilometres south of the capital, and became known as the Mona Lisa of the Southern Hemisphere.

In less than a year, in an almost-inexistent market, the value of the painting soared 40 times over. But that was only the beginning. Soon Victorian art came back in vogue, and in the 1980s prices began to rocket. Auctioneers flew over to Puerto Rico every year, futilely entertaining Mr Ferré, who was by then the island's Governor, to lavish dinners. There were other suitors, and one of them presented a blank cheque, but Ferré tore it up. Lord Lloyd Webber ("I write music to buy art"), is said to have sent dozens of emotional letters to Ferré. He even flew over to the island, played the piano and sang songs, but Ferré was not swayed.

In 1996, after three decades of absence, *Flaming June* returned to London as the centrepiece of Leighton's centenary exhibition at the Royal Academy. By then, Ferré had it stripped from its frame, and Arnold Wiggins & Sons made an exact replica from Leighton's original mould that they still had. Huge blown up images were hung on the façade of the Royal Academy, making the Leighton exhibition a blockbuster. At the end of 2003, when Ferré died a year short of a century, it was hoped that his young widow and his many sons and daughters would agree to sell the painting. But by now it had become the island's national treasure. It rarely left Puerto Rico, though it came for fleeting visits in 2009 to the Tate in London, the Prado in Madrid, and in Hague, Stuttgart and Vienna. In 2015 *Flaming June* visited the Frick Collection in New York, and a year later arrived at Leighton House, London, where she was created.

This 19th century masterpiece is currently valued at about £14 million. The attempt to get as close as possible to the real thing had an impact on the art market. In June 2001, Sotheby's offered for sale a tiny oil sketch – a square of 10 by 10 centimetres – of Leighton's study for *Flaming June*. In 1916, it was sold to Lord Leverhulme of Sunlight Soap for a mere £26, and now the hammer went down on £104,700. The new owner of the small colour sketch became John Schaeffer, an Australian tycoon who made his fortune (and lost it) in cleaning and security services. So another *Flaming June* left Britain. The iconic work continues to cast its spell, and in July 2015, a small pencil and white chalk study of the model's head took the art world by surprise when it was sold to an American collector for an unprecedented £167,000, four times its estimate.

The Victorians adored *Flaming June*, but had to console themselves with paper engravings hung on walls or placed on the mantelpiece; their great-great-grandchildren do the same with a hand-painted reproduction on canvas at £215, a true-size wall tapestry at £110, a wrist watch at £30, IPhone cover at £25, a necklace at £20, a pillow-case at £18, wall-clock at £15, a thousand-piece puzzle at £12, a mug at £12, a mouse-pad at £8, hand painted window cling at £7, a fridge magnet at £3, and the Tate Gallery Shop used to sell scented soap and candles, pins and a disposable camera, all stamped with the image. If you are brave you can order a tattoo of *Flaming June* to be etched on your back.

The orange beauty became an inspirational icon for artists (Gustav Klimt's *Danaë*) and photographers; the 2013 Christmas *Vogu*e cover was Annie Leibovitz's photo of actress Jessica Chastain morphing herself into Flaming June's pose and colours. It was the album cover of Malcolm McLaren's *Waltz Darling,* and the Royal Philharmonic Orchestra's *The Gift of Music*. It is one of the most popular Valentine Day greeting cards. In the annual list of the top 10 best-selling artistic reproductions, (headed by a Van Gogh), Frederic Leighton is the only British representative thanks to *Flaming June*.

The painting's immense popularity would have surprised even Leighton himself. He worked harder and longer on other pictures which were more significant to him, but eventually, this became his most famous painting. The image gained a life of its own and is better known today than its maker. Leighton was often criticised because his art ignored the social upheavals of his time: "reform bills, strikes, socialism and the Salvation Army...but then it has the virtue of helping us, for a while at least, to forget these things," as *The Sewanee Review* wrote in 1899. What appealed to the Victorians appeals 120 years later. No less than her erotic allure, *Flaming June* reflects a form of escapism, a yearning for peace and tranquillity, the ultimate poster for life away from it all.

The girl who posed for it never managed to get away from it all. Dorothy Dene always felt she had too much to achieve.

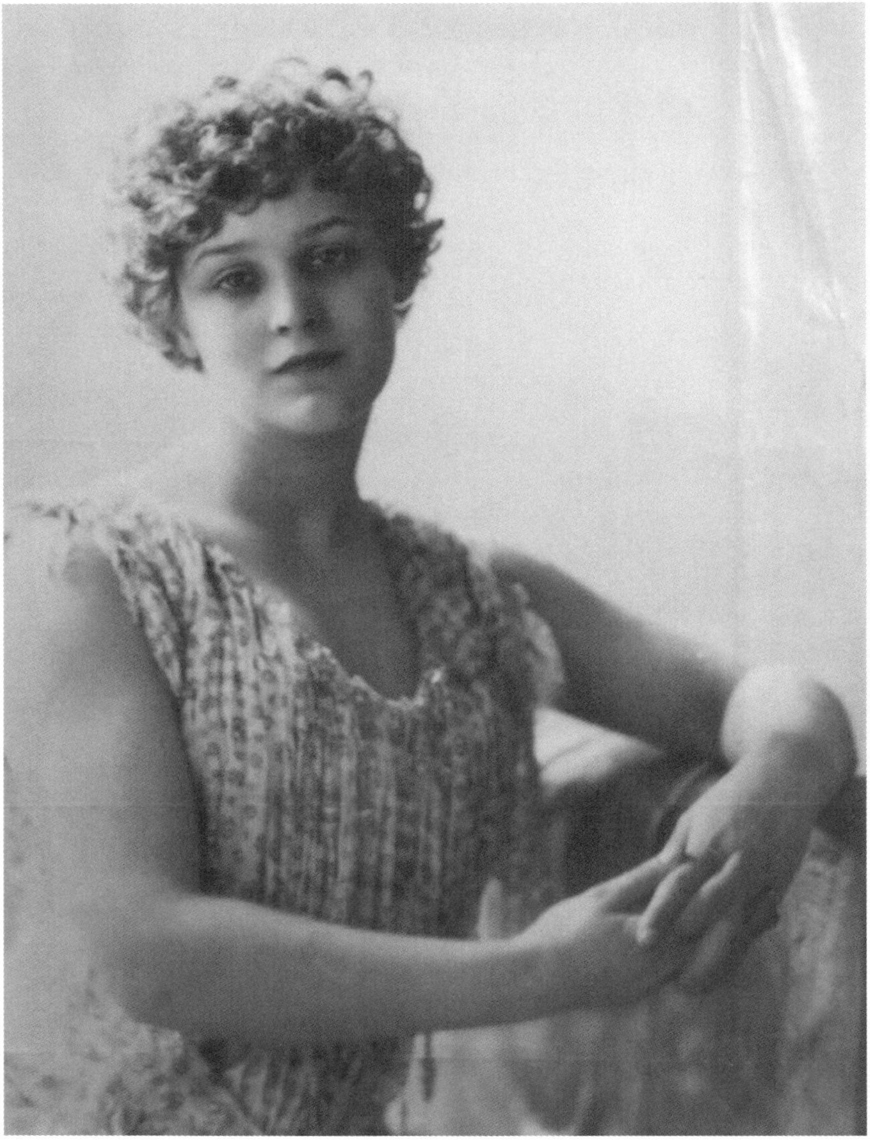

Dorothy in summer dress
Photo by Hernry Van der Weyde

Chapter Two

On becoming Eliza Doolittle

Dorothy Dene was the stage name of Ada Alice Pullan.

She is usually portrayed as a poor Cockney girl from London's East End. Luckily for her, she was picked up and groomed by the President of the Royal Academy, who turned her into a Fair Lady, a dramatic actress, a prolific model, and a celebrity who was crowned "the most beautiful woman in England." However, Ada never was "a squashed cabbage leaf," "so deliciously low – so horribly dirty," as George Bernard Shaw described Eliza Doolittle. Eliza also had an accent that would doom her for her "curbstone English: the English that will keep her in the gutter to the end of her days." Ada Alice Pullan did not fit the Eliza Doolittle cliché, though.

Better models for Eliza Doolittle would be the illiterate Clare, whom F. G. Stephens, painter and art critic, taught reading, writing and proper manners, before secretly marrying her. Or fifteen-year-old motherless Annie Miller, "dirty and covered with vermin," who worked as a barmaid. She modelled for William Holman Hunt, who promised to marry her once she had some education and etiquette. He paid for her tuition but discarded her when she had an affair.

Then there was the fishmonger's daughter Sally Higgs, whose mother sold flowers at Victoria station. "But fairer than any flower found in her basket, with a wild beauty all her own, was the sweet, bare-footed child who trotted by her side and made herself useful by hawking penny bunches of violets," remembered painter Edwin A. Ward. Sally was spotted by Frank Miles who was struck by the underage beauty, made her his model and took her to live with him in the Chelsea house he shared with Oscar Wilde. Dressed in a Japanese kimono, Sally "presided over the tea-serving business, there being no lady of the house to act as hostess." She married a young Etonian, a banker's son, despite his family's objections.

Shaw could find an even better candidate for Eliza among his intimates: Jane Burden was the daughter of a stableman and a laundress, and would have become a domestic servant had not her beauty caught the attention of Rossetti and Burne-Jones. William Morris, Shaw's friend, fell in love with Jane, but before marrying her, he had her privately educated, to fit in with his worldly friends. She became an avid reader, an accomplished pianist and fluent in French and Italian. And she changed the way she talked as Shaw would have deemed necessary and adopted a refined accent.

Ada was not a low gutter girl. Her mother, Sarah Eagle, was born in the village of Hurworth-on-Tees, Durham in 1833, the second daughter of a millwright-carpenter. In her teens, her father took his family of seven and moved to London. He rented an expensive house in New Cross, Deptford, and just minutes' walk from the poet Robert Browning's family home.

In 1850, the 16 year-old Abraham Pullan, son of a wool merchant, left Bradford to seek better prospects in London. The Eagle brothers, engineers at the New Cross foundry, introduced him to their sister Sarah, who was by then, a house maid in affluent Park Lane. Abraham and Sarah were married in August 1856, and he moved in with her family. Ada Alice, their second child, was born on April 11th, 1859.

Ambitious, bright and driven, Abraham Pullan soon became chief engineer at Gardiner and Mackintosh. He specialized in steam locomotive engines and was constantly working on how to improve them. By the time he was 25, he already had his first patent registered, and several more followed.

With a child born every two years, life with the Eagles became too crowded. Abraham's good wages allowed him to rent a spacious house at 306, New Cross Road, close to his parents-in-law. Most of the neighbours were skilled workers, upwardly-mobile like himself.

In interviews, Ada described herself as a very ambitious, delicate child, "the product of a serious family." Hers was not the destiny of a flower-girl: her father, she said, was "a well-known civil engineer" and her mother an "intensely intellectual woman – possessed of great beauty and grace of person – and devoted to the fine arts." Education was the Pullans' priority, and financially secure, the children completed school and were not forced out into the labour market.

When she was six, Ada chanced to hear a drawing room recital and was enthralled. At school she learned music and drawing, English, grammar and composition, and was captivated by Shakespeare, even learning Macbeth by heart. She would get up at night to practice scenes in front of the mirror, and "spouted it to the moon through the nursery window." These lunar performances were her formative experiences. She visited theatres several times and her idol was Kate Vaughn, with her "exquisite dancing and deft manipulation of her skirts." But Vaughn's vaudeville and burlesque performance was far from the genre that the solemn Ada would eventually embrace.

As much as the Victorians loved the theatre, hailed its stars, collected their photographs, copied their dress and savoured their flings in the gossip columns, they did not wish to see their sons, and especially not their daughters, on the stage. The theatre was said to be the home of women of loose morals, and the profession itself seemed dangerous, rife to every vice. Veteran actresses warned against seeming gentlemen who used to ambush stage doors, take off their hats and bow low to novice actresses, tempting them with flattery, and soliciting "young girls who were perfectly innocent." The physical and mental strains on an actress, particularly in demanding roles, seemed to endanger her mental stability and cause depression and breakdown; one admitted that she had worn herself out, body and soul after twenty years on stage.

Many plays and novels of the time dealt with the theatre, portraying exhausted and diseased actresses. Except for the stars, most actresses were poorly paid; they could not afford proper accommodation, especially on long tours around the country. They had to live for weeks from a crate packed with their personal belongings that they had to shift, at their own expense, from one town to the next. They had to buy their own costumes and pay for their lodgings and food. The job was insecure and there were long periods of unemployment, which made them vulnerable.

Newspapers relished juicy accounts of actresses who were arrested for being "drunk and behaving in disorderly manner" and were also robbed, raped or murdered. These were usually the only mentions these actresses got and they were never in the arts page, only in the crime columns. A typical example was one who had a child out of wedlock and attempted suicide when deserted by her lover. An actress was "a frivolous and almost irresponsible being, without conscience, principle or self-respect, and incapable of understanding the serious duties and responsibilities of life," blasted *The Diary of an Actress.* The book vowed to be "a plain record of real life," but since the introduction was written by a pastor, it preached a very conventional morality. Indeed, it was written to put off girls, and especially their parents, from considering the profession. Ada knew her parents "held theatres in abhorrence" so she kept her ambitions to herself. She was, however, undeterred – "the opposition served only to incite her to the accomplishment of her wish."

Actresses rarely managed to marry. When the teenage Ellen Terry met George Frederic Watts, the elderly painter was determined to remove her "from the temptations and abominations of the Stage, give her an education and if she continues to have the affection she now has for me, marry her." She complied, but her affection for him was apparently non-existent; within a year of a disastrous marriage, they separated, and she went back to the perils of acting – and became a legend of the theatre.

Marriage was a contradiction; they were already married – married to the stage, in the words of Gordon Craig, Ellen Terry's son. "I don't see how you can rock the cradle, rule the world, *and* play Ophelia perfectly, all in the day's work," he wrote in his mother's biography. Those who did marry faced pressure from their husbands, jealous of the stage and especially of the fact that their wives expressed passion for another man in front of an audience. They usually demanded that she abandon her career, which she often did. The divorce courts and the penny dreadfuls rollicked with the details of the infidelities of actresses. The stage was an arena for sin. And sin sold papers.

Many girls' desire to become an actress caused domestic crisis when the parents failed to block their daughter's stage-craze and it "threw gloom and sadness" over the household. Parents often feared that men might not like to marry their daughters if one of them, or even an aunt, became an actress. The Pullans – who had six daughters – were not prepared to pay the price. Disobedience or running away from home was not in Ada's character. Dutiful and prudent, she waited for a crack to open.

The crack appeared sooner than anyone had expected.

In May 1876, the firm of Gardiner and Mackintosh was dissolved; Abraham Pullan lost his job. In this crisis he trusted his ingenuity; he was already working with his son Thomas, a mechanical draughtsman, on improvements to locomotives and other engines, and they registered their first joint patent.

In February 1877, the Pullans' tenth child, Samuel, was born. The delivery went terribly wrong, the pressure damaged Sarah's spine and she was left paralyzed. 18-year-old Ada became the mother of the family, running the household of twelve, and raising her siblings, three of them younger than six. Then in November, they were all heart-broken when eight-year-old Dorothy got the measles and died after three painful weeks.

The next blow shattered the family; Abraham Pullan was declared bankrupt in September 1878 and left home. He fled his creditors, the threat of prison, the burden of an invalid wife and a house crammed with children. His desolate family did not see him again, although he was moving from one rented room to the other in the vicinity. He was still developing patents but hardly eked out a living. Sarah Pullan and her children were forced to give up their home. They managed to stay in the neighbourhood, but from a large, comfortable house, the ten of them had to squeeze into a flat in 23, Station Road, Deptford.

With no father and an invalid mother the children could easily have lapsed into destitution, child-labour, and every misery and danger of the city. The two eldest children, however, were very capable and took control. 20-year-old Thomas became the head of the family, with Ada at his side. Any personal aspirations had to be postponed until the younger siblings were all on their feet. The shock and anxiety pulled the family closer, and created a bond, especially among the sisters, a bond which would stay with them all their lives. It was a household run by children, and their first decision was to ensure the well-being and education of the young ones – eleven-year-old Henrietta-Sarah

(Hetty), seven-year-old Kathleen-Blanche, four year-old Isabel-Helena, nicknamed Lena, and baby Samuel, just a year old. Thomas and 17-year-old Henry worked as assistant engineers, and 15-year-old Arthur as an apprentice. Despite the long hours that the three boys put in, their wages were simply not enough.

Ada had to do her share of breadwinning and thirteen-year-old Edith replaced her at home. Ada's options were not exciting: a shop assistant, an apprentice dressmaker, a milliner, a florist, a telegraph clerk, and least appealing of all, a domestic servant.

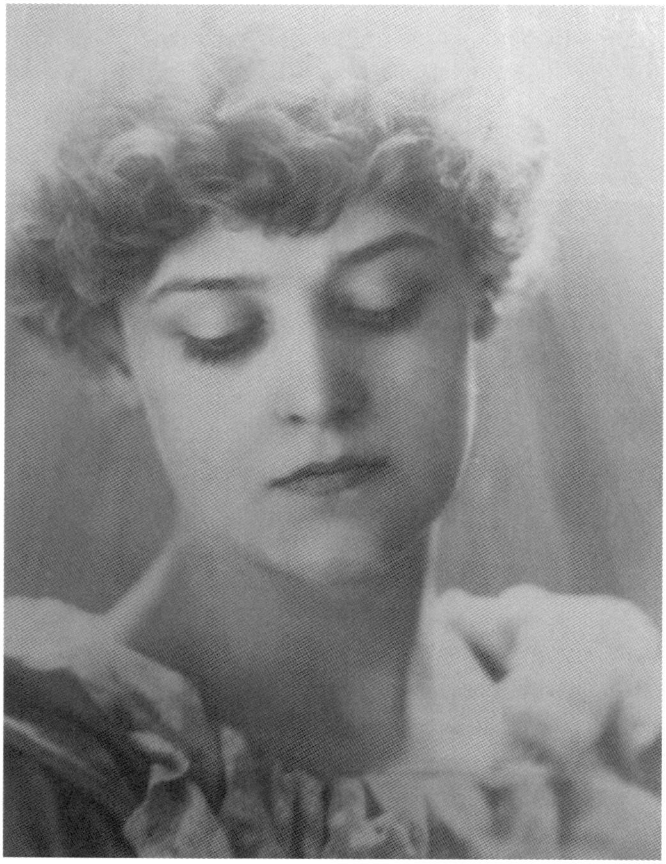

Dorothy Dene
Photo by Van der Weyde

Chapter Three

The new Galatea

All five Pullan sisters were exquisite and the spitting image of one another: wavy fair hair, classical features, clear, glowing skin, a dimpled chin and a graceful neck. In a later group photo, it's easy to get confused despite the large age gap: is Ada, the eldest, the one on top, or is it Lena, the youngest? And which one of them is Hetty, Edith or Kathleen? They were all smartly-dressed – their aunt was a dressmaker – but Ada was the most beautiful of them all.

Starvation and despair brought many girls to modelling, wrote journalist Joseph Howard: "Happy is she with the flashing eye and the pretty head. Fortunate is she with the outlines of beauty to whom comes the suggestion: 'why not offer yourself as a model? You are sure of respectful treatment, of cash on delivery, of the wherewithal not only to keep the wolf from the door, but to have a door from which to keep the wolf'."

A girl began her working life earning 5 shillings a week for 80 hours' hard labour, which only after years would be raised to 20 shillings. In comparison, an artist's model's day earned her 7 shillings for only a third of the hours, plus her travel fare and two meals at the artist's expense. That seemed a much easier and pleasant way of earning a living, just sitting perfectly still and doing nothing, in a well-heated studio, usually in an opulent house in one of London's better neighbourhoods. At the end of the week you had 30 shillings – all for being admired for your well-shaped hands or the expression in your eyes, a tiny curve of your chin, or some subtle charm in the carriage of your head. On top of that, "between employer and employed, between capital and labour, there is no such equality of relation as subsides between artist and model," wrote the widely-read daily *Standard*.

Working fewer hours would also enable Ada to keep an eye on her mother and young siblings, and in the summer, she would have plenty of free time when the artists usually went on holiday.

Being an artist's model, however, was risqué. If actresses had a bad reputation, models were even worse, and associated with depravity. The widespread impression, wrote the contemporary artist Harry Furniss, was that anyone could be a model, "that is, anyone who has lost her self-respect." Alone with a man, behind closed doors, sitting, standing, or even lying on a bed, subject to his probing gaze. On occasions, veiled only in flimsy transparent drapes or even without anything on. People believed that artists made sexual advances, exploiting the model's physical vulnerability and financial dependency. The nature of the experience and the easy earnings led some models to squander the "shame money."

There were models born to the profession, "their mothers and grandmothers before them knew no other life than that of the studio, and the children learn to pose as soon as they can toddle," reported the *Manchester Courier*. Many were working class girls and immigrants "tired of the ill-paid drudgery of the unskilled occupations." Some took to modelling after a family crisis. Mary Lloyd, who would be Ada's rival, was brought up in luxury in Shropshire. When her father went bankrupt, however, her best hope was to move to London and earn her living by modelling. The three Pettigrew sisters lost their father, who left them destitute. Their mother took them from Portsmouth to London. The girls soon became coveted artist's models and earned the family's living, in the same studios where Ada would work.

***

Ada did not decide to try modelling lightly. She had the striking face and figure, but was demure and thoughtful, and no bubbly extrovert. She would not have dreamt of offering herself as a model if her father had not left the family. The failure of Abraham Pullan was her opportunity. From the studio she knew she could catapult herself on to the stage. Dreading poverty, her brother Thomas had to agree, but they must have kept it a secret from their now bedridden mother.

There were no modelling agencies, and girls didn't advertise themselves in newspapers, since it was expensive, frowned upon by family and neighbours and could attract the wrong kind of attention. For their part, artists rarely advertised a vacancy. They saved money by using their wives, mistresses, daughters, sisters, their housemaids and fellow female artists as models. If they wanted a new face or figure, they preferred to pick a girl up in a street, in a shop or in the pub, or to rely on their colleagues' recommendations.

Competition was tough. It was estimated that 500 models were working in London – and artists would have many girls knocking on their doors daily. Ada was cautious and choosy. She only called on the most respectable addresses: no less than twenty painters and sculptors were living on just two streets in Holland Park, in a dense artists' quarter dubbed "Paradise Row." Some were Royal Academicians, others exhibited in prominent galleries. Sensibly, Ada skipped, for now, the most eminent, like Leighton or Watts. She also made it clear that she would sit only for the head. And just in case some male artist wanted more, she first sat for a woman painter. The 33-year-old American-born Miss Louisa Starr grew up in England, was admitted to the Royal Academy School when only 16, and became the first female student ever to win the gold medal. Portraits were her forte; she kept an atelier in the newly-built studio complex close to the palatial mansion of Sir Frederic Leighton, the artistic sovereign of Holland Park.

You could not pass through Holland Park and escape the radar eyes of Emily Isabel Barrington. She was an amateur painter, and had always dreamt of establishing an artistic salon. Male painters rather liked her company as she was vivacious and admiring, but the women couldn't stand the sight of her. She was the local busybody, and Miss Violet Paget (the writer Vernon Lee) stamped her as "a rumpled, scrumpled little brown paper woman of uncertain artistic pretensions, a sort of King Charles' dog of the neighbouring studios." For Mary Watts, the painter's young wife, she was "a poisonous snake."

Louisa Starr's studio was one of six red-brick houses arranged around an oblong courtyard, with a wide arched entrance from Holland Park Road. The ground floor was the living quarters, while the spacious studios sprawled on the first floor, to get the most of daylight. One wintery day in 1879, at the onset of her modelling career, Ada was standing on the porch of Miss Starr's studio. Emily Barrington spotted her: "A young girl, with a lovely white face, dressed in deepest black," she noted to herself. Bewitched by the "vision of beauty," she just knew that this girl would be perfect for Leighton. She rushed to tell him. Leighton, ever eager to procure good, experienced models, asked for the girl's details. His letters to new sitters were informal and friendly, but precise: "I should be pleased to see you tomorrow morning at nine o'clock sharp," he wrote on his headed notepaper. An invitation to sit for the President of the Royal Academy was not just a sign that Ada was a good enough model, but an honour and a promise of better pay. Meeting Leighton would change her life. More remarkably, meeting Ada would change his.

***

Artists often carped models were lazy and unpunctual. Leighton was known to be especially fussy about his schedule. It was a long and tiring travel from Deptford, nearly two hours by train, tram, carriage and a good deal of walking, so Ada got up very early. The butler showed the 19-year-old girl into the entrance hall and went off to inform his master. Any visitor to 2, Holland Park Road would be overwhelmed by its sumptuousness, and Ada could not have found herself in more different surroundings to the stuffy, drab flat she had just left. Leighton's architect-built house was a revival of an Italian-Renaissance palace, made to impress. It was a theatrical display of expensive and elitist taste, "a good advertisement, as the English public especially believed that wealth meant success," commented his friend the poet Robert Browning.

Artists wanted their models to be silent, not to peep at the canvas and offer suggestions or criticize the way they were portrayed. Modelling being tedious and difficult, Leighton preferred a sympathetic model, intelligent enough to understand the required pose, because "when the model is sulky or a dolt, stiff, stupid, and idle, the process will not bear description. I have often expected madness or murder to ensue during its performance," affirmed his friend F. G. Stephens in an essay about Leighton. For their part, models grumbled that artists were rude, inconsiderate and miserly, but Leighton was known to be kind and generous. Gaetano Valvona, who began modelling for him at about the same time, recalled that on his first day of work, the butler took him to the kitchen, sat him at the table and put out coffee and milk, eggs, bacon, cold ham, tongue, butter and several kinds of cheese: "I thought, giving me a dinner at eight o'clock in the morning, but still anyone can put up with this sort of fun," he wrote in his unpublished memoirs.

The man that Ada was waiting for was said to be a "modern Adonis". He was "the paragon of manners in the highest society of the mind," extremely clever and an ideal man. He loved to dress in silk and velvet, and the painter Julius M. Price wrote, "I don't think it would have been possible to find a handsomer specimen of manhood ... for he was of fine presence, above the average height, about 5 feet 11 inches I should say, and built in proportion – but it was his head chiefly that arrested attention ... and his long hair and pointed beard, which were just turning grey, gave him a most striking appearance. He had the eye of a dreamer and student." Leighton dreaded getting old and already at 40 he informed his sister that he was doing physical exercises every day – "I should like to try getting ten or twelve years younger." To a friend he confided that "I pray God I may die before I am seventy."

Leighton worshipped beauty, and especially beauty of form. His art "exists to create beautiful images. Often beauty is their sole motive," wrote William Cosmo Monkhouse, the poet and art critic. When Henriette Corkran showed Leighton one of her paintings, he remarked: "but why choose such an ugly subject as a grimy street boy? Art ought to be beautiful." For him, the classical ideal was an antidote to an age of rapidly changing values. His ideal models, male and female, were those whose features resembled the classical sculptures, masterpieces of perfect human beauty.

Young Italian women ruled the modelling scene in London with their build and proportions, their natural grace and dignity and "for their hands and feet which were considered much more refined than those of English models." Leighton found them on his Italian holidays and in the flow of immigrants to London. John Millais rebuked him for reverting to old-fashioned classical art: "what can be more beautiful than an English girl, an English child or landscape? Nothing like painting one's surroundings and time."

Leighton could follow his fancy though. His paintings were selling well, his investments in the stock market were successful and he had always been supported by his wealthy father. He was free to paint with no financial pressure, and he must have disliked the critique that his "fancy pictures" were mere pot-boilers. He was taken as a typical example of a first-rate artist who, once he had a fine reputation, received many commissions and could immediately sell every canvas he produced, began to hurry over his work. In the recent Royal Academy exhibition of May 1878, two of his works infuriated the critics: *Winding the Skein* (two Greek girls on the roof of a house, winding a basket of wool) and *Nausicaa* (a pensive Italian girl leaning against a wall). Tom Taylor, the famous art critic of *The Graphic,* complained that "I'm quite at a loss to understand by what steps a painter so endowed and so earnest in his work as Mr Leighton has come to substitute wax for flesh and blood ... this waxiness is a serious drawback from the beauty, as substituting a poorer and weaker for a nobler thing, and as suggesting effeminacy in the painter." Leighton was always proud of his meticulous study of the human body but now he was mocked. The anatomy of his figures was "full of bad drawings": the feet of the young woman "are so distorted they are scarcely human ... the face and head are those of a lady; the arms are those of a stout country girl." He must have been glad to set off for Italy for his annual, long Mediterranean vacation.

When he got to Rome, he received a telegram. Sir Francis Grant, the President of the Royal Academy, had died. Anxiously, Leighton hurried back to London – the Royal Academy presidency was his life-long ambition, and he was not going to miss the opportunity. The Prince of Wales supported his candidacy. So did many artists but not because they thought he was the best painter in Britain; they judged that his sincere devotion to art and his ability to fulfil the public duties of the Presidency made him a good choice. It also helped that no scandal muddied his name.

On November 13th, 1878 Leighton was elected president and knighted. Now that he achieved such eminence, "he at last felt free fully to express through his canvases a depth of emotion he had previously denied himself," argues the art historian Stephen Jones. Ada arrived at a turning point in his life. Her timing was perfect.

***

Ada waited in the dimly-lit entrance hall, painted *café au lait.* The hall opened into a larger hall with beams painted brilliant blue with silver incisions, and a wall of dazzling blue and white ancient tiles brought especially from Turkey and Syria. A fountain gurgled softly in the Arab Hall, to her left. A stuffed peacock with outstretched wings of brilliant hues stood guard by the stone staircase which led to the studio on the first floor. The stairs were "about as wide as the flights in the Palaces of the Cæsars – of which the carpetless white is pleasant, as well as artistically effective," enthused the design-guru of the day, Mary Eliza Haweis. The walls were studded with paintings; a portrait of the master of the house done by his friend Watts was prominent. Leighton sat informally with his head resting on his hand, sporting a full beard, wearing a brown velvet suit with his white shirt open – a picture of a confident man in his prime.

The studio showed off the owner's taste and artistic standing, spacious enough to entertain a large party of guests. A plaster cast of the Parthenon frieze, with a row of young men, women and horses, dominated the room. The walls were painted dull Egyptian red; broad, rich rugs covered the floor. Easels with paintings in various stages of progress and small clay models with drapery arranged on them dotted the room. Tables were crowded with books and sketches, portfolios with studies of nude and scantily clad figures. Tall wide windows faced the black entrance door; the model's platform was in the centre to get the best soft natural light, and a cosy fire burnt nearby, to keep the model warm.

"His manners were courteous and easy, and his voice well-modulated and suave," remembered painter Henrietta Ward. "Indeed, his entire personality was charming, particularly, perhaps, to ladies." The 48-year-old bachelor scrutinized Ada when she stepped into the studio. Her colour was exceptional, "a clouded pallor, with a hint somewhere of a lovely shell-like pink," remembered Mrs Barrington. "But such a mere hint, it was difficult to localize it in the very even smooth texture of the surface. It seemed under the skin, as colour lies under the smooth surface of the inside of a shell."

Ada offered Leighton the perfect type of Greek beauty, which would draw poetry from the pens of journalists; "her form and features would not be out of place in a gallery of antique sculpture." Her head was crowned "with a glory of curls that seemed to have somehow caught a stray glint of God's glorious sunshine in their soft meshes." She had an oval face, and her eyes, wide apart "were brilliant and light blue of the Scandinavian rather than of the English face." Her pupils were set in a haven of blue, and gazing into them you became mesmerised, bewitched, "entrapped in their depth." Ada had a strange fairy-like look, and her nose was of a Grecian perfection "preserved even rarely in our statues." The soft down upon her cheeks, "the veins like faint threads that gave to her skin its tints of transparency, the coral of her curved lips, the colour that came in her cheeks to add to this harmony of nature's painting". Actress Mary Anderson remembered that Ada had lovely, white teeth, and her wondrous throat, round, full, long and exquisite was the crowning glory which "appealed so strongly to the imagination of Leighton that it haunted him for years." She looked much younger than her age, a miracle of teenage beauty.

Till then, Leighton had found his ideal beauty only in models with Italian or Greek roots. Suddenly, there she was, his sought-after woman, a girl with Yorkshire ancestry. Like himself.

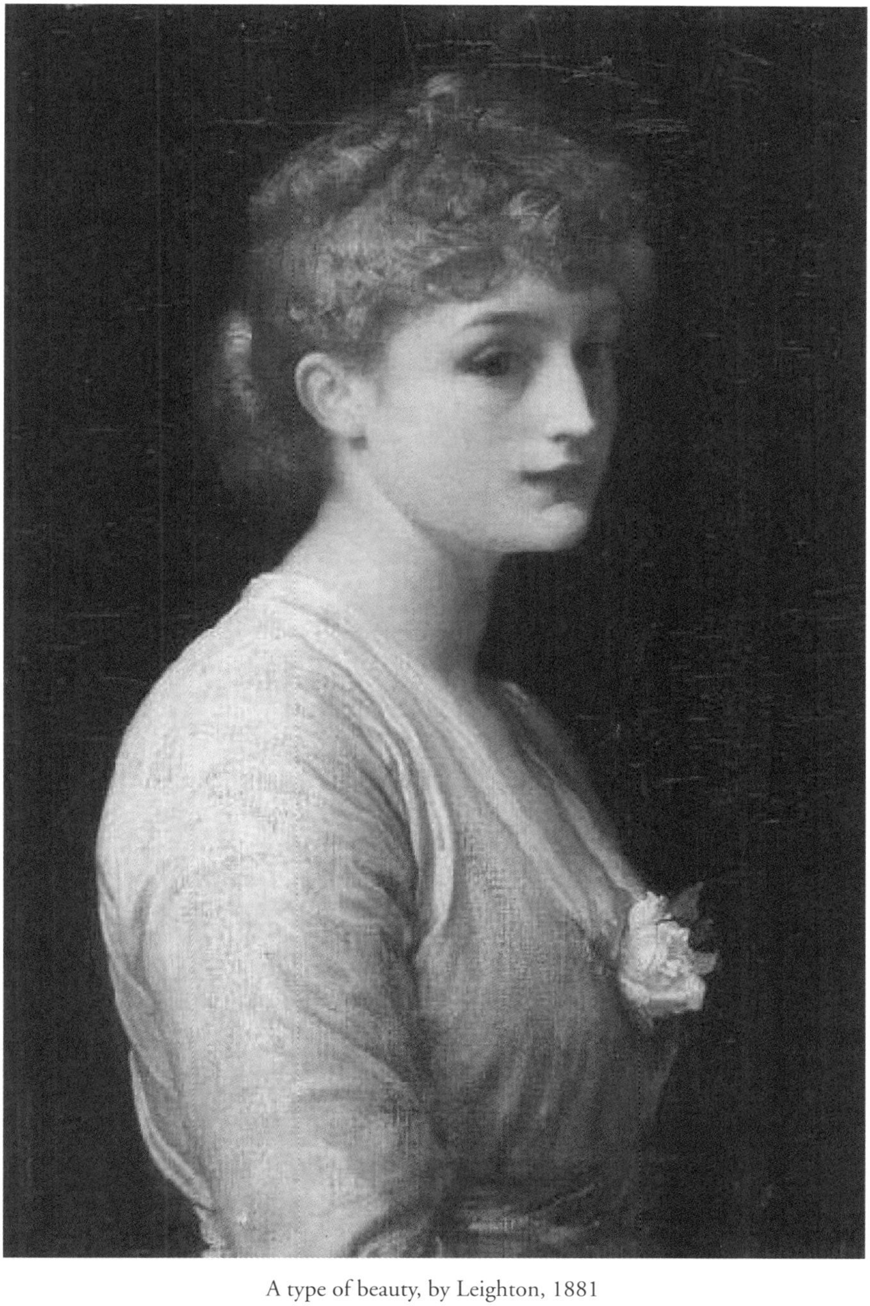

A type of beauty, by Leighton, 1881

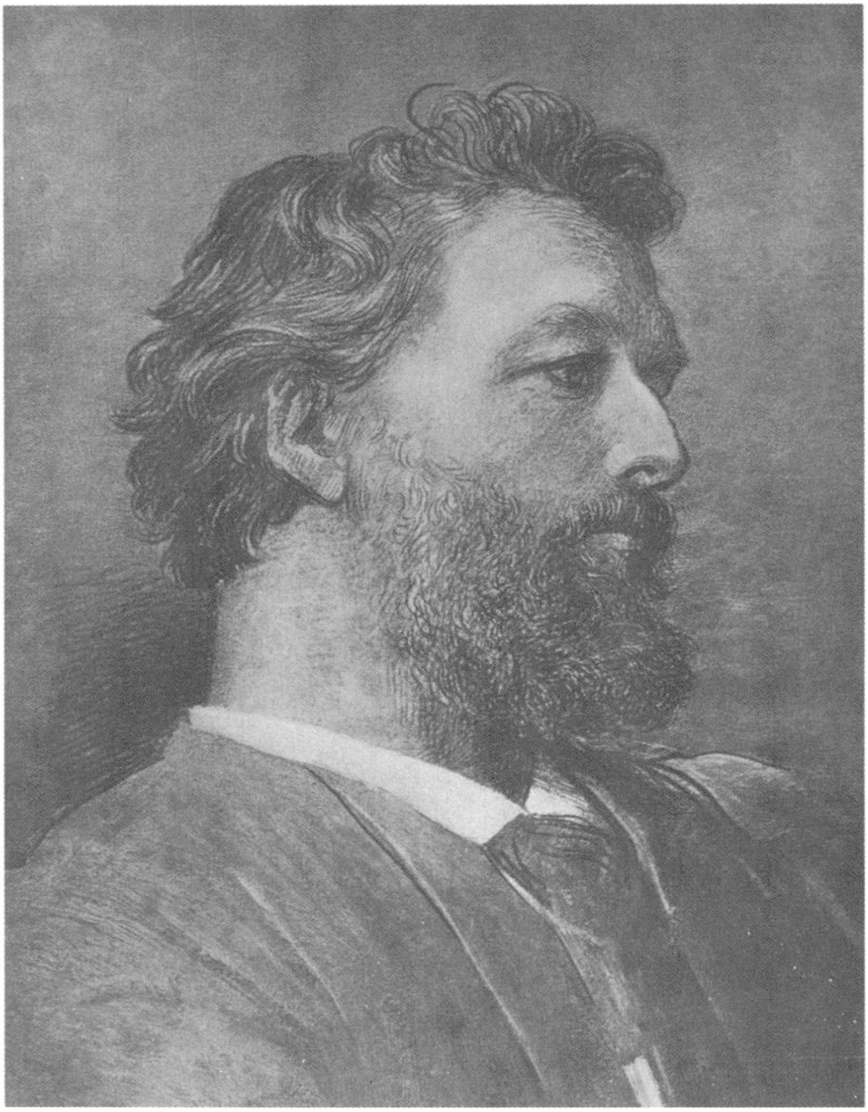

Frederic Leighton, 1881, engraving after a portrait by G.F. Watts

Chapter Four

A Nymph is Born

Leighton could afford to be selective in his choice of models. They should look poised and anything but decadent or cheap. Fallen women were ruled out, since they could not be his adored ideal beauty. Worse, using such women might lead to seduction and scandal, which was the last thing he wanted. Ada seemed naïve enough for him to trust her.

He made some quick sketches and Ada tried a few poses as they talked. He was authoritative, but informal, amiable and seemed dependable. He clearly enjoyed the *tête-à-tête* and did not give the impression that he was conducting an interview. A Prince Charming with an engaging smile, he instantly put her at ease, and listened to her.

He was interested in past experience, personal background, and was sensitive to hardship. But what was for him most interesting was the fact that she had four sisters, all of them younger versions of herself. The most appealing were seven-year-old Kathleen, and five-year-old Lena. He preferred the youngest, whose rare refined charm was captivating. Lena was cute and friendly, unlike the restless Kathleen; eventually, she would be the only Pullan sister he never painted.

Lena was a godsend, in fact. Connie Gilchrist, Leighton's long-term child-model, had just left him to become a skipping-rope dancer on stage. In a way, her departure suited him as well: he had painted her since she was six, but now, at the age of 14, at puberty, she was no longer useful. "She is losing her beauty," Charles Dodgson wrote in his diary after photographing Connie. Dodgson was Lewis Carroll of *Alice in Wonderland.* Losing her beauty apparently referred to the loss of her childhood innocence. Connie Gilchrist would have a short stage career, quickly marrying into the aristocracy. Years later, the story goes, she surprised Leighton and burst into his studio, uninvited. "Don't you know me? I used to sit for you for the figure," she said after an awkward silence. "Oh! Is that all? – then strip," Leighton snapped, without moving a muscle.

Little Lena was almost a carbon-copy of Connie: slim, fair-skinned, with long, silky blond hair tied up in a bun, and a fringe over her forehead. She would be his new child muse. All of Leighton' friends knew that he adored children, and it was typical that when he saw a baby in a pram, he "instantly dropt on one knee and kissed the baby's hand," recalled the painter George Dunlop Leslie. Leighton's files contained sheets upon sheets of paper covered with drawings of children, many done as the child model was playing in his studio. The children would climb up on to his knees, stroke his beard and daub his face with colours from his palette. "He entered hugely into all their plays, dolls, balls, horses, hide-and-seek, pick-a-back, and games and romps, none came amiss. Wherever he was and whatever he was doing children seemed drawn irresistibly to him," remembered his biographer, Edgecumbe Staley. "He loved little things, little children, kittens," wrote Mrs Barrington. "Everything lovely that had in it the unconscious grace of helplessness seemed specially to touch him."

Though Leighton was busy with a huge fresco for the South Kensington Museum, and finishing half a dozen paintings for the summer exhibition – mostly genre pictures of young Italian girls in peasant dress –he made time to sketch and work on Ada or Lena, and on the two together. For the Pullans, it meant substantial extra income, since good-looking and disciplined child models were hard to find and were paid as much as adults. Now five siblings were contributing to the family's livelihood, and they were no longer in danger of poverty.

***

The bond between a little girl and a young woman had always intrigued Leighton. Already in 1862, he exhibited *Sisters* – a young girl stretching her hand towards the unsmiling face that bent towards her in a formal embrace. In *Mother and Child* (1869) a girl was feeding her mother with cherries, and in *The Music Lesson* (1877), two sisters in rich silks sat on a marble bench, the older teaching the younger to finger the lute. And a year later, he created the two sisters *Winding the Skein.*

Leighton boasted that he always had the image complete in his mind's eye, before drawing the first line. He was exaggerating as on several occasions, it seems he was influenced by an incident in his studio. This may be the case of *Sister's Kiss*, which celebrated the tenderness between Ada and little Lena. He sketched them in several poses: Ada leaning over and turning Lena's head towards her for a kiss, and the reverse – Lena standing on a low wall behind Ada, clasping her older sister's neck and planting a surprise-kiss on her lips.

In July 1879, *Sisters' Kiss* was well advanced. Charles Dodgson visited the studio and was impressed by "a standing figure in green drapery, with a child leaning over and kissing her, painted from two sisters," he wrote in his diary. In the past, Leighton gave Dodgson the details of his eleven-year-old model, Ada Smith, and Dodgson photographed the child in the nude. But now Leighton withheld little Lena's name.

Still, Leighton felt that it was safe enough to hand over Lena to Miss Emily Gertrude Thomson, for her illustrations of naked fairies. Soon he painted Ada and Lena again. For nearly a decade he was working tirelessly on his large fresco, *The Arts of Industry as applied to Peace.* One scene depicted a half-naked Greek beauty gazing at a mirror held by a small girl. He tried various poses with several models, and in one early sketch, the eight-year-old Connie Gilchrist – the girl holding the mirror – was nude. When Ada and Lena became permanents in his studio, he developed the composition into a separate picture, *The Light of the Harem*, moving the scene from Greece to an Oriental palace. Silk dresses were made out of the sumptuous fabrics that he purchased on his travels to the Middle East. Ada, graceful and stately, was not half-naked as the model in the fresco, but wore a majestic, gold-embroidered white gown with a low décolletage. He made Ada the sole figure, the Emperor's favourite, chosen from all others – wives or concubines. She would become his inspiration, giving his work the energy it had started to lack.

***

More than any other English artist of his time, Leighton excelled at nudes. Victorian England has often been portrayed as obsessed with respectability and "the artistic nude implicated a general spread of vice," according to the art historian and curator Dr Alison Smith. Students at the Academy were allowed to paint a nude female only if they were over twenty or married. Leighton was a physician's son and was taught anatomy by his father, who hoped that he would continue the family's medical tradition. "I owe my knowledge to my father. He would teach me the names of the bones and the muscles. He would show them to me in action and in repose; then I would have to draw them from memory; until my memory drawing was perfect, he would not let it pass," Leighton told Emily Barrington. He said that he knew much more anatomy at fourteen than he did as the president of the Royal Academy. His artistic education in Germany, Italy and France, let him approach nudity with fewer inhibitions than English artists. He completed his first two nude paintings – *Pan*, and *Venus & Cupid* – in Paris when he was 26 years old, but at home they were deemed improper. He could not find a buyer, and for better luck, sent them to an exhibition of British Art which toured New York, Philadelphia and Boston. To his bitter disappointment, they were not exhibited there either "on account of the nudity and stored away in a cupboard."

Leighton learned and took the advice of his intimate friend, Henry Greville, to stick to "well-covered limbs, and paint no more Venuses for some time to come." Although Greville's advice might have had a hidden agenda – he was homosexual – Leighton only returned to the full scale nude after becoming a member of the Royal Academy. *Venus Disrobing for the Bath* (1867) caused a sensation, encouraging others to paint nudes, and earned him the title of "the most sensuous painter of the time," who produced voluptuous pictures, usually of beautiful women, and occasionally of beautiful men.

In every cycle of his nude paintings, Leighton portrayed dangerous femme fatales –in the 1850s it was *The Fishermen and the Siren,* who dragged him down into the water in a deadly embrace. In the 1860s it was *Actaea, the Nymph of the Shore*, who murdered her groom on their wedding night.

Ada saw female nude and semi-nude studies in Leighton's studio, as well as a current work in progress: *Psamathe*, a woman sitting lazily on a stretch of golden sand with her bare back turned to the viewer, as her gauzy drapery has slipped off her. So she should not have been that surprised when he asked her to take off her clothes. In the months that they had spent together, she had grown to trust him, and wishing to be part of the art world, she could not refuse. Behind the models' partition she found a flannel dressing gown. When Leighton finished arranging his tools, he called her in.

Ada was trusting but still very embarrassed to face him naked. Leighton saw her bashfulness, her head bowed, with downcast eyes and quickly made sketches, peering at her through a pair of large spectacles with divided lenses, the upper part to look at her from a distance and the lower to look at his canvas.

The best way to make nudity respectable was to use the cloak of mythology. "If the nude figure must be given, give it as some classic figure – some heroine or goddess of ancient times," wrote the *Liverpool Mercury*, criticizing Laurence Alma-Tadema's frontal nude, *The Sculptor's Model*. "We object to any girl or woman being degraded to be stuck on a common three-legged table, naked for the purpose merely of being stared at." Leighton sheltered Ada under a mythological halo. He conjured up an obscure nymph and elevated the embarrassed naked London girl, into Crenaia: a fountain-nymph who pretended to follow her many suitors, but always deserted them.

Ada stood with her arms modestly crossed over her bosom, huddling enough diaphanous white drapery, which covered only half of her body, and exposed a breast, her curves and hips. She was not just a chaste nymph, but Leighton's *Venus Pudica*, the goddess emerging from the water trying to cover her nakedness. The choice of background reflected Leighton's experiences: some years earlier, he stayed with his friend, the 7th Viscount of Powerscourt, at his estate in Wicklow. There he made several sketches of the river Dargle with the Powerscourt Waterfall, the tallest in Ireland.

That summer, Adelaide Sartoris' health was deteriorating. The former opera diva was sixteen years Leighton's senior, a wife and a mother, and for all the 26 years of their relationship, she exercised more influence over Leighton than any other woman ever had. Augusta, his younger sister, noted in her diary, "She is a creature who can never age, and before whose attractions those of younger and prettier women must always pale." Immediately after Adelaide's death in August 1879, a mournful Leighton travelled away to Italy. Ada would soon become, as Adelaide had been, his closest female confidante and friend.

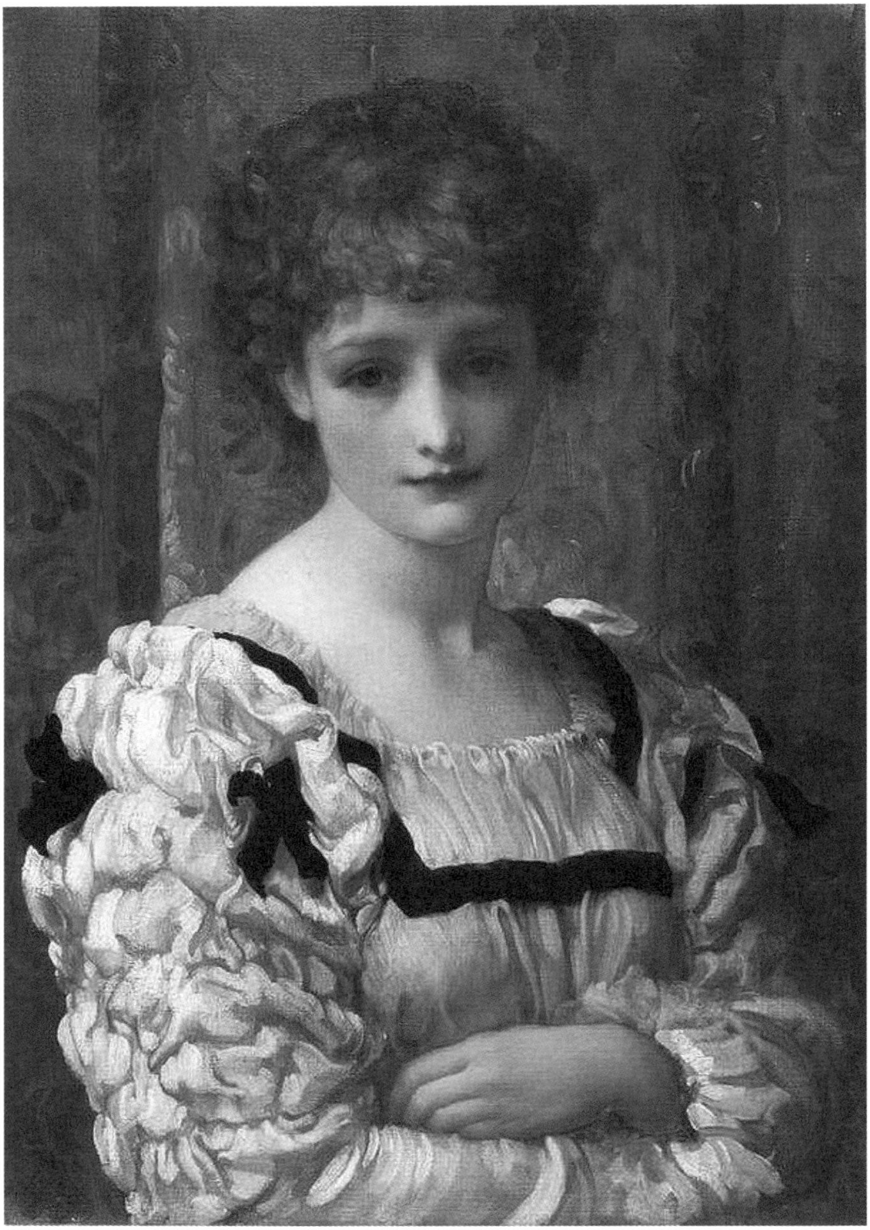

Dorothy as Bianca, 1881

Chapter Five

Roses and Thorns

While Leighton was in Italy, Ada sat for Luisa Starr, Emily Barrington, and the young Herbert Schmalz. But her most famous employer was Sir Edward Burne-Jones. For four years, he exhausted himself over a monumental painting, a procession of 18 garlanded nymphs fluttering down a flight of winding stairs, holding musical instruments. He already used his own daughter and those of his close friends, but he desperately needed more; he asked his colleagues to recommend "a nice innocent damsel or two [to fill] the staircase picture." The candidates had to epitomize the aesthetic ideal of beauty and also offer an air of subdued and chastened melancholy. So, Ada, who could look tender and sad, came to his studio, which was not far from Leighton's.

In Burne-Jones' *Golden Stairs* (now at Tate Britain), she is the one stooping barefoot halfway down the stairs, almost falling, wearing a pale-white Greek-style pleated gown girdled at the waist.

"What Is Burne-Jones like?" she was asked years later by an American journalist.

"He is a man, I was going to say, you would not look at twice; but yes, you would," she answered candidly. "He has a distinctive personality, although he is small. He has large blue eyes, a long, pointed, sandy beard and long, straight hair of the same colour, and he speaks in a most caressing voice, more like a woman than a man."

At the beginning of November 1879, Leighton returned from the continent and started painting Ada again. By the time he woke up in his austere bedroom, she already started on her long journey to Holland Park. He had his breakfast, glanced through the *Times* and opened his mail: he never "left a letter unanswered even for a day." Zealously guarding his privacy, he was one of the first artists to build a special side entrance for models. Ada was among the very few allowed to ring the front door bell. After having her breakfast, she would climb up the stairs to the studio where Leighton was waiting for her.

"I never give my whole attention to one picture at the same time," he said. "I invariably have six or seven canvases going, and I find it gives me all the rest I need to go from one to the other, working a bit here and a bit there." Leighton was "a perfect slave to duty," wrote Edgcumbe Staley. He laboured assiduously on each painting, practicing techniques of the Old Masters. Reviewers believed that too much education abroad restricted and undermined him. Even if the figure appeared fully dressed at the finished painting, he started with the nude. If you look my paintings, he said, "you will in places be able to trace the forms beneath." He first positioned the model in his mind's eye, and then tried some variations in the studio. He would make dozens of drawings before moving to the canvas. The model was called again to pose in the nude, and then again, while he would exhaustively arrange the folds of fabric on her naked body: "I can paint a figure in three days, but it may take me thirty to drape it," he said. The French art critic Robert de la Sizeranne pointed out that Leighton's nude female figures were French, but "draped they are English."

Each painting went through seven or eight stages, and the process took months, sometimes years, to complete. This, argued his critics, destroyed Leighton's spontaneity. His pedantic methods were different from those of many of his contemporaries, who dashed off canvasses fast to feed the market. Leighton was wealthy enough to take as long as he wanted on each work. He demanded reliability and Ada had to be at his disposal whenever he needed her. For her that was no ordeal. He was interesting to be with, and she seemed absorbed in his work. The many long sessions also increased her earnings considerably.

Holding a fixed pose was excruciating. "You must think as little as possible while sitting," advised an experienced artist's model: one must get into a sort of waking sleep, a mental blankness in order to maintain the pose. Models often complained that "Sometimes the artist will hardly let you rest a minute, but let you keep an uncomfortable attitude for hours, till you feel ready to drop, and pins and needles begin to shoot all over your body": the words of an anonymous artist's model published in *The Girl of the Period Miscellany Magazine*. Ada's first employer, Louisa Starr, once had a model sit for her for nine hours without moving, without resting, so as not to lose the pose, Miss Starr fed the model and blew her nose.

Leighton, however, took care of his models. He ensured that they were warm enough, did not tire themselves, and allowed them to take a rest whenever they needed. He himself supervised a break every twenty minutes or half an hour. Ada would step down from the podium and pick up the dressing gown she had dropped on a side chair, wrap herself and lie on one of the couches. At noon they stopped for lunch. Gaetano Valvona recalled that he ate by himself from a tray that was brought up to him to the studio. Leighton, "the Michelangelo of Great Britain," would come up for coffee and pastry, and then would lay down on a sofa. "There's another there, lie on it," Leighton told the Italian youth, taking a quick after-lunch nap. Ada most likely ate with Leighton at the dining room downstairs and he would then continue painting her for as long as daylight permitted.

With many duties to fulfil, and so many seeking his advice, time was a priceless commodity for Leighton. He was methodical and regular; his entire year was planned out beforehand and noted in his small diary. He made a mosaic of his days, "on which he received visits, those of work; the hours in which he would see his few intimate friends, and those in which he would return their visits; even the day and hour to go and see his father," recalled his close friend, the Italian painter Giovanni Costa. His schedule being so tight, he often allocated just 15 minutes to a meeting. Ada spent more time with him than anyone else did.

***

While modelling in the studio, Ada could not fail to see on one of the easels, the self-portrait that Leighton was working on for the gallery of eminent artists in the Uffizi, Florence. Like his predecessor, Joshua Reynolds, he wore the red cloak of a Doctor of Oxford University, with the gold medal of the President of the Royal Academy hanging on his chest. "It is like, very like!" he boasted. There were no further references to his profession, and "the portrait gives us the impression of a man self-contained, magnanimous, of magnificent intellect. We feel the force behind that serene aspect, the critical insight behind that splendour of contemplation. He does not look unconscious. It is the face and figure of a man accustomed and aware of being the centre of observation," wrote his biographer and friend, Alice Corkran. Leighton looked older than 50 and could have made himself look younger, but chose to emphasise his gravitas.

Establishing their *Gallery of Beauty*, the weekly illustrated *Graphic* magazine rented a space in Grafton Street and commissioned twelve eminent artists to submit works under the title "Female Types of Beauty." For the exhibition in February 1880, Alma-Tadema painted a portrait of his wife, James Tissot of his mistress, and Leighton, of his new flame. A year after meeting Ada, Leighton found her suitable to represent his concept of beauty. Not long before, he painted a series of young Italian girls in peasant costumes: *Catarina, Amarilla, Nicandra* and *Serafina.* He called his portrait of Ada *Selene.* It was her first exhibited portrait. She looked very natural. She glanced sideways, absorbed in her thoughts. Her features and expression were those of a teenager, and Leighton dressed her in an appropriately modest, light blue dress topped with a white rose. The *Morning Post* identified *Selene* with the moon goddess, and praised the painter and his model for realizing "the description given of her in the mythologies, that she is 'tender and timid' and that 'it is only in secret that she loves beautiful youths and kisses them in sleep'."

The exhibition was popular and attended by several members of the royal family. The Princess of Wales who saw Ada's *Selene* "seemed disposed to award [her] the palm of loveliness." *The Medical Press and Circular*, though, published a somewhat startling if intriguing review from a physician's point of view. This doctor diagnosed the beauties on show as suffering from depression and "bodily, as well as mental feebleness." Anaemia was traced on several faces, and emaciation in more than one. The doctor saw the pink on Ada's cheeks as a sign of ill-health, and diagnosed the colour on her ear as "a suspicion of eczema."

The pictures were shown again the following year, and for its Christmas edition of 1881, *The Graphic* prepared a special double-spread supplement of Leighton's engraved work. The title *Selene* was dropped in favour of *Type of Beauty*, a change made without his consent. He disapproved and in a letter to the editor, William Luson Thomas, he wrote: "I confess that I regret very much indeed, though it is now too late to say so, that my head of 'Selene' should figure of my notion of a type of beauty. I painted as *pretty* a head as I could from a *pretty* model, but nothing could be more removed from my notion of a 'type of Beauty'."

Leighton's outrage seems over the top. In less than a year, he painted Ada obsessively, in five different paintings, something which he had never done before with any model. Was he protecting himself, by reducing her to just one pretty face of many? Or was he implying that she was unique, and not typical of anything?

Selene was a hit making Ada a poster-girl. An estimated half a million copies were sold. In a few years' time, more of her posters would decorate shop windows, people would collect her photographs, and tobacco companies use her image to boost sales. All this gave Ada confidence, and she was ready for the next challenge.

***

This painting was a step further: Ada reclined languidly on another woman, lulled by a young shepherd playing the flute. Leighton had enough confidence to cast her as an equal partner to Lillie Langtry. He knew the mistress of the Prince of Wales well, and the royal fancy did not object to being paired with an apparently common girl. Langtry was "a vision of that divine loveliness dreamed of by painters and sculptors since Art began," according to the contemporary painter Graham Robertson. When Leighton approached Lillie, the Prince had already decided to end their three-year affair.

To restore her wounded pride, Lillie needed to be back in the limelight and Leighton was more than willing to help. He decided to make an intimate composition of the two 'stunners' of their day.

Lillie had already been painted by Leighton's' friends – she was Millais' *Jersey Lily* in the plain black dress that was her trademark, and Watts painted her as the respectable *Dean's Daughter*. Edward Poynter's *Portrait of Lillie Langtry* was more sensational: she was reclining on a red armchair and holding up a yellow rose – symbolizing adultery –

with a discarded white rose – the symbol of her broken marriage vows. Leighton was more daring. He was not afraid to use her in a provocative pose, which could offend the Prince of Wales. She was a nymph lying on her back with a flimsy dress, one nipple tantalizingly exposed, while Ada rested her head on her bosom.

Idyll contrasted the two ethereal forest-nymphs with a muscular and tanned shepherd. He was playing the flute when, bewitched by the power of music, the nymphs emerged from their shadowy world and lay beside him under a fine old English oak. The shepherd is unaware of their presence, and they will disappear as soon as the music stops. Leighton was probably inspired by the *Idylls* of Theocritus and a pose from the Parthenon Frieze, a copy of which he had in his studio. The two nymphs were typical of his women, with "hands that have done no work, and hearts that have known no sorrow; soft robes that have never been soiled by rain or torn by storm," sniped the art critic Harry Quilter in the *Spectator*. "Is it any wonder that they have little appeal for us who live, girt by the beating of the steely sea, in an age which has certainly little in common with that of Arcady?"

***

At the Royal Academy summer exhibition of 1880, the President's paintings were hung in the central gallery and drew much attention. Ada appeared in three of them. "A beautiful girl, slender and supple, though of course abnormally tall, with bare feet too beautiful to tread on anything but rose-leaves," wrote the *Art Journal* of *Sister's Kiss*. Her attempt to cover herself in *Crenaia* was seen as "a pretty action and has been expressed with taste and much spontaneity." In *The Light of the Harem*, she was admired for her graceful and voluptuous figure, but one reviewer called her a "soulless creature," and the *Pall Mall Gazette* was even more insulting: "a brilliant piece of furniture-painting, in which the figure is the central and most precious piece of furniture." The reviewer thought that Leighton's subjects were not interesting enough and too detached from modern reality. The statement in the *Art Journal* had a double edge: "we should grow old in disappointments if we sought in real life for such forms and faces ... because we see them only there."

Running Leighton down was in fashion and Ada became a victim of the critics. "A superb decorator and a superb piece of decoration, [he] paints poor pictures of the correctest idealism, of orange tawny naked women against indigo skies," wrote Vernon Lee.

Most reviewers thought that Leighton "is hardly at his best this year" and detested the too refined finish: "the face, hands and feet are more like wax than as if composed of flesh and blood." The *Manchester Courier* summed it all up: "These are rather studies than pictures, and neither pretend to nor possess any emotional qualities." It was not easy to determine whether the blame was entirely Leighton's, and what part Ada played in the 'failure'. All three paintings disappeared into private collections.

Crenaia was rechristened by its owner, Viscount Powerscourt, as *The Nymph of the Dargle*, after the river that ran through his estate. His heirs later sold it to an American art dealer, and a succession of tycoons owned it, including the press mogul Randolph Hearst and then Walter Chrysler. Perez Simon, a Mexican telecommunications tycoon, owns it now. In 1996 *Crenaia* visited London for the first time and did so again in 2014.

When Leighton returned from his annual Continental tour, he learned that Mrs Langtry had left her Mayfair home and returned to her parents in Jersey. She was pregnant by one of her several lovers and wanted to carry the child discreetly, away from the ever prying press. Although he was disappointed, he nevertheless proceeded with *Idyll,* assisted by a clay model of the two women. While playing her role as the hedonistic nymph in *Idyll,* Ada had not yet grown out of her shyness, as reflected in the next painting she sat for, *Bianca* wearing a virginal white dress. Leighton emphasized "the delicate porcelain whiteness of her unblemished skin, the deep flush of her small rosebud mouth, the intricate curls of her fair hair ... her eyes carry little indication of emotion or attitude, perhaps just a meek expression of acceptance or awareness that she is the mute object of our inspection."

Ada might not look emotional, but she was about to face a major crisis in her life.

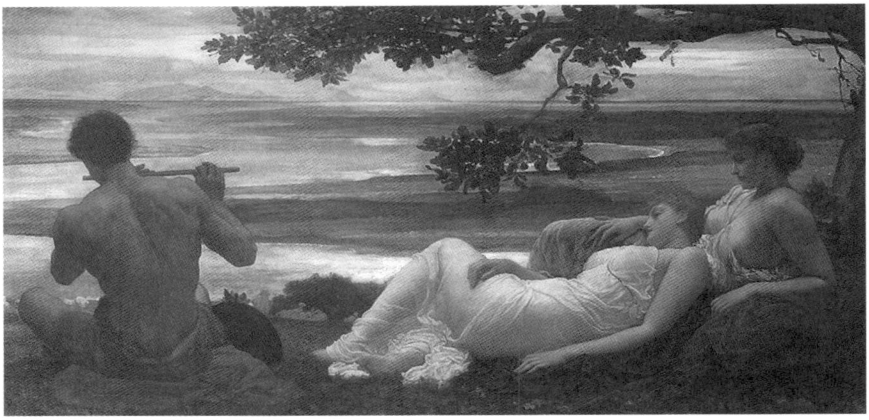

Dorothy and Lillie Langtry in *Idyll*, 1881

Chapter Six

"Impossible! with that voice!"

For two years, Leighton had been paying Ada in cash, for her sittings and for Lena's. That changed at the end of January, when he wrote her a cheque for £10: equivalent to two months' work. Most probably, it had to do with her mother's deteriorating health. Four years of spinal disease and being confined to her bed had taken their toll. Ada's mother caught double pleurisy; both her lungs were flooded with fluids. On February 2nd, 1881, Sarah Pullan died at home, surrounded by her children. She was 48 years old.

Ada and her six siblings, the youngest only four years old, were completely on their own now. Henry, aged 20, had just got married and moved out. At the end of February Leighton wrote another cheque, for the hefty sum of £25. This time it was drawn to the new head of the family, Thomas, Ada's older brother. Leighton had paid the sisters generously all along the way, but now it was not a fee for work done, but to help them in their pressing needs.

In April, when she filled the form for the census, in the column headed "occupation," Ada stated that she was an art student; but she was not studying anywhere and was not an apprentice to any artist. Some girls proudly identified themselves as artist's models, but she was too embarrassed to do so, it seems.

In his thirties, Leighton painted a few scenes of young lovers, the last one, in 1868, idealised the nymph Acme and her sweetheart Septimius, embodying ideal love. In the exhibition catalogue Leighton used the following quote from the Roman poet Catullus:

> "Then bending gently back her head,
> With that sweet mouth so rosy red,
> Upon his eyes she dropped a kiss,
> Intoxicating him with bliss."

It was the most popular picture of the year.

Thirteen years later, with Ada as his model, he returned to the idyllic youth-and-maiden love scene. The lovers were again seated on a marble bench and holding hands, the half-naked muscular Gaetano Valvona whispering tenderly in Ada's ear; she responded with dreamy eyes and a soft smile. Leighton first named it *Betrothed*, and then changed it to *Whispers*. No one knows where the painting is now, but in the surviving sketch and photoengraving, the fair, curly-hair and the bowed head are almost identical to Ada's in *Crenaia*. The moral code demanded that Ada and Gaetano modelled this intimate scene separately, on different sessions; they were united only on canvas.

The summer exhibition of 1881 was Ada's second appearance at the Royal Academy: now she was the wistful *Bianca*, Mrs Langtry's cuddle in *Idyll*, and the beloved in *Whispers*. Once again, though, Leighton failed to please his critics: "Leighton's women may be like what are in the heavens above, but they have no counterparts in the earth beneath," wrote the *Nottinghamshire Guardian*. Even Alice Corkran complained that "they have not much character; they have nothing of the spice of the devil in them which proves so attractive. They belong to an ideal world where they have never wept passionate tears or have ever rejoiced, laughing for mere laughter's sake; where they have never been moved by wild joys and hopes. They are parted from their sisters of strenuous workaday life by a mist of dreams." It was a harsh critique of Leighton's perception of women, and Ada, who had endured much tragedy, had hardly lived in "a mist of dreams."

Society's *crème de la crème* attended the opening night, and William Powell Frith saw it as an opportunity for another of his grand-scale panoramic scenes. In his memoirs he wrote that in making *The Private View*, "beyond the desire of recording for posterity the aesthetic craze as regards dress, I wished to hit the folly listening to self-elected critics in matters of taste, whether in dress or art." Set in the largest gallery of the Royal Academy, the pivotal figure of the painting, "a well-known apostle of the beautiful, with a herd of eager worshippers surrounding him," was not the President but the young Oscar Wilde. Oscar had his back to Mrs Langtry in a white dress; Leighton was in a brown frock coat, talking to the Countess of Lonsdale, who sat on an ottoman.

Many of the figures in *The Private View* are unclear and it's difficult to identify Ada. As yet, she was not the fashion icon that she would soon become, nor a celebrity whose relationship with the President made tongues wag and gossip columns froth.

***

Ada divided her time and attention, also sitting for Herbert Gustave Schmalz, Leighton's new protégé and neighbour. He was three years older than she was, the son of a Scottish mother and a successful Prussian businessman who settled near Newcastle and became the German consul there. Herbert boasted of his maternal grandfather, the marine painter James Wilson Carmichael. A tall, flamboyant and handsome young man, Herbert studied at the Royal Academy School. He then moved to the Holland Park Studios, to be close to his mentor. He gave his paintings intriguing but sentimental names like *I cannot mind my wheel, mother, The love that hopeth all things* or *The love that feareth all things.*

Apparently, it was Schmalz, not Leighton, who sensed that Ada had dramatic qualities, and cast her in her first narrative role. She was the pale, large-eyed nun kneeling before Sir Galahad and tying a girdle made of her own hair to his belt. The critics ignored *Sir Galahad* when it was shown in the 1881 summer exhibition, but it attracted the attention of the public and had immediate commercial appeal. *The Graphic* and the *Illustrated News* made an engraving which made Ada yet more famous.

With keen business sense, Schmalz instantly realized that he would not earn as much from his paintings as from their reproductions, and he published these at prices people could afford. "The artist's danger is that his works will become too sweet and pretty," wrote the *Liverpool Mercury.* Ada was comfortable in the young dandy's studio, and in a white gown with one breast exposed, she was sweet as the flower-crowned maiden who leads a procession of youths carrying rose wreathes and torches to the *Temple of Eros.* Schmalz even put his huge black German hound in the picture. With an eye for publicity, he would take the huge dog to private views at the Grosvenor Gallery, and chain him outside the entrance hall. The dog was the message; everyone would know that

Herbert Gustave Schmalz was inside. His somewhat eccentric charm opened many doors, and one day, as he was leaving one of Lady Wilde's salon gatherings, he bumped into her son.

"Leaving mamma so soon?" asked Oscar.

"Yes, I have a picture I must get on with."

"Might one ask what subject?"

"A Viking picture," Schmalz answered.

"But, my dear Schmalz," Wilde said, slowly gathering himself for a witticism, "why so far back? You know, where archaeology begins, art ceases." The central figure in this Viking picture was Edith, Ada's younger sister.

Schmaltz's paintings were melancholy and a little artificial; "his young ladies, with their pale faces and darkly-shadowed eyes, are sad for the want of fresh air and something to do, – sad, perchance, from sheer delight in sorrow," wrote the *Spectator*. Schmalz would become a permanent fixture in the Pullan family life, and continue to paint Ada and her sisters.

The news of the new beauty travelled around Holland Park, and Leighton's next-door neighbour Val Prinsep took Ada for his *At the Golden Gate*. He dressed her in a flaming orange sari, accentuating her auburn curls and marble neck which was becoming her trademark. She was leaning against the locked golden gates of her paradise, passively looking down. "His drawing of the well-developed maiden ... has much of Sir Frederick Leighton's union of precision and suavity; but the robustness is of Mr Prinsep's own," wrote the *Evening Standard* in May 1882.

***

Ada was now Leighton's favourite model and he refrained from exhibiting her in the nude or in transparent dress; he kept her as his ideal chaste beauty. He found her too inhibited to portray Phryne, the most famous courtesan of her time, and the model and mistress of the great sculptor Praxiteles. Facing a death sentence, Phryne's body is exposed to arouse the pity of the judges and to show them how irresistible she was. Leighton cast one of his Italian models for the part. Ada was spared the repercussions – classicist Walter Perry thought that such an image "lowered the tone of national morality" and the *Art Journal* feared that Leighton's work would lead to a deluge of nudes on the walls of the Royal Academy.

She was left out of Leighton's next work, *Wedded*, in spite of the sentimental subject: a young bride leans backwards, her groom's arm around her waist, "whilst the impassioned kiss of fervent love united two lives which are made one for the other," Edgcumbe Staley wrote. Enthused by the scene, Leighton said: "all the world is at their feet," and Robert Browning exclaimed, "I find a poetry in that man's work I can find in no other." The engraving of *Wedded* was a huge commercial success for decades to come.

Gaetano Valvona was the lover. Dr. Robin Flower, a deputy keeper of manuscripts at the British Museum, recalled that Valvona told him that posing for *Wedded* was the hardest work he had ever done. The girl was so sexy, and the pose so close and intimate, that he had a continuous erection. Richard Ormond, Leighton's biographer, doubts it: "it was against normal Victorian studio practice to allow mixed modelling, and certainly when there was any question of partial undressing. The least hint of anything untoward would have been extremely distasteful to the fastidious Leighton."

Then at long last, Ada was given a dramatic, tragic role: the moment that Antigone learns King Creon has sentenced her to be walled up alive as punishment for burying her brother. It was a radical departure from her usual ethereal porcelain beauties. But Leighton did not make it easy for her. He was focusing on her best feature – her neck – to portray the impending tragedy: Antigone was soon to hang herself. Many of his compositions were inspired by the theatre, of which he was a great fan; but apparently, in *Antigone*, he was not much of a director, and Ada was too much of a novice to impress the critics only with her twisted neck and agonized face. They dismissed it as just another "fine female head and bust."

All those years in the Holland Park studios, Ada was waiting for the right moment to realize her childhood dream. Many models made a leap to the stage: they gained experience and confidence in performing before an audience of one, portraying different characters. They established connections in the world of art, could be credited for working with leading artists and had a portfolio to show. They also knew that few models lasted after they were 25 years old, and so would need another source of income. Theatre managers were always on the lookout for the fresh and the flesh as long as the flesh was beautiful.

Emily Barrington stepped in. She was not content with just chronicling Leighton's life, but made a point to be involved in it; in fact, to emphasize her own contribution for the future hagiography that she would write. She took the credit not only for discovering Ada, but for realising her stage dream and helping her to achieve it. One day, while sitting for her, Ada confided "that she longed greatly to find something to do more interesting and remunerative than spending her days as a model. She thought she could act. I consulted Leighton. His first exclamation was, '*Impossible!* with *that* voice! How *could* she go on the stage?' I thought the voice, which had a singularly unpleasant Cockney twang in it, might be trained, as I had observed how very eager, she was to learn to speak in a more educated manner, quite realising her own shortcomings." The voice might seem harsh to the upper class ears of Leighton but he did sympathize with Ada's ambitions. He had known something like it as a child.

"As far back in my boyhood as I can remember, I was determined to become an artist," he told the celebrity journalist Cornelia Rockefeller, who had married into the aristocracy and became Baroness von Zedlitz. "My father was at first, averse to the idea of my adopting a profession which, in those days, appeared to his strict notions synonymous to the life of an idler." He was twelve when his father showed some of his drawings and paintings to the American sculptor Hiram Powers. Leighton remembered that Powers "probably detected in the youthful aspirant some symptoms of artistic possibility."

"Shall I make him a painter?" the father asked.

"Sir, you cannot help yourself; nature has made him one already," answered the eminent sculptor.

"What can he hope for, if I let him prepare for this career?"

"Let him aim at the highest," answered Powers; "he will be certain to get there."

***

By now, the theatre was alluring and lucrative, offering women freedom, excitement, and the promise of better pay and social mobility. When Ada was born, about 800 women and 1300 men were registered as actors. Ten years later, the number of women had doubled, and in the census of 1881, there were already 2368 registered actresses and 2197 actors. The actual figure of women in the profession was higher, and sometimes, 200 of them had to fight for one minor part in a new drama.

In the late 1870s, London had 50 licensed theatres and there were 203 in the provinces. 155 new plays were staged one year in London and 95 more in the provinces. Paris premiered just 79. "There is no question that at the present moment the English people are much more constant playgoers that they have been for many years past," said Lord Wharncliffe, who chaired a public meeting of theatre managers, actors, playwrights and critics. In the past, when there were few theatres, managers could select the best actors, "but since the increase of theatres it must result that the supply of properly trained and good artists must prove insufficient to the demand for them, and, as a consequence, actors are not up to so good standard in the lower rank of the profession as they ought to be."

Aspiring actors learned their craft by playing non-speaking parts or watching and imitating more experienced cast, often at the expense of the audience. Actresses usually entered the profession between the ages of 16 and 18, financially supported by parents, or ready to endure long, hard years of apprenticeship.

Several veteran actresses gave private or group lessons, but the fee was so high that only girls from the middle or upper middle class could afford it. These aspirants had a great advantage over Ada: they had the best education, privately at home or in girls' school, which taught singing, dancing and recitation. These girls were also articulate in the language of their social class. Nevertheless, to go on stage, they still needed lessons in elocution, gestures, the "grand manner" and how to act in classical plays and Shakespearean verse. Ada was a late starter, but looked younger, and the experience she gained as a model compensated for her age: already 23 years old.

Once Leighton realized that she was set on preparing herself for the stage, he "showed himself as ever the most unselfish and untiring befriender," Emily Barrington noted. Ada was sent to the veteran actress Fanny Stirling to judge if she had any talent and to teach her. After her second lesson, Mrs Stirling told her that she would do well if she worked hard and said that "No one can make you an actress, but many can help you." Ada took two more lessons, but Leighton believed in formal schooling, the kind he himself had in Europe: "the fundamental stone upon which to build up a thorough artistic nature should be by necessity an all-round and sound education," he said.

The Royal Academy Schools was established in 1769, the Royal Academy of Music in 1822, but there was no academy for actors. "The training, if any, is a mere chapter of accidents," complained Mrs Stirling. Several attempts were made, but it was only in May 1882 that the School of Dramatic Art was established in London and began to recruit students. No scholarships were offered to talented but penniless applicants and the exorbitant tuition fee of £40 – more than the annual income of a working girl – meant that only middle-class parents could send their children. Ada, however, did have Leighton and he made sure that money would not be an obstacle.

Ada was not the first to enjoy his generosity. The actor-manager Henry Irving professed to have "known of many whom Leighton has helped, not merely with his purse, but with his time and personal exertions on their behalf." He also helped fellow artists in need, by buying their work and recommending them to his rich acquaintances. When his friend the painter George Mason died, leaving a young widow and five children, Leighton supported them generously throughout his life.

But he was mainly attentive to those who were trying to make a name for themselves. John Hanson Walker started modelling for Leighton as a young boy: "Leighton made the sittings enchanting; he whistled like a bird; he sang songs for me; he told me the most wonderful stories. He drew from me that it was my ambition to be a painter. He spoke of the difficulty of art and of the splendour of it." One day a large crate was dropped at the Walker family door. "There were all the treasures I longed for: plaster casts of heads, hands, and feet. There were drawing-paper and drawing-boards, pencils and chalk, everything a boy could want whose longing was to be an artist."

Leighton was generous to strangers as well. Once a student in despair wrote to him with some specimen of his work. Leighton invited him to his home, "advised him to study more, and gave him two letters of introduction. As the young man was leaving, Sir Frederic handed him an envelope, remarking: 'here is an example of the best kind of drawing. No doubt one of these days you'll be able to do as well, if not better'. It contained a cheque for fifty pounds" – which the student lived on for almost a year.

Leighton was also deeply generous to those who worked for him regularly. On Gaetano Valvona's first day in the studio, Leighton advised him to leave off "that shepherd costume and dress like us, so you will not attract the attention of the stupid curious people and children and having a crowd following you wherever you go laughing and yelling." He assured Valvona that he would pay the bills and sent his butler to accompany the newly-arrived Italian to High Street Kensington, "and you may have your own choice in the way of clothing."

He also helped Valvona find accommodation near Holland Park, so that he would not waste money and time to get to his sittings. The handsome youth would remain Leighton's favourite male model for more than a decade and would sometimes accompany his patron in his travels throughout Italy.

When he identified genuine talent, Leighton responded with sympathy, encouragement and advice, but "to those who are destined to fail, he does the greatest kindness in his power – he dissuades them from a career for which they are unfitted, and in which it is impossible for them to excel," wrote the *Review of Reviews.*

Leighton clearly believed in Ada, and his generosity towards her was second to none. To let her prepare for her new career, he cut down significantly on her modelling assignments. In *Vestal*, he made no more demands on her than on a shop-window mannequin head, featuring the luxuriant curves and creases of the veil of white and gold that hid her hair.

***

The studio podium was now occupied by eight year old Lena. The rosy-faced child, with her fine honey-coloured hair, was cast in *Kittens*, and Leighton dressed her in a splendid garment of oriental purple and fawn. He sat her on a couch and she turned "sidelong and stoops over a pretty tiger-like kitten, her own type, which gambles at her side," gushed F. G. Stephens in *The Athenaeum*. There was only one kitten in the painting, so the title clearly included Lena as well. John Ruskin, the leading art critic of the time, who was fond of real and painted little girls, was excited by *Kittens*. In a lecture he praised Leighton for "condescending from the majesties of Olympus to the worship of this unappalling powers which, heaven be thanked, are as brightly Anglo-Saxon as Hellenic; and painting for us, with a soft charm peculiarly his own, the witchcraft and the wonderfulness of childhood."

Lena was also the dancing girl in a dark yellow pleated tunic in the frieze commissioned by the banker Stewart Hodgson for his drawing room in Mayfair. She was chaperoned to Leighton's studio by Edith who had just finished school. Modelling was often a family affair; mothers introduced their children, sisters followed one another. So Edith was the next in line. For the melancholy scene of *Memories*, she had to act much older than seventeen. Dressed in black, with a dark shawl patterned in gold, her head rested on her arm, eyes moist with tears. She was a sad widow as the title of the work suggested.

Leighton made sure that the Pullan household income was not affected by Ada's studies, and he wrote generous cheques to her brother Thomas. Before leaving for Cairo, he paid Ada's tuition fee, and as a further investment in her future, increased his payments to the Garrick Theatrical Club. He had been a member since 1864, but now, he gave the club an additional £30 or £40 a year as a good-will donation.

Chapter Seven

"The sensitive and prickly Tragic Muse"

When Ada began to train for the theatre, there was less stigma surrounding actresses. "It has long ceased to be a maxim, even in fastidious circles, that 'going on the Stage' is the last phase of social deterioration. Acting is more recognized as a fine art than it ever was before," wrote Arthur Talbot Vanderbilt in his *What to do with our girls*. The popular handbook listed professions open to young women; for those with some artistic gifts, "probably none is more attractive and dazzling than the Stage." Recommending the new School of Dramatic Art in 7a Argyll Street, the guidebook emphasized that it was safe for ladies of refinement and education, and that the management reassured

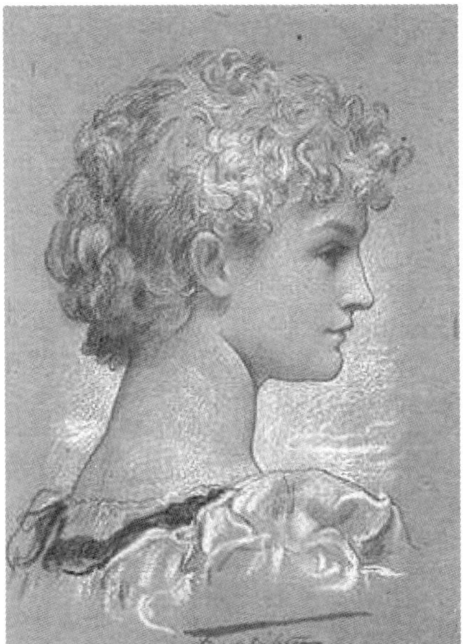

Dorothy Dene in the *Court and Society Review*, November 1886

parents that every effort was made "to enable Lady Pupils to pursue the entire course of study under the same careful control and supervision as they would be subject to be in every high-class School or College." Classes for women were to be separated from those of the men. The sexes met only at rehearsal, when "the ladies are under the immediate charge of a Lady Superintendent who is always present." There were no public spaces like a library, cafeteria or lounge, where the sexes could mingle without chaperones.

The School professed to be the English equivalent of the French *Conservatoire;* it had an impressive list of benefactors headed by the Prince of Wales and the Duke of Cambridge, and a board composed of the most celebrated men and women of the profession. Leighton knew them all: Henry Irving, Mrs Fanny Kemble (Adelaide Sartoris' sister), Clement Scott, George Augustus Sala and Alfred Lord Tennyson, all useful links for a hopeful actress. Nevertheless, it was first and foremost a commercial enterprise. There were no auditions and anyone who could supply some sort of reference letter was accepted. Students could join at any term, quit at any time, or take partial courses. In fact, anyone who could afford the exorbitant tuition fee could enrol, and they were kept in class as long as they continued paying. The *Era*, a weekly dedicated to the arts and the theatre, was alarmed by the potential dangers of flooding the profession with mediocrity and criticized the management's indiscriminate approach. Unlike in any other professional institute, a student was never called to the principle to be told, "We've given you a fair trial, and you appear to have no natural aptitude to the profession you have taken a fancy to, so we cannot allow you to waste your, and our, time here any longer."

Ada began her first term on October 4th, 1882. It was a full five day week: elocution classes every Monday and Thursday between 11 and 1, with veteran actresses Mrs Dallas-Glyn and Mrs Chippendale. A short break followed by two hours of dancing in the magnificent ball-room. Tuesday and Friday mornings began with two hours of stage gestures, expression and pantomime, followed by two hours of fencing in the afternoon. On Wednesdays there were workshops and lectures on subjects of dramatic interest by the celebrities of the profession, including advice on diet and clothing. Once a day, both sexes – seated separately – would meet for rehearsals.

Seventy-five students enrolled that year; the youngest being the 14-year-old Bessie Hatton, daughter of the well-known newspaper editor and novelist, Joseph Hatton. There were a few married women, some clergymen's daughters, and a handful who had come all the way from the USA. Plenty of homework was given, and the short breaks between terms left little time for anything else.

Leighton supervised Ada's progress closely, and received constant reports from her teachers. It was not easy, however, for Ada to give up modelling entirely. Leighton, who thought that if she were to make a successful actress, she had to put in more serious and concentrated study, wrote to Mrs Barrington:

"I want you to help me in a little conspiracy against (?) our young tragic friend. Mrs Glyn frequently urges that she ought, at all events for a time, to give her *whole* mind and being to the study of her art. I need not say I share that opinion, and I have at last, after infinite trouble and persistence (my *nose*, you know) induced her to leave off sitting for a *month*, in the hope, if you will all help, of making it a *quarter*. This would, I am confident, be of the greatest value to her, giving her time also to read a little and concentrate her thoughts. I am quite prepared to give up painting from her for three months; but she is in mortal dread lest her other friends should think her unkind and ungrateful for their sympathy. I have told her I believe no such thing, and that I feel sure that Schmaltz and you (who work most from her) will, as willingly as I, postpone your studies in order to aid her in so important a matter. She is going to call on you to-day; if you agree with me, *be very firm* – have a *nose*! *Refuse* to paint from her for three months."

The plot succeeded and the Holland Park Circle made "the little girl work exclusively at her acting." Lena was the only sister who was now modelling for Leighton, and his *Letty* again excited John Ruskin's admiration. "One of the sweetest and freshest studies of seductive maidens, with a soft English beauty; her pale brown soft-toned hair is crowned by a black hat, and about her neck is a saffron-coloured kerchief," echoed Alice Corkran.

Leighton, as well as Watts and Mrs Barrington, came frequently to see Ada and her fellow-students perform. She was the hope and pride of the school, and felt indebted to Isabel Dallas-Glyn, her elocution teacher, who, she said, worked her like a slave. The teachers looked to mould their students in the tradition of the 18th century tragedienne Sarah Siddons, whose pathos was effective and her death scenes terrified the audience. This old-fashioned style would eventually prove to be a major obstacle in Ada's career, however.

Students who were "sufficiently advanced" took part in Speech Days and Dramatic Representations in the 600-seat concert hall or in the small school theatre. They were cast in roles suited to their temperament and personality. Ada delivered a tragic monologue from Shakespeare's *King John.* She played Constance, Duchess of Brittany, grieving over her 16 year-old son Arthur, who should have become King of England, till bad King John had him killed in prison to make sure the boy would never get the crown.

Ada also recited Juliet's two most tragic scenes of the play, "banished" and "the potion." In stark contrast, she played the gushing sentimental 17 year-old Florence, whose ideas of life came entirely from romantic novels. This one-act comedietta *Cousin Dick* was written by Val Prinsep, who had painted Ada not long before.

On the brink of her stage career, Ada reinvented herself. Actresses often chose a stage name, to save embarrassment for their families, erase any traces of their origins, and, most importantly, to have a catchy name that would impress agents, theatre managers and the public. Ada changed her first name to Dorothy, in memory of her deceased young sister. Pullan had a too-strong Yorkshire flavour, so it had to go, and with Leighton's approval, she doubled the initials and made Dene her surname. She never changed officially into Dorothy Dene, and in all legal documents she remained Ada Alice Pullan. Her sisters and her younger brother followed her, all adopting the surname Dene. Ada had become Dorothy.

On top of their keep, Leighton upgraded the family's lodgings, and in the summer of 1883, he gave Thomas Pullan the mighty sum of £400 to buy the lease of a house. All seven Pullans moved to 83, The Chase, Clapham, [now number 103], so from a working-class neighbourhood, they settled in a well-to-do, even wealthy area. It was a modern red-brick house three times larger than their previous home, and they had all four floors to themselves, with a proper reception room to welcome guests. They enjoyed all the up-to-date Victorian luxuries – a modern toilet and hot water, marble fire places, ornate plaster works, and even bell pulls to summon their housemaid. The new home halved the distance and travelling time to the West End theatres and to Leighton's studio.

***

Being a classicist, Leighton urged every aspiring artist to experience Italy and its treasures, and as a graduation present, he surprised Dorothy with a trip to his favourite country. It was an uncharacteristic gesture for such a ferociously private person, who dreaded gossip. His past financial gifts were kept between himself and Dorothy, but here he was going public. The trip would also serve as an audition to find out if she would be able to fit in with his artistic and titled friends. Leighton usually travelled on his own, with not even a servant to cater to his needs. His duties in London involved so much bustle and so many people demanding his attention, that going abroad was a relief, to have time just for himself. How would he and Dorothy manage the close intimacy for days and nights, for the first time under one roof, and in a foreign land? And what would they say behind his back about the beautiful young woman beside him? But no second thoughts made him change his plan.

In September 1883, he and Dorothy were already in Siena, where his friend Giovanni Costa was spending the summer. While Leighton made some landscape sketches, Dorothy sat for Costa. He painted her defiant profile in tempera, accentuating her long neck adorned by strings of pearls, and her short, shiny curls. The painting earned her the nickname of "collo di cigno" – swan-neck – and she became a local sensation. When "Ritratto di donna di profilo" was exhibited in Rome, it was praised by the critics, and inspired the poet-painter Giuseppe Cellini to write *Dorotea*, praising Dorothy's Leonardesque beauty: "O forehead, eyelashes, profile, pure and rare, white neck…"

Later the painting was exhibited in Earl's Court as part of an exhibition of modern Italian paintings. The well-known photographer

Paolo Lombardi took several portraits of her in profile, looking to the left and to the right. He displayed his "Dorotea in Siena" in his shop window, the first in a long series of fan postcards of her.

Throughout her time in Italy, Dorothy was preoccupied with her forthcoming career; how she would take centre-stage and step into the lives of tragic heroines? Hysterical, mad women intrigued the Victorians, and actresses competed for choice parts. She later told the *Dramatic Peerage* that a strange fancy possessed her to study madness from life, and she "found this weird cult so fascinating, that even during a holiday trip on the Continent, she squeezed in a visit to a madhouse when she could. In this way, she laid up for herself treasures upon earth, which proved an excellent investment."

Dorothy passed the 'test' of the Italian trip and Leighton felt assured enough to leave her with Costa and return to London on his own. His departure was a relief for Costa, who loved Leighton dearly but was irritated by his fussiness. He wrote to a friend that the President "will remain with us for thirty-six hours, sixteen minutes and forty-nine seconds, and then I shall go with him to Florence for two days. After this Olympic visit, peace will be restored."

Dorothy and Costa travelled to Perugia and then to Rome where she stayed with the MP William Cornwallis Cartwright and his daughter Roma. Already on his way home Leighton sent Costa a letter signed with one of his nicknames, Gaffer, and adorned it with a sketch of his own head. He concealed his concern for Dorothy under a playful tone and inquired "how the wild Roma gets on with the sensitive and prickly Tragic Muse." It was an allusion to great dramatic actresses of the past, painted by his predecessors: *Mrs Siddons as the Tragic Muse*, (Joshua Reynolds), and *Mrs Yates as the Tragic Muse* (George Romney). The phrase also alluded to Dorothy's touchy temperament. Leighton did not mention Dorothy by name, and his use of the nickname implied intimacy, though it might have been more paternal than anything else; he would invent several nicknames for her, often using "Tragichetta."

***

When Dorothy got back to London, Leighton was eager to resume her sittings for him, to proceed with an important painting he had begun earlier. *Cymon and Iphigenia* was based on a tale from Boccaccio's *Decameron*, in which the uneducated son of a nobleman "fell into brutish and savage ways" and was hence called Cymon – meaning "the brute." He chances upon the maiden Iphigenia, fast asleep in a meadow under a tree. Mesmerized by "the fairest creature that had ever been seen by a mortal eye," he is transformed; the power of beauty and love turns him into an elegant courtier, who wins Iphigenia's heart and marries her. Leighton put all his study of beauty into this work because it conveyed his "creed of creeds ... the ennobling and elevating influence of beauty in the lives of men and women," as Mrs Barrington noted. Wishing the viewers to experience the same transformation, he changed his Cymon from an idiot into a meditative youth, and put Dorothy in many poses, until he found the right one: on her back, her arms above her head and her face and body turned towards the viewer, making each one of us a Cymon, a voyeur falling in love and being transformed by a radiant beauty. The sleeping Dorothy, in the nude sketches and in flimsy dress of the final work, seems relaxed and confident, having lost all her inhibitions. Her serene expression and body language reflect the intimacy between the artist and his model.

Boccaccio described Iphigenia "attired in such loose garments as hid very little of her white body." Cymon admires every inch of her, her forehead, nose, mouth and neck, "but, above all, her breasts, appearing as yet but only to show themselves like two little mountains." No wonder that from the Renaissance onwards, Iphigenia was always painted in the nude, (Rubens, Reynolds) or at least with fully exposed breasts, (Angelica Kaufmann, Millais). But not Leighton. In the finished painting he made Iphigenia "fair as an angel" but covered her naked body with a loose cream-colored robe. He was so excited about this painting that he invited Alice Meynell of the *Art Journal* to his studio and described his method of working in great detail. He allowed the magazine to print three of his preparatory clay models, all in the nude. One nude clay was missing from the article though: that of Dorothy. Her modest Iphigenia suggests that he did not want to jeopardize, however slightly, Dorothy's respectability at the start of her acting career. Lena was also in the picture, as one of Iphigenia's attendants, sleeping at her feet. "We recognize a child whose pallid and pure colouring, light eyelashes and delicate forms, the painter has frequently studied," wrote Alice Meynell. Leighton was so mesmerized by Lena that he did not mind over-using her.

Cymon and Iphigenia, an enormous painting of 163 by 328 cm, drew great attention even before it was exhibited, and Leighton sold it off-the-easel for £4000 to the Fine Art Society, who resold it immediately for a large profit. It is regarded a major masterpiece of European Symbolist art and was much admired by Watts. It is now in the Art Gallery of New South Wales in Sydney, Australia.

The indefatigable Emily Barrington then introduced Dorothy Dene to Watts. His style, technique and working methods could not have been more different to Leighton's. Watts believed that "drawing from the model, for instance, is like looking in the dictionary for a word; you will not write poetry till the words come to you without having to turn them up in the dictionary every time." He did not need the model for more than a few hours, so for Dorothy not to lose her full day's pay, she sat for Mrs Barrington in the mornings, and after lunch, crossed the lawn and stepped into Watts' studio. In the evenings, Mrs Barrington used to drop on Watts to see and discuss his and her daily work with Dorothy. Back at home, she would struggle to improve her portraits of Dorothy, and always failed. She was not the only one.

Although Leighton had spent so much time with Dorothy – in his studio, at home and elsewhere, he painfully realized that he never succeeded in getting her "particular texture and colour," recalled Mrs Barrington in her biography of Watts. "He got much else from Dorothy Dene in the way of dramatic expression and gesture, and for these qualities he mainly worked from her, but, as far as likeness went, he always maintained that he had failed to satisfy himself. No other model had he found so tantalizingly difficult to paint from. Watts, in a couple of hours, produced a head of Dorothy Dene which was, as a mere portrait of her, more like than any Leighton ever achieved."

Leighton's personal involvement with Dorothy Dene, it seems, stood in the way of his depiction of her. For Watts, she was just another model, and he could see her as she was – vulnerable and exposed, as in his *Portrait of a Young Lady* dressed in black and saffron of 1883. Mrs Barrington claimed that Dorothy – and not Watts' ex-wife, and child-bride, Ellen Terry – was also the bored girl on a sofa who has dropped her book and wearily looks out of the window in *The rain it raineth every day*. A year later he painted Dorothy as *Uldra*, the Scandinavian spirit of the waterfall. It was a half-length female nude, ethereal rather than sensual, seen through a rainbow-hued mist. He also made a similar image of Dorothy, now as Aphrodite, in his *Olympus on Ida*.

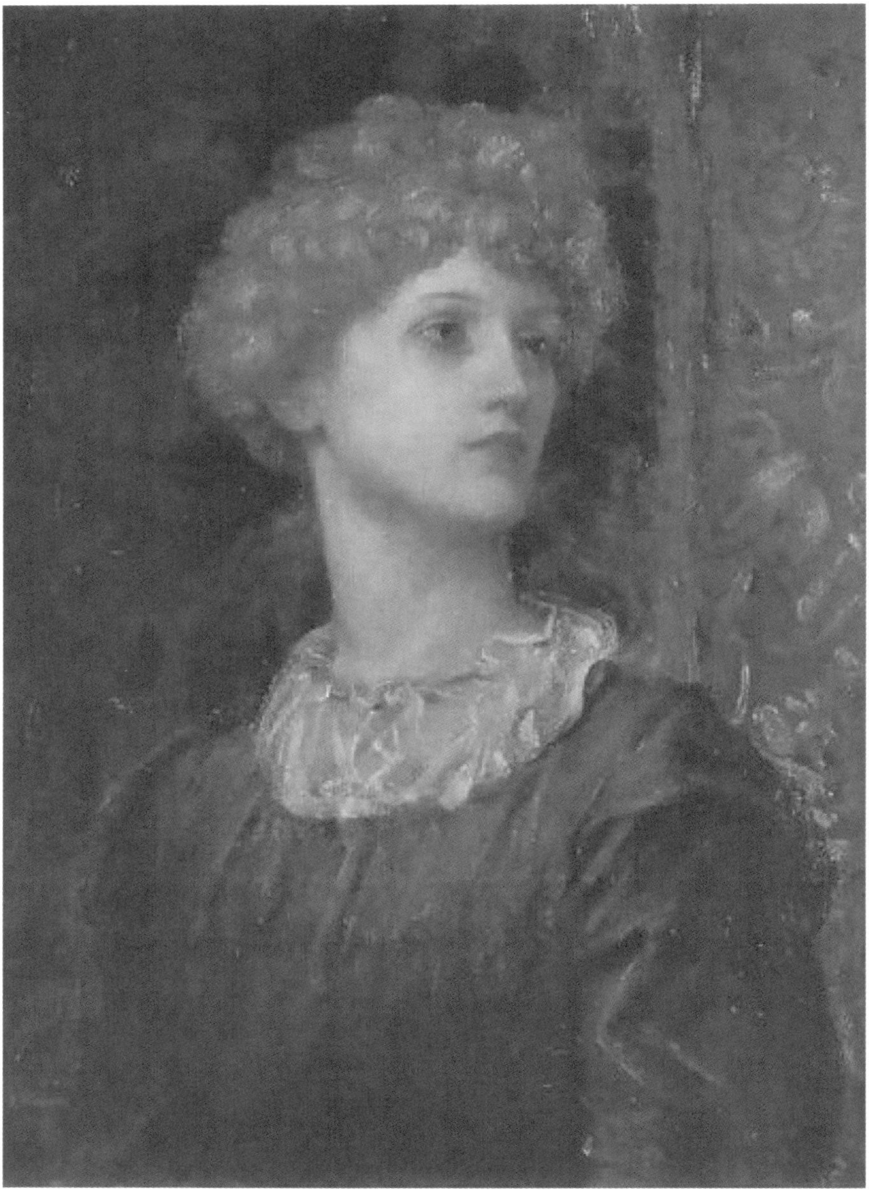

A portrait of Dorothy Dene by G.F. Watts, 1884

Chapter Eight

"A very promising debut"

The School of Dramatic Art guaranteed that upon graduation, novices would earn 30 shilling which could soon rise to four or five guineas a week "and thence to any amount, according to the ability and popularity of the Actress. There never has been, indeed, such a mania for acting as now, and there seldom has been a time when higher salaries were paid to really moderate talent," Vanderbilt wrote in *What to do with our girls*. But in fact, only a third of the graduates got work in London or in the provincial theatres. Those who could do comedy, burlesque or farce and had a singing voice, had better chances of finding employment, as well as those who were willing to play any part. Dorothy Dene was none of the above.

Dorothy's distinction at school gave her a head start. She did not have to play walk-on parts like other novices, but started right at the front. Her first public performance was on February 23rd, 1884, in Sheridan's *School for Scandal*, at the *Olympic*; she played the beautiful young Maria who was courted by two brothers: the one truly in love, the other after her inheritance. All the characters in this comedy of manners were nasty schemers, greedy, vain, slanderous and lecherous, except for the virtuous Maria. Her integrity led her to a happy and prosperous marriage, putting an end to a vicious circle of family disgrace.

The part was quite a challenge, since Dorothy was the only newcomer in a cast of veteran and well-experienced actors, including some of her teachers. She received better reviews than most of them: "A very promising debut," wrote the *Graphic*, while the *London Daily News* applauded the "extremely pretty young lady, whose features are, we fancy, traceable in the pictures of one or two distinguished painters ... having profited by careful teaching, should soon fill very usefully the place on the stage for which she is well fitted by her personal attractions." From the outset of her career, the critics stressed her striking looks and curvy figure and her reputation as an artist's model, for better or for worse.

Dorothy knew that the Italian tragedian Tommaso Salvini, who was appearing that week in Covent Garden, was sitting in the auditorium. Salvini's career shows how odd the Victorian theatre could be. He had been praised for his performances as Hamlet, Macbeth, Othello and King Lear in New York and London, though he recited his lines in his native Italian while the rest of the cast spoke English.

Dorothy asked Leighton to introduce her to Salvini. He obliged as ever; "Do not tell her anything untrue," Leighton told him and added, "She wishes to be a worker, and knows well that with her youth and inexperience, she has not mastered so difficult an art as acting." After the show, Salvini shook hands with her warmly and said, "I will tell you candidly what I think. You have the links of a beautiful chain in your hand, and only have to learn to put them together."

The School of Dramatic Art was always losing money and benefit performances were regularly held to raise funds. One of them was *Lady Dedlock's Secret*, a very popular tragedy in four acts, staged at the *Opera Comique.* John Palgrave Simpson based his play on an episode in Charles Dickens' *Bleak House*, where a respectable lady is falsely accused of murder, and sinks into a life of shame. She is finally reconciled with her long-lost daughter, who has no idea of her past. Dorothy got good notices for her portrayal of Esther, the daughter, "in a manner which reflected credit upon that institution, having not only a pretty face and a lissome figure – the usual attributes of the ingénue – but a knowledge of stage business as is only to be acquired by experience," wrote the *Yorkshire Post.*

The London Serio-Comic Journal *Judy* was excited about that "very pretty, sweet-voiced young lady, called Dorothy Dene. Her name sounds like that of the heroine of some rustic idyll, and her graceful presence would have well suited such a part. She will do well." *The Stage* praised her as "pretty, confident and intelligent. Her voice is rich and resonant, and she is uniformly graceful." Apparently, Leighton's earlier judgment and concerns about her accent and voice, was too harsh. After a year and a half of elocution classes, she was already commended for her speech.

The Stage, the most largely circulated theatrical newspaper, had always been critical of the School of Dramatic Art and derided its approach, which emphasized "the grand manner"; Dorothy was caught in a battle between proponents of the classical theatre and the modern one. She was seen as a victim, an example of an "extremely ill-taught and over-trained" actress. "She has spoken each sentence with deliberate and painful emphasis, as if she were engaged in a tragic lesson. Miss Dene has evidently so well-drilled in Shakespeare and blank verse plays that she feels she is at sea with simple prose. If the School is organized to revive the old-fashioned bow-wow, princely and wealthy style of art, then the sooner it ceases to encourage these pernicious habits the better. In cultivating art, we must not forget nature altogether. Still Miss Dene may be recommended to persevere." The stuck in the past School did not survive for long, and closed down after three years.

***

Leighton attended all of Dorothy's performances, sitting in the first row with his friends, applauding fervently. As helpful as he was to other budding artists, he was more dedicated to her than to anyone else. He acted like a diligent agent, or rather like an anxious, pushy parent, praising his prodigy, sending letters to anyone he knew in the profession, and urging others to intervene on her behalf. Asking for favours from so many people made his feelings for Dorothy clear and could make him indebted, but he was not deterred.

One of the most influential gate keepers was Henry Irving, not just the greatest actor of his time, but a manager, who turned his *Lyceum* into a national theatre in all but name. His verdict could make or break a career. Acting on Leighton's behalf, the Irish writer May Hartley wrote to Bram Stoker, the author of *Dracula* who was Irving's assistant:

"Miss Pullan wants to get in the Lyceum Company somehow or anyhow, and to do understudies – she would have been a right good Viola just now – she is extremely beautiful – very clever and hardworking good girl – she is only 21 or 22. Sir Frederic Leighton has painted her in all his pictures for three or four years and takes a strong interest in her – so do I – for I know all her circumstances – she has been well trained and is competent. I know very well a manager cannot take risks – there is far too much money involved to try perilous ventures in a theatre – but I do think if you were to bring Miss Pullan before Mr Irving – let him see her and hear her once in action."

When a cautious reply came from Stoker, Leighton told Emily Barrington: "I certainly did not mean to seem churlish in regard to that letter from Irving. *If Miss Pullen is now ripe for him to hear her* – this is the most important point (for to go to him *too soon* would be the most unwise thing possible in view of her getting a good engagement) – and if, having declined a letter on a previous occasion, she has any unnecessary scruple about now asking for one, it will be quite enough for you to tell me from her that she wishes for one, and I will at once write it. *Kemp* [his butler] *will always be able to tell you where to get at me.* I can write as easily from Vienna or Constantinople as from here." Knowing Dorothy inside out – her stubbornness, her fretfulness – Leighton stepped aside, making himself available whenever she decided to make a move.

"I should have written to you sooner," Dorothy finally wrote to Irving, "but have been so very busy preparing for an engagement I have with Mr Bruce to act in the provinces. It will be impossible for me to call in the daytime, but I shall be very pleased to do so on Thursday evening." And she signed Ada Pullan (Dorothy Dene). Irving was the Laurence Olivier of his day. For any novice, an invitation from him was a fairy's wish that came true. Far from dropping everything to meet him, however, Dorothy acted as if she and Irving were on equal footing. Nothing ever came out of it, and she never played for Irving.

That summer of 1884, she was indeed occupied with rehearsing her dream lead as a mad-woman. Edgar Bruce, the actor-manager of the newly-built *Prince's Theatre*, had just struck gold with his latest production, *Called Back*. The novel, by Hugh Conway, was a mystery/romance which sold 75,000 copies within four months. It was immediately adapted for the stage and ran for more than 100 sold-out performances. Nine different companies toured the provinces simultaneously with unauthorized versions of the play. Dorothy joined Bruce's touring company in the original production.

Gilbert Vaughan, the hero, was a young Englishman of fortune who was totally blind as a result of a cataract. One midnight he strays into a strange house and walks in on a murder, hearing a scuffle and a woman's shrieks. Two years later, the cataract is operated upon and he recovers his sight. In a trip to Italy he falls in love and marries a young girl of extraordinary beauty, Pauline March. Her face "was fair as the moon; her figure as perfect as that of a Grecian statue," but her mind was flawed, "as much missing as a limb may be from a body." She seems to have lost her memory and has a "puzzled, strange look in those beautiful eyes ... sorrow and delight she seems incapable of feeling ... it was a child's mind in a woman's body."

Vaughan realizes that she is suffering from deep trauma, and the only cure is to find the cause. After many twists in the plot it turns out that she had witnessed the murder of her beloved brother; the same murder that he had witnessed. Horror-stricken, she lost her mind and blocked the past.

The leading part of Pauline had everything Dorothy could wish for. Pauline, seemingly mindless and often shrieking got up at night, and, moonstruck, sits at the piano and plays musical preludes brilliantly and faultlessly, or sings in a wonderful voice. Dorothy had to yo-yo from sanity to madness and back. She now did something few actors did then – some research. The previous year, in Italy, she visited a mental hospital to study madness. Now she went to the most famous asylum for the mentally ill in England, the Bethlehem, whose name gave the English language the word Bedlam. She visited the wards several times and spent hours witnessing the outbursts of dangerously ill mental patients.

The play opened at Exeter on August 22nd, 1884, and her first night reviews were triumphant: "in the poetical touching *role* allotted to her [she] evinces the delicate appreciativeness of a true *artiste* and the generous ardour of a heroine," wrote *The Exeter and Plymouth Gazette*.

Dorothy instantly shared her exhilaration with Leighton:

"Don't be frightened that I shall let all this praise turn my head. I know how much better it could be done, and after every scene a great weight falls on my heart that I have done no better. But I like you to warn me; it is good for me, so don't leave off, please. I am sorry that your friend, Lord Mount-Edgcumbe, will not see me, and that you had the bother of writing for nothing. Please do not fash yourself about finding out anyone else. I must leave off now, as it is time to go to the theatre, and you will not get this any sooner if it were posted to-night than to-morrow."

The following morning she resumed writing:

"To continue, our lodgings are very comfortable, and nearly opposite the theatre; the food is good, and very fairly cooked, but I am very pleased with the tuck parcel; we had one of the birds when we arrived, the other things we have hardly touched. I thought it better to save them for places where the food may be bad. Please send me Mr B. Tree's letter. [Herbert Beerbohm-Tree, a famous actor]. I thought as you think about its advice. Thank you so much for *your* kind advice and gentle reminders, I shall try so hard to remember all you have said to me at different times; and if I do become anything in the future, I shall owe all the best part of it to you."

Unfortunately, the letter did not survive in its entirety, and vital passages which could shed light on their relationship are missing. Did Dorothy feel close enough to address him as Fred or Freddy, and how did she sign? Did she use her nicknames or any terms of endearment? The letter was censured by Emily Barrington or by Leighton's sisters. Still, it is clear that they were very close and she felt free to share with him the trivialities of her daily life. She gave Leighton her itinerary telling him when she would be back in London, so that he could block in his diary the times she was free to meet and sit for him. He also had the addresses of the hotels where she was staying so that he could write and pamper her with parcels of delicacies. He wrote to his friends who lived in the countryside, urging them to go and see her. He also continued sending letters of recommendation to acquaintances from the profession, in an effort to secure her next employment.

Called Back was Dorothy Dene's first commercial appearance, and for the next eight months, she shuttled between Gloucester, Lancaster and Leighton's hometown of Scarborough. In each city, she was called again and again to take her bows: "a magnificent performance," "dramatic force and fire," her madness "was rigidly maintained with a reality which was most impressive." The *Citizen* found her physically suited to be mad Pauline: "we cannot imagine a more polished, and yet, vigorous representation of the part. It is perfect in every particular, and the audience was not slow to testify its approval." She was praised for avoiding the tendency to exaggerate: "Miss Dene, a lady who, although hitherto not well-known in York, has now earned a good reputation for herself by her delineation of the arduous and exacting character placed in her hands. Throughout, her acting is very powerful – in her natural self she is forcible in her scenes of madness. She gives one the impression of the dread reality," wrote the *York Herald*.

The review intrigued Oscar Wilde, who was visiting York on a lecture tour: "I've heard so much of Miss Dene's genius and beauty that I'm extremely anxious to see her," he wrote in a letter. "After my evening lecture I will be very glad to visit the theatre." His impressions did not survive.

Working continuously in the same company was every actor's dream, and Dorothy became part of the William Duck Company, under the auspices of Edgar Bruce. In Joseph Hatton's *The Vicar*, she was again a naïve ingénue, hesitating between two suitors. The pretty and virtuous Maggie, the ward of a vicar, is courted by two men: one is the vicar's son, the other an attractive lord, who is older than herself. Innocent and kind-hearted Maggie is trapped into an engagement with the vicar's son, not realizing that he is, in fact, an evil seducer, a gambler and a thief. Eventually, she discovers the truth and helps bring justice, finally marrying the true and kind lord. The *Era* commented that in just ten months on stage, Dorothy had wonderfully improved and has evidently "chosen a profession wherein she is likely to attain a good position. She struck the note of melancholy too soon, perhaps, but displayed unlooked-for emotional power in the last act. Beside the undoubted charms of a pretty face and figure, Miss Dene has a voice of varied modulation and expression. She is, perhaps, a little too fond of the lower register of her voice, but she was altogether a charming heroine."

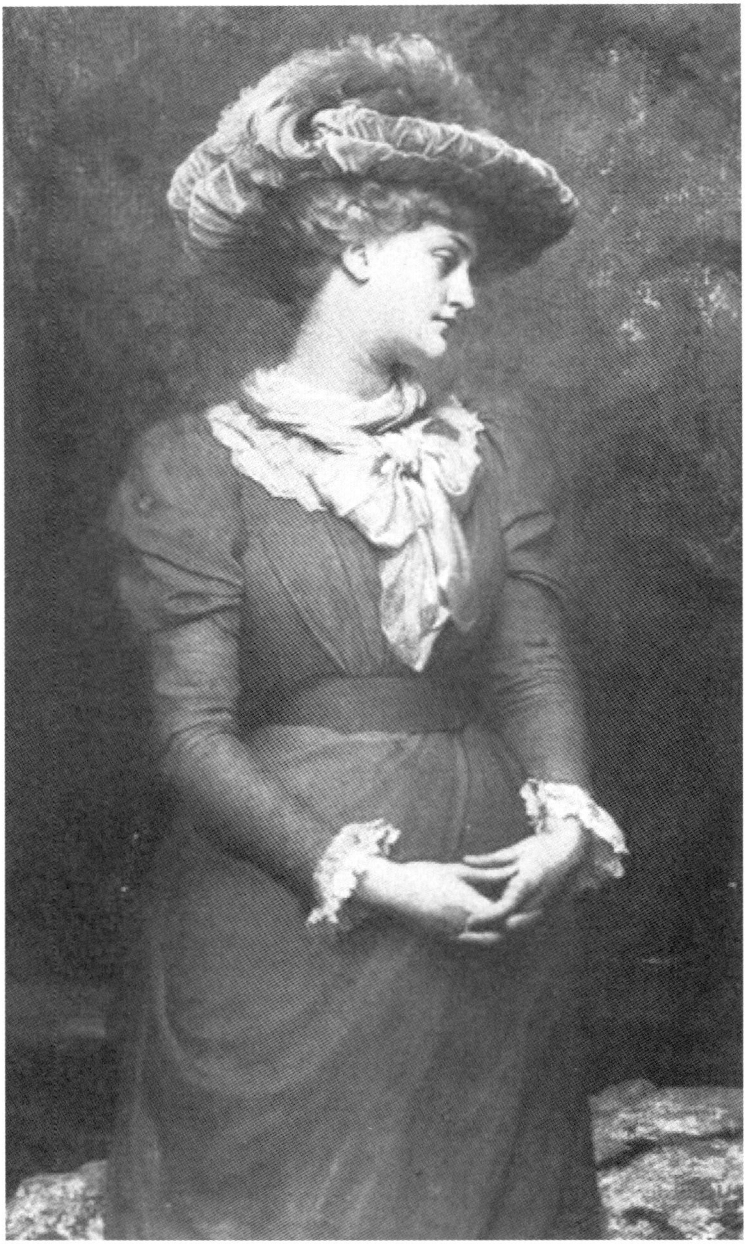

Serenely wandering in a trance of sober thought, 1885

Chapter Nine

"Too good to be true"

In the winter, Leighton made for Dorothy a sort of advertisement to be exhibited in the Royal Academy annual exhibition, perfect timing as a preview for her London stage debut in June. London's elite would be there.

"It is a figure of a beautiful girl, life size, half length, in an attitude of meditation by a stream – she is in a picturesque modern dress," he wrote to a prospective buyer. Leighton ordered for Dorothy a steely-blue outfit with a matching light silk bow which accentuated her neck. A belt hugged her slender waist. His generosity enabled her to develop an addiction for clothes, and a fetish for large picture-hats, so much so that he teasingly called her "the mushroom." It was not his only term of endearment – in fun he called her "the little teetotum."

For the sitting, Dorothy bought a wide-brimmed spectacular hat of velvet and feathers. She stood with her hands clasped before her, and in her pensive face there was a dreamy sweetness and languor. At this stage in her career, it was premature to expect the painting to bear her name. Leighton chose a poetic title which quoted a line from a love sonnet that the enamoured Keats dedicated to 18-year-old Georgiana Augusta Wylie, his young brother's fiancée:

> "Nymph of the downward smile and sidelong glance,
> In what diviner moments of the day
> Art thou most lovely? When gone far astray
> Into the labyrinths of sweet utterance?
> Or when sere serenely wandering in a trance
> Of sober thought?"

Weeks before the opening of the summer exhibition, Leighton would invite colleagues, friends, potential buyers and members of the press to his home, to give them a preview of his new works. The *Athenaeum* identified the model for *Serenely Wandering in a trance of sober thought* as Mary Anderson. The beautiful American actress was Dorothy's age and had become very famous since she had arrived in London in 1883. As a rule, Leighton did not disclose the identity of his models, perhaps because he did not want to make too much of their contribution to the work. He did not admit to having a preferred model and claimed that he was using several for each work. He might have ignored the *Athenaeum*'s blunder had it not been harmful to Dorothy, and he used the mistake in her favour. He wrote to the editor, F. G. Stephens, complaining that "I cannot of course contradict such a trifle myself – I who never rush into print – but if you care of your own reason and knowledge to correct the error in your gossip column it will perhaps be as well that the truth which does not always prevail should be made known." He identified the sitter as Miss Dorothy Dene and added that she was about to make her London stage debut. His letter was published in full in the next issue, and to appease the President, the editor added that "the sitter was a newer competitor for fame than Miss Anderson." The grapevine began to buzz. Gossip columns picked up the story. The painting stopped being that of an anonymous "nice quiet looking girl," but of an upcoming actress, the President's beautiful protégée.

Now that she was an actress, Leighton could invite Dorothy more easily to his soirees, musical events and "at homes," and to the gala nights at the Royal Academy. However, he was careful not to give her a lift in his carriage, and they arrived separately; she was usually accompanied by her sister Hetty. She was not overlooked though as he introduced her to his friends and became a welcome weekend guest at their homes even if he was not present. Society was curious as to the bachelor's next move. "It was somewhat amusing to observe at Academy soirees the greeting between the President and the professional beauty, who perhaps followed on the heels of a Bishop," wrote the journalist Mrs Frank Elliot. His circle noted that the twinkle in Leighton's eye was reserved for Dorothy.

Mary Anderson, who enjoyed the extra publicity, graciously told a journalist that "Dorothy Dene is the prettiest of them all. She is exquisite, charming ... I met her first at the reception at Sir Frederic Leighton's house. He was painting her portrait at the time, and was enthusiastic over her; indeed, it was he who made her fame. He exhibited her portrait at the Royal Academy, had people to meet her at his house, and continued to praise her until everyone joined in the chorus. You always feel with Dorothy Dene that she is too good to be true. She looks like an ideal head which some artist has painted, dreaming of a beauty he never hoped to see realized."

The paint was still wet when Leighton got an offer for *Serenely Wandering*. "The price without the copyright will be 800 guineas, with the copyright 1000 guineas", he wrote to the collector. "I mention these things so that you may be able when you have seen the work to say whether you desire to possess it." The work is untraced today, and only a black and white reproduction remains.

Next to *Serenely Wandering* Leighton showed Dorothy's pearly-white skin from her other, even softer profile. For this painting she sat on a red armchair wearing a large warm green velvet hat and a shawl of white silk trimmed with gold. Although Dorothy was in modern dress, Leighton named it *Phoebe*, after the Greek goddess of prophecy.

"To look at her is (for the male heart) to succumb instantly, and despair for evermore; whilst the bosoms of the fair would beat with a rare hatred, but that she is only a picture, this Phoebe, and not a woman," wrote the *Lloyd's Weekly*. *The Magazine of Art* implied that the artist had fallen in love with his creation: "There is about his work that odd, same haunting suggestion of the romance of Pygmalion." The current owner of the painting, the art expert and collector Fred Ross from New Jersey, is impressed with her regal elegance, which "accentuates her subtle expression of bemused interest and curiosity. The viewer is at once also curious about her circumstance and entranced by her vivid glowing features and riveting beauty."

The curtain rose on Dorothy's much-anticipated London debut in *Gringoire* on June 22nd. "Poor Dorothy was paralyzed with terror yesterday, but I hope that intelligent people will have seen through that," an anxious Leighton wrote to Mrs Barrington.

The press had no such anxieties declaring that Dorothy Dene "promises to become a rival to Mary Anderson and Mrs Langtry." In the English premiere of this successful French drama, Dorothy was again a beautiful innocent maiden, ten years younger than her actual age, courted by an evil French king, but finds her true love in a young romantic, idealistic poet. It was not much of a role, but the *Era* recognized her as "the one bright and shining light reflecting credit on the School of Dramatic Art," while *Bell's Life* complimented her talent and looks with which she "did full justice to the part of the impulsive and lovely Louise."

***

Since Dorothy's appearance on the Royal Academy walls as the naked Crenaia, there had been a marked increase in nude paintings, which provoked much objection. Already in 1857, the government brought in the Obscene Publications Act which professed to discern between nudes created for artistic purpose, and images used for sexual stimulation – mainly photographs imported from France. The architect of the anti-pornography statute, Lord Chief Justice Campbell, promised that serious works of art were not in danger, only those whose "single purpose of corrupting the morals of youth and of a nature calculated to shock the common feelings of decency in any well-regulated mind."

Opponents of the Act feared for free artistic expression. Lord Lyndhurst, son of the painter J. S. Copley, imagined a scene in which a policeman sees a print of Van Dyck's *Jupiter and Antiope* in a shop window. For the policeman, it is a picture of a stark naked woman held down by a rapist. So the law seizes the print, and the owner is summoned to court. When Leighton heard that T.C. Horsfall, co-founder of the Manchester Art Gallery, banned nude paintings, he wrote to him furiously: "that you should lay down a cornerstone of your scheme an enactment which would exclude by implication more than half the loftiest works we owe to art – nearly all Michelangelo, much of Raphael's best, Sebastiano del Piomba's *Raising of Lazarus*, Titian's *Bacchus and Ariadne*, Botticelli's *Birth of Venus* – this is indeed a measure from which I must most distinctly dissociate myself."

The dispute brought together diverse interest groups: the Church, social reformers, social purity groups and feminists. They all wanted to regulate what they saw as vice and immorality. In early 1885, the

Christian women's journal *Seeking and Saving*, launched a campaign to save female models, who were "always the poorest, the weakest in the great battle for life, the most likely to be vanquished by men's money ... constantly employed against woman's modesty." The public were urged to discourage any girl from entering the profession.

The arguments were not just in print. The opening of the summer exhibition was marred by a "scratching fiend" who damaged more than fifty paintings. A second and third attack followed. The Royal Academy listed the works, including two of Leighton's and gave details where exactly each cut was made, and how large it was. Dorothy's *Phoebe* suffered "a strong mark along the crimson leather of the chair and across the third finger of the hand," while Schmalz's *Elaine*, which featured her sister Edith, had "three scratches on the dress and another about an inch and a half long crossing the heel of the boot." To avoid scandal, the Academy withheld the identity of the one most affected: *White Hydrangea*, a frontal nude by Albert Moore.

Moore was unlucky. In 1869 he stopped painting nudes after his *Venus* was criticized for being repulsive. Now, when he had finally braced himself to do another nude, he was accused of depicting a voyeuristic scene as the young lady of the house went to the bathroom wearing only her cap, and surprised her parents' guests. It took him a week to repair his painting.

No one claimed responsibility for the attacks so theories spun wild. One blamed careless bonnet-wearing ladies getting too close to the paintings and scratching them with their hatpins; another pointed to spiky gentlemen's umbrellas. Some fanciful rumours suspected that at night the grand halls of the Academy saw cats chase rats and mice.

On May 20th 1885, two days after the first attack, the *Times* published "A Woman's Plea" signed by "A British Matron"; she complained that any woman who visited the Academy or the Grosvenor, hanging on the arm of a father, brother or lover, was bound to feel a burning sense of shame when suddenly confronted by so many nudes, causing visitors to "turn from them with disgust." The British matron was actually a man – J.C. Horsley, the treasurer of the Royal Academy, who had never painted a nude, and lost to Leighton in the race for presidency.

The incidents fuelled the debate over studying the nude in art schools. Old tropes returned. The nude model was described as a social victim, much like a prostitute who excited the animal passion of her male viewers. Some called on the public to boycott museums and galleries which exhibited nudes.

Another mysterious break-in occurred in October, when 150 nude drawings by life-class Academy students competing for the gold medal disappeared from a locked-up room. It was suggested that the British Matron came at night, dressed as a Greek Fury, and stole the key, but it was no joke for "the poor and struggling students who have looked to them for their chance of a first upward step in their profession."

Although he was due to preside over the prize giving, Leighton still kept silent. He was challenged again at the Church Congress at Portsmouth that month, when the melodramatic local vicar Frederick George Lee read a long letter he had written to Leighton. The vicar described the case of a wretched woman on the London streets, hearing that she could make easy money by modelling at a life-class at the Royal Academy, but the woman did not have the slightest notion of what would be required of her. When told to take off her clothes, she first refused, but then was bribed to consent. Finding herself "under the glare of gaslight, naked before 40 or 50 students, the poor frightened creature threw up her arms, and with a wild shriek fell fainting on the floor." When she came to, she flung the money on the ground and rushed from the life class in a storm of passion – "the outcome of a few remains of modesty she still possessed," thundered the vicar.

Everyone was waiting for Leighton's reaction, but although it was an attack on the institution that he was President of, and linked models and prostitution in a humiliating way for Dorothy, he said nothing. Others spoke on his behalf. His friend Marion Harry Spielmann, editor of the *Magazine of Art*, reprimanded Horsley for criticising Leighton for his nude paintings: "think of it! – the most statuesque, the purest, the most ideal painter of the human form in England, bombarded with the missives of this apologists for God's handiwork." The war of words went on.

Finally G.F. Watts gave an interview, stating that he speaks "not for myself alone, but also for Sir Frederic Leighton and others of my profession." Watts warned that "to abolish the model is to abolish all true art," and that it was absurd to consider sitting for a nude portrait as debasing. All the models he had known were extremely well-behaved women, "quite modest in their manner, and I have always treated them as I would treat any lady in the land." He had never known a girl to go wrong as a result of being a model; to think otherwise was an insult.

That autumn, however, saw juicy reports from Berlin regarding the Graf trial. Professor Graf, member of the Royal Academy of Art, was a distinguished historical and portrait painter. He had been in prison for six months, awaiting trial for taking liberties with a 14-year-old girl who was his model, and for having another girl "related to him in the double capacity of model and mistress." The 65 year-old artist "did not seek to deny that he had parted with very large sums of money to her and her family, and that he had also made other social sacrifices on her behalf; but contended that all this was done from purely platonic motives, and from the desire to secure the artistic services of so suitable and inestimable a model." He had been labouring for six years on *The Marchen*, a full length nude figure of exquisite and fairy-like beauty, but only when he met the 14 year-old girl, did he feel he had found a model who could realize his ideal. So, he had been obliged to bind her to him "by methods of fascination which, though naturally calculated to excite the suspicion of the world, were altogether harmless and honourable."

After nine days in court, Graf was acquitted, but "nothing can compensate him for the terrible torture of mind inflicted on him," concluded the *Times*.

***

Leighton's next assignment would become a kind of experimental laboratory with Dorothy. The American banker Henry Marquand was building a chateau-like mansion on Fifth Avenue and for the hefty sum of £2000, Leighton agreed to decorate the ceiling of his ostentatious Greek-style music room. Marquand was not just an important art collector and patron, but the president of the Metropolitan Museum, so it was a significant commission. As a subject, Leighton chose the Muses, all life-size, surrounded by cherubs and designed a monumental triptych.

He cast Dorothy in all five major roles: in the central panel, enthroned and leaning forward with one leg crossed over the other, she was Mnemosyne, the thoughtful mother of the muses. On her left Dorothy was Melpomene, the muse of tragedy – draped in slate-blue, her head bowed as she clasped a scroll in her right hand. She was also Thalia, the muse of comedy, in plum-red, looking upwards. In the right side panel, Dorothy was pirouetting and holding a tambourine as Terpsichore, the muse of dance, in a robe that left her right breast and shoulder bare. In the left panel she was Erato, the muse of lyric poetry, in pink and holding a garland of roses above her head. Lena had roles of her own as a cherub, standing on her toes, or playing the lute.

It was "one of the happiest things Leighton has ever put together," marvelled Alma-Tadema, who supervised the entire project. Leighton used the opportunity to demonstrate his protégée's full potential, as his great muse and as an actress who could do anything. In the coming years, he would work, and re-work, the same poses with Dorothy in several major works.

Leighton had made clay models as preparation for his more elaborate compositions, but had only made one statue so far, in 1877, the life-size and imposing *Athlete Wrestling with a Python.* Now he made two more: *The Sluggard* was inspired by Gaetano Valvona as he stretched his limbs after posing a long time. In contrast to the massive bronze muscular man was Lena's statuette, named *Needless Alarms*: it was identical to one of her poses for the ceiling of the music room. Leonora Lang of the *Art Journal* described it as "a little naked girl who is shrinking in wild terror from a toad – perhaps the toad who afterwards turned into a fairy prince." It was quite a comical scene since the girl's panic was exaggerated. The pose was very uncomfortable for Lena, who had to stand upright, looking over her shoulder while her body was twisted.

There was a growing market for small-scale sculptures to decorate bourgeois homes, and Millais admired the piece so much that Leighton swapped it with him for his *Shelling Peas* painting and made another for himself. However, there is something unsettling in this image of the eleven-year-old Lena, "just passing from the slenderness of girlhood to the fullness of womanhood," as the *Athenaeum* noted. It seems that

Leighton was racing against time to make the best of Lena before she reached puberty. She had been posing for him in the nude since she was five, but until now, it was always in the privacy of his studio as studies, and never for public display.

Who could permit a child to pose nude? Lewis Carroll photographed the three Hatch sisters, aged seven to nine, and the two Henderson girls, aged seven and eight. He had their parents' permission to photograph them but did not publish the photos during his life. As she had no parents, it was Lena's older siblings who gave consent for her. In the statuette, she holds her hands close to her chest, hiding her nipples, and her thighs are held together, guarding her still innocent sexuality. In the Victorian eye, however, *Needless Alarms* was applauded. "Sir Frederic has never done anything more charming, or that appealed to a large number of hearts in its familiar grace." The critics identified Lena as the model of Leighton's other work for the 1886 summer exhibition, the portrait of *Gulnihal*, looking bashfully sideways, in rich oriental silks: "more luscious than sugar, more fragile than Dresden china." *Fun* magazine still dismissed it as "an abominably bad example to students by exhibiting such a wretchedly-drawn piece of rubbish."

Lena's statuette paved the way for other artists to portray pubescent girls and boys, "showing the beauty of tender, undeveloped forms." After Leighton's death, it was cast in two dozen more copies in dark bronze, to answer collectors' demands – the latest was sold in December 2016 for £27,500.

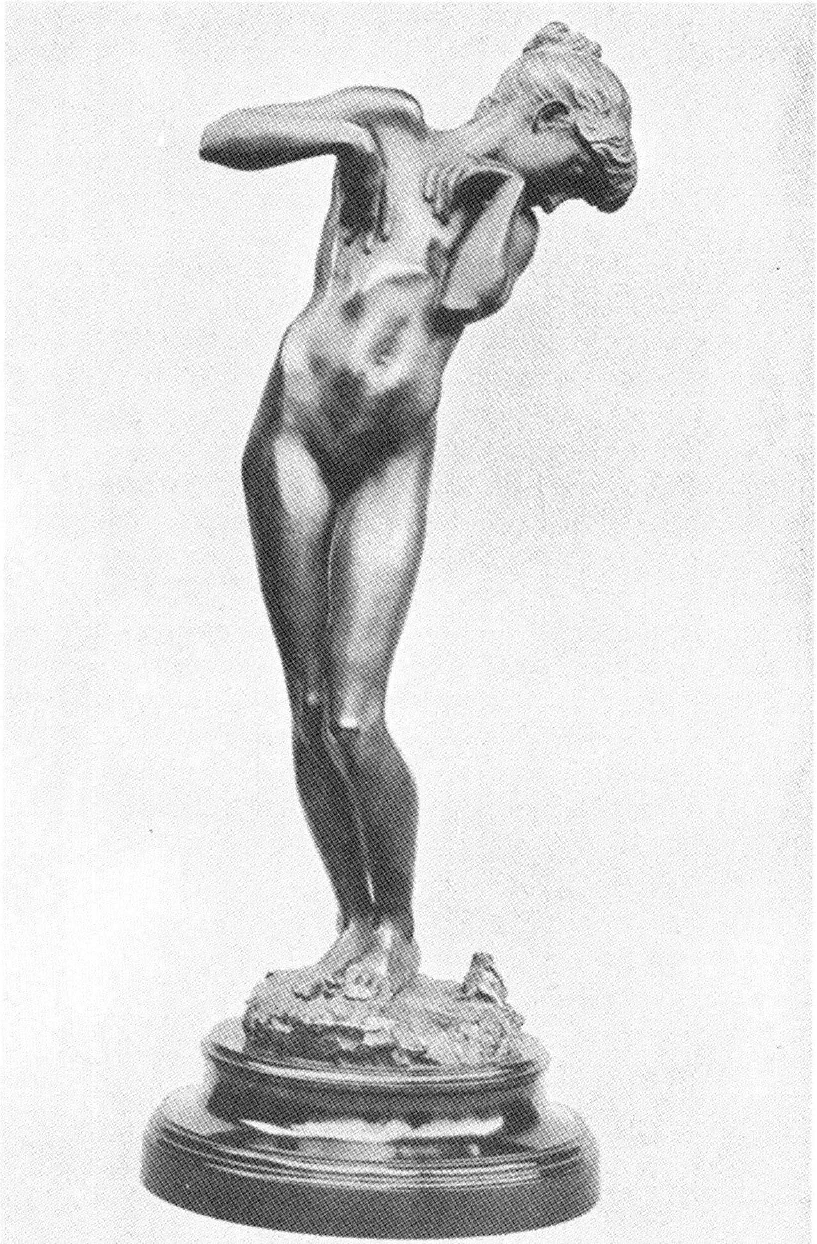

Lena in *Needless Alarms*, 1886

Chapter Ten

"Because of her personal worth"

Dorothy aspired to play tragic heroines, preferably Shakespearean, dying slowly and painfully, but she was not offered one. Instead, she was given sensational, sentimental, shallow roles which usually had a happy ending and were very popular at the box office. In Mark Quinton's melodrama, *In His Power*, she played a young wife living blissfully with her husband, who had no idea that she had been married before to an Italian crook who had deserted her and came back to blackmail and expose her as a bigamist.

Touring England and Scotland from September to December 1885 with the William Duck Company, Dorothy scored great reviews. "She acquitted herself admirably in the transitions from the joy which she feels in the possession of her husband's love to the despair which seizes her under the threats of her secret being revealed," marvelled the *Scotsman*, while the *Stage* described her "sweet sympathetic voice, not without the power on an intelligent audience."

Dorothy's two professions were inseparable. "To lovers of pictorial art her face will, doubtless, be familiar as the original of many of Sir Leighton's beautiful creations," wrote the *Hampshire Advertiser*. "If, as seems to be the case, her fame attends her as far in dramatic as in the sister art, her name as an actress bids fair to become as well-known as her beautiful presentment on the walls of the studio." Despite the excellent reviews and the press exposure, agents and theatre managers did not sign her up, not convinced that the hundreds of thousands who admired Dorothy Dene on canvas would flock to see her in the flesh. For the first months of 1886, she had no theatrical engagement. Leighton's financial support enabled her to be choosy and wait for a substantial classical role. In the long run, this strategy had its drawbacks, since it involved long periods of sitting at home missing out on the experience and connections that would have come if she had taken a more active part in theatrical life.

So she retreated to modelling and sat for Watts. It is challenging to recognize Dorothy in his iconic painting *Hope*. Watts always maintained that he never documented reality, was "above any particular model," and painted not the model's features but the impression that she made upon him. But Emily Barrington points to Dorothy in all but name: "A beautiful friend of mine." Barrington thought that "no ostensible portrait ever gave the essence of her personality, nor the suggestion of the dainty refined distinction which emanated from everything she was or did, as does the '*Hope*'."

Watts had been contemplating the subject for years but could only start when he was in despair; the one-year-old baby girl of Blanche, his beloved adopted daughter, had died. "The rare and distinguished personality of the lady who gave him sittings for *Hope* was the originator of the picture in Watts' brain, the inarticulate motive of the painting," wrote Emily Barrington. Aware of the way Dorothy had dealt with her family tragedies, Barrington and her friends "found her very intelligent and conscientious... and she enlisted our sympathies entirely." Watts painted a blindfolded and stricken young woman with short, fair hair, coiled on a globe, her head resting on a wrecked lyre, "all the strings of her instrument are broken but one, and she's trying to get all possible music out of the poor tinkle," he described it to a friend.

The picture was received with such enthusiasm when exhibited at the Grosvenor Gallery in May 1886, that Watts decided to give it to the nation; he then made a second *Hope*, which was somewhat less optimistic and without the faint star above the girl's head. It immediately acquired iconic status and still has it; it comforted Holocaust survivors, and Nelson Mandela hung a reproduction in his prison cell. The second-year Harvard law student, Barack Obama, heard a description of the painting in a sermon, given by Reverend Jeremiah Wright: though the harpist, sitting in rags, looks like "a victim of Hiroshima... the woman had the audacity to hope." Obama changed the phrase into "the audacity of hope", and made it the title of his keynote speech at the Democratic Convention in 2004, as well as the title of his second book.

One version of the painting is kept at Tate Britain, and another was sold by Christie's in 2001 for a million dollars.

Leighton admired the work so much that Watts gave him an oil sketch, which he hung in the silk room. Ten years later, he adopted *Hope* "as one of the sources for his late masterpiece *Flaming June*, in which the embryonic anticipation of Watts' coiled figure is released into a warm and sensual world of dreams," according to Dr. Nicholas Tromans, the chief curator of the Watts Gallery.

***

The fast pace of change – in sixty years the railways, the telegraph, the elevators, the telephone had been invented and people were flocking to growing towns where there was work – produced a yearning for the origins of civilization. Leighton was a major force in the revival of classicism in British art, dubbed "South Kensington Hellenism." He often painted mythological figures and was perceived as the artists' Zeus. In a caricature by the *Punch* cartoonist Edward Linley Sambourne, Leighton sits on his Olympian throne, attended by Royal Academicians, and to his left stands his female model in Crenaia's pose, trying not very hard to hide her nakedness.

Recent Greek archaeological discoveries were exhibited at the British Museum, and also had a profound influence on art and fashion. Greek dress was the new chic, "a rebellious reaction against an unhealthy orthodoxy in fashion," according to the classical expert Dr. Debbie Challis. It was said that letting women move freely without squashing their bust, buttocks and waist in corsets and stays was good for their health. *Liberty* department store sold Greek tunics and other comfortable costumes, inspired by sculptures in the British Museum and the Louvre, and endorsed by the wonderfully-named "the Rational Dress Association."

The explosion of neo-classicism in art and in fashion did not influence the theatre, and classical plays were not in demand. George Warr, Professor of Greek at King's College tried to change that. In 1883, using his own translations, he compiled a selection of the most dramatic scenes and monologues of Homer's *Iliad* and *Odyssey*. He named it *The Tale of Troy*, added songs and music and invited well-known artists, including Leighton, Poynter and Watts, to design sets and costumes.

Three years later, Warr added scenes from *The Story of Orestes.* At that time, a rival production was in preparation, John Todhunter's play, *Helena in Troas*, and Dorothy was invited to take part. It was tempting to share the stage with the celebrated acting duo Mr and Mrs Beerbohm-Tree and with Hermann Vezin, her former teacher; but she declined, since she was offered only a walk-on part. Her refusal paid off, for she got a much better deal from Professor Warr.

Leighton designed the opening scene in Warr's production, "Aphrodite's pledge redeemed," and at his suggestion, Dorothy received the two major roles. She was Cassandra, the tragic prophetess who foresaw her own death and the fall of her beloved country, Troy. "Nobody noticed her looks, as she was made up to look haggard and terrible" one critic wrote. She wore a wig of long dark hair – the Prince of Wales carped that it was "too black." In her other role, as Princess Nausicaa, she was dressed in a white tunic and purple cloak, a gold fillet round her hair. She was dancing and laughing with her maids when she stumbled on the naked Ulysses who was struck by her beauty. There were only few rehearsals, most of the cast were amateurs, and the director, Walter Crane, was really a painter. No one could give Dorothy any guidance, and she had to develop the two opposing roles all by herself.

On May 12th, 1886, a day before the premiere of Cassandra at the *Prince's Hall*, Dorothy rushed a letter to Crane:

"I write to ask your sanction for an alteration which I wish to make as far as my attitude is concerned in your beautiful tableau. If that tableau stood alone, I should not think of doing so; but it does not: it is a moment in a continuous dramatic action of the greatest difficulty, and which I have considered with the utmost care ever since the part has been in my hands – every step in the action has been considered, and one *must*, as I need hardly say to such an artist as you, flow out of the other. I propose to stand precisely where you place me, upright, and if possible, *statuesquely* my gaze riveted with intense prophetic emotion on Clytemnestra, but with my arms *down*, not *up*. This is to me of the utmost importance as a link in my performance – action comes later on, at the 'Woe, woe.' I feel sure that you will be willing for the performance as a whole to sacrifice this little detail, on which certainly your tableau does not depend."

Dorothy must have been desperate, having to make her suggestions in writing, at the very last moment. She comes across as polite but determined, pedantic up to the minutest detail, and not afraid to speak her own mind. She emphasized the value of the pose, the gaze, over action – the qualities needed on the model's podium. But although Crane thought that Dorothy distinguished herself by the passion and feeling that she threw into her role, he turned down her small request.

Leighton was busy promoting Dorothy, urging his many friends to buy tickets. To Robert Browning, who was about to attend the second night of the play, he wrote that he, Watts and a good many of their friends were interested in Dorothy, "not only on account of her abilities & her devotion to her Art but because of her personal worth." It was a rare intimate comment from the secretive Leighton. Dorothy was, for him, much more than a gifted and inspirational model and a talented and dedicated actress that should be nourished. It was her "personal worth" that won him over.

Leighton saw her in rehearsal, and probably heard her recitations in his studio; he assured Browning that he, too, would be very much struck by the manner in which Dorothy flung herself into the weird character of Cassandra. He asked Browning for a favour: "if you are, and of course only if you can do it in entire sincerity – would you grudge putting a word or two to that effect on a postcard which I may show her? it would be a great encouragement to a young artist at the outset of her career and would therefore I am sure be a grateful act to yourself – but she is too much of an artist to wish for a syllable said *only* out of kindness."

On May 13th, 1886, the *Prince's Hall* was packed with a fashionable audience headed by the royals and their entourage. The proceeds of the three shows would go to the Endowment Fund of King's and University Colleges, to enable men and women from poor backgrounds to study there. The *zeitgeist,* of the budding women's emancipation, corresponded with the depiction on stage of clever and beautiful Greek heroines, whose power was suppressed in a domineering male society.

The audience enjoyed watching dozens of pretty maidens in flowing drapery. One critic remarked that the costumes were rather revealing, and that Miss Dene stood out as not in the least embarrassed of her body. Her body, however, did not move much due to the tediously dry academic approach of Professor Warr. For him the text was all. The motionless cast recited endless monologues in verse. The audience yawned and fidgeted. "Boredom was writ large – boredom polite, but unmissable," wrote the *Era*.

Everything changed the moment Dorothy/Cassandra stormed on to the stage. "The delighted audience, released from an imprisonment of dullness, broke out like schoolboys into the fresh air of applause," the *Punch* critic reported. "Miss Dorothy Dene electrified them with her prophetic warning."

This was too much for Professor Warr. "Up he jumped, indifferent to the presence of the Prince and Princess of Wales, and to the beaming countenance of Sir Frederic Leighton, all of whom were vigorously applauding the delightful Dorothy. His face glared in the gaslight. His spectacles glistened like balls of fire. His classic forehead shone with indignation, and then he gave vent to these words, 'No! Applause! I won't have it!'"

Warr's behaviour startled the audience into silence. They thought they had been guilty of some shocking faux pas. "Recovering a moment later, a shameless old gentleman clapped his hands under his opera hat. The Professor popped up like a Jack-in-the-Box. 'I tell you! You mustn't!' A young lady tapped her fan against the opposite seat. 'This is shameful!' shouted the Professor. A graceful youth knocked his stick against the floor. The Professor leaped to his feet. 'How dare you do it! No applause!' Whereat the Royal Highnesses roared with laughter."

Dorothy's exceptional acting and the battle between the hysterical professor and the cheering audience were the talk of the town. *Punch* capped its review with a quarter-page drawing of *Serenely Wandering*: Dorothy's hat, face and shoulders, with the caption "An Ideal 'Rural" Dene', or Cassandra *chez elle*." Her roles united her two professions, modelling and acting: a freeze-framed image in the artist's studio, breathed into life on stage.

When she played Nausicaa, "everybody was astonished at her great beauty, especially when somebody recognized her as the model from which Sir Frederic Leighton, president of the Royal Academy, painted a strikingly beautiful female figure last year."

In her brief two-year career Dorothy had played only six roles, three of which were at a one-off matinee and three with a touring company in the provinces. So she took the London critics completely by surprise – no one expected the depth of her performance. They poured superlatives on her ability to lose herself in the character of Cassandra. It was tragedy as it should be acted, and poetry as it should be spoken.

"She had the accents of fire borrowed from the mysterious power of a prophetic spirit, flashes of terror, of hate, and of vengeance in her large eyes, sometimes filled with tears by the vision of the unhappy destiny of her country; she had a voice rich and melodious, and action broad and noble. These elements formed a harmonious whole of lines ably drawn, of meaning skilfully conveyed, and of feelings which, by their intensity, could not fail to meet at once with the sympathy of the spectators, and to find an echo in their hearts. Such a masterly creation would have done great credit to the most experienced of our actresses," wrote the *Town and Country Journal*.

After taking her bows, Dorothy changed out of her Greek robe into her little white dress, and slipped in among the dignitaries in the reception. Robert Browning spotted her and congratulated her warmly. "To listen to Miss Dene's blank verse is to me like listening to sweet music," he later said. That night, he wrote to Leighton enthusiastically that he had seen nothing like it since the days of the legendary French tragic actress, Mademoiselle Rachel. Leighton was quick to respond: "It was very kind of you to send me a little lively Pun about Miss Dene & kinder still to tell *her*, as she says you did, what you wrote to me– it will be indeed a pride and an encouragement of a high order to a young artist who is wholly devoted to her art & who tho' full of high aspirations is very humble in regard to what she yet can do." And he gave Browning's letter to Dorothy for keeps. Hence, the revered 74 year-old poet joined her growing fan club, and she joined the "Browning Society." The widowed poet was "a great flirt and proud of his conquests" and surrounded himself with a host of beautiful "lady friends." Their friendship ended only when Browning died three years later, "or not ended," as Dorothy told a reporter softly with pathos, "for I believe such friendships are eternal."

"Dramatic London is suffering from a Greek epidemic," noted one critic, when two days after Dorothy's triumph, the other production, *Helena in Troas* was performed, to nearly the same audience. "Happily, the Greek form of drama, as exemplified by culchaw's [culture's] latest fad, is not likely to become popular," wrote the London correspondent of the *New York Mirror*. Audiences needed modern plays as "our own drama fits us best." Plans to extend the production were dropped.

Still, there was one clear winner: a star was born. "When next Miss Dorothy Dene has an opportunity of showing her undoubted talent in a play that demands thought to conceive a character, and power to execute it, may I be there to see her. I promise to applaud her and shall not be deterred from that pleasant duty by fifty Professors of Greek or any other dead language," wrote *Punch*.

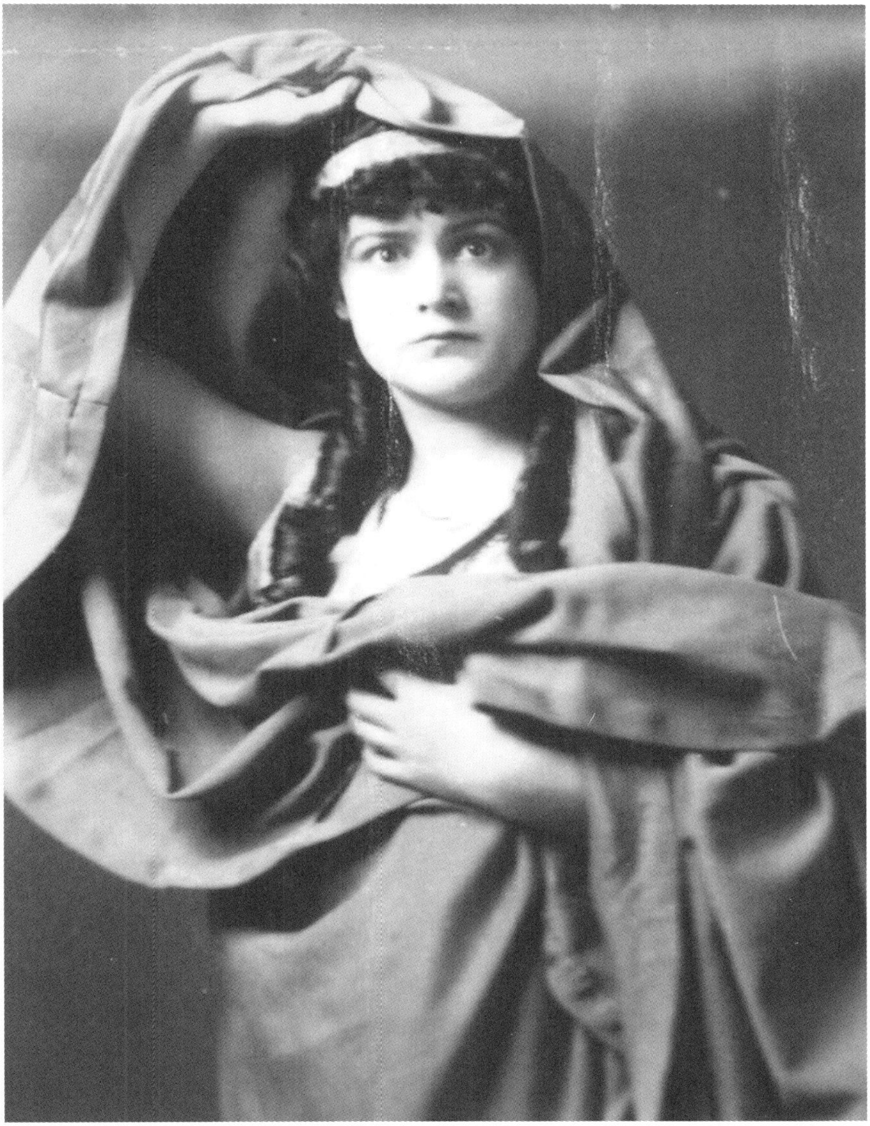

Dorothy Dene as Cassandra, 1886
Photo by Van der Weyde

Chapter Eleven

London went mad over her

Now, wherever I go, or wherever I've been,
I am met by the face of Miss Dorothy Dene;
By photographers' windows whenever I pass,
Fair Miss Dorothy Dene's is the face at the glass.
There are crowds that encumber the pavement I walk,
And Miss Dorothy Dene is their subject of talk;
All the papers are "solid" that Tragedy's queen
Is – or will be most shortly – Miss Dorothy Dene.
As a graceful Phoenician she charms us no less
Than when raving the *role* of a Trojan Princess;
And the fairest Nausicaa ever was seen,
Or the wildest Cassandra's Miss Dorothy Dene
There are Deans that reside by Cathedral Close greens;
There are blameless Deans Rural and Faculty Deans,
But the sheep of *their* pastures are scanty and lean
When compared with the flocks of Miss Dorothy Dene.
(*The Globe*, May 18, 1886)

Head of family, model, actress – Dorothy Dene now added Celebrity to her list of roles. She had to be a spectacular fashionista in order to be noticed and praised by the gossip press; she faced fierce competition from ladies born and bred to gala nights and who had rich husbands in tow.

Looking as if she had just stepped out of a painting gave her an advantage, and the elaborate descriptions of her outfits travelled as far as America and Australia. Women journalists acknowledged her picturesque taste and learned to distinguish between the different shades of her and Leighton's beloved colour; they usually liked what they saw. "Her gown was of blue satin, with fine stripes of white, and she wore a big shady Liberty hat, covered with silk of the same blue, and trimmed with long plumes of blue Ostrich feathers," wrote the *Whitby Gazette.* A bunch of Neapolitan violets flattered her swan-neck and gave this costume a final touch. She gloried in matching accessories for each outfit: jewellery, hats, furs, gloves, stockings and shoes. None of this came cheap.

Even in a crowd of 12,000 people who attended the annual fete of the Royal Botanic Society at Regent's Park, Dorothy was instantly spotted by the press: "Miss Dorothy Dene in one of the big hats (almost as large as a tent) which she generally affects looked not so well as usual." In a charity bazaar at Spencer House, she was singled out for her rich red flannel with a faint white line, a Norfolk jacket and an immense black-lace hat with a touch of red. The tiniest details inspired imitation: "This lady also wore a lovely Norwegian silver chatelaine. Chatelaines are coming into fashion again, and when of good quality, are a charming addition to any toilet."

At another charity bazaar, Dorothy presided over a stall that did a nice trade in engravings, "and I saw Sir Frederic Leighton glance with a look of recognition at an engraving of his own picture, for which she was the model," wrote the widely-syndicated columnist "Penelope." Leighton was nearly always there, "accidentally" passing by, nodding, exchanging a smile; Dorothy was always accompanied by one sister or another, who were also dressed to the nines.

Leighton encouraged her to adopt the aesthetic dress code for her everyday clothes, wearing simple-cut, comfortable, free-flowing dresses; for formal evening appearances she usually wore tight-fitting costumes corseted with frills and bows. When she dared to appear in aesthetic dress at the Grosvenor Gallery winter exhibition, the fashion police snapped: "Aesthetic, saucer-eyed, powdery-faced, Miss Dorothy Dene, who was clinging, as usual, to one of her limp sisters, Miss Dene's Liberty silks and gay gauzy garments are, no doubt, all right in the summer, but at this time of the year, they positively make one shiver."

***

Dorothy would often be recognised on the street and greeted, having to shake hands "with some or other Society friend". Celebrity made her accessible not only to the upper crust that frequented the Royal Academy and Theatre Land, but also to the 'masses'. "Everybody who is in the habit of walking about the regions of the fashionable shops and enjoying their attractions which they so kindly place on free exhibition in their windows must know the face of Miss Dorothy Dene," wrote the *New York Tribune*. Photographers began taking photos of her in July 1885 when she was revealed to be Leighton's darling model and made her London theatrical debut. In the thirst for fresh beauties, they were quick to spot a face that would sell a thousand photos; hers became hot-sellers, so she was asked to return to the studios again and again, to provide new poses in new outfits. By the summer of 1886 she was "the most be-photographed person in England at present. Neither Ellen Terry nor Mrs. Langtry approach her in popularity." The top of the profession courted her. She recreated *Serenely Wandering* with a wide-brimmed hat for William Downey, and was seen in her Cassandra gown in Henry Van der Weyde's studio. Van der Weyde, the American photographer who moved to London, pioneered the use of artificial light, which, shining behind her, allowed close-ups that enhanced Dorothy's large, lustrous eyes.

For the studio sessions, Dorothy did not wear the most ostentatious dresses and left her jewellery and accessories at home. There were some conventional romantic poses, such as a girl in her boudoir reading a love letter, but mostly head and shoulder shots. As a model, Leighton's admiring eyes made her taller, sensuous, and contemplative but somewhat detached. Van der Weyde stripped her of the frozen, grand gestures of the stage. As a result, Dorothy seems free and relaxed. In her flowing sleeveless summery dress, she looks straight at the viewer, not trying to bewitch or bedazzle.

Shop windows were filled with her photographs, and of all "the dangerous army of beauty, she has attracted the wandering gaze of passers-by of all ranks, from the haughty aristocrats to the admiring butcher-boy – for the pavement, 'equality' is no fable," wrote the *Court and Society Review*. Between her roles on stage and on Leighton's canvas, she scored the highest ratings as herself on camera. Art connoisseurs

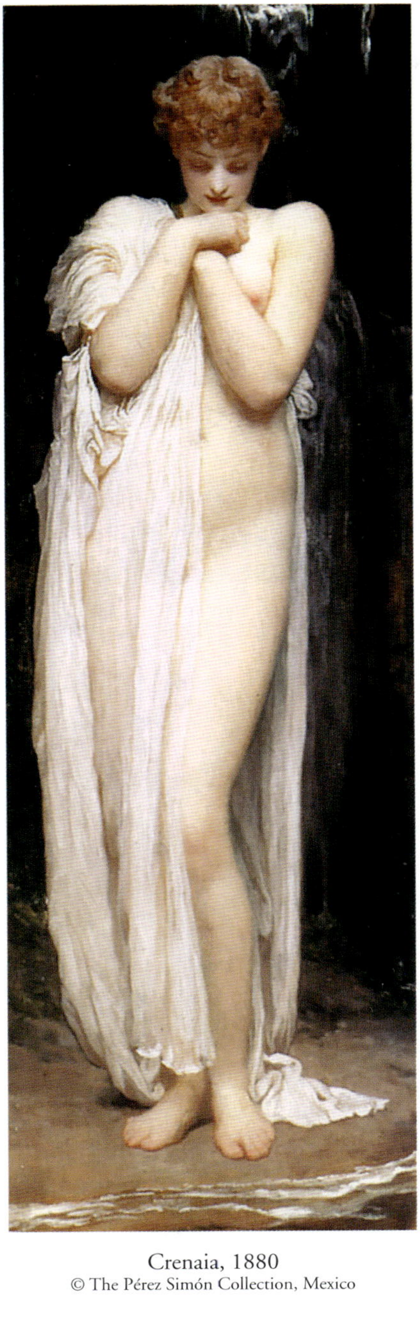

Crenaia, 1880

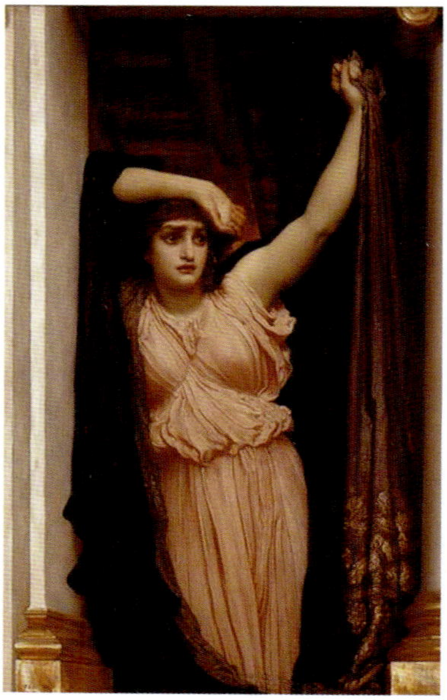

The last watch of Hero, 1887

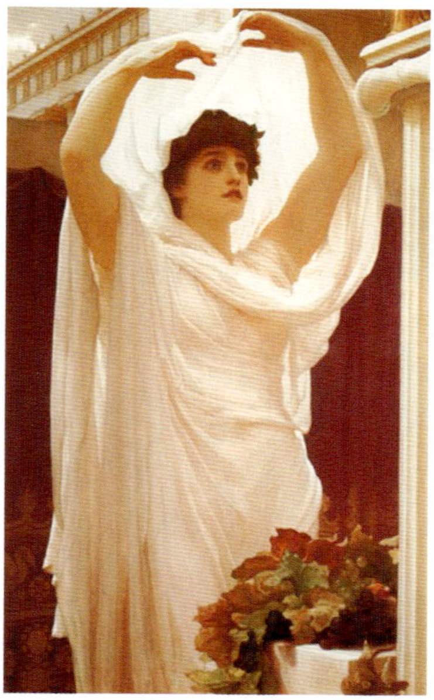

Invocation, 1889

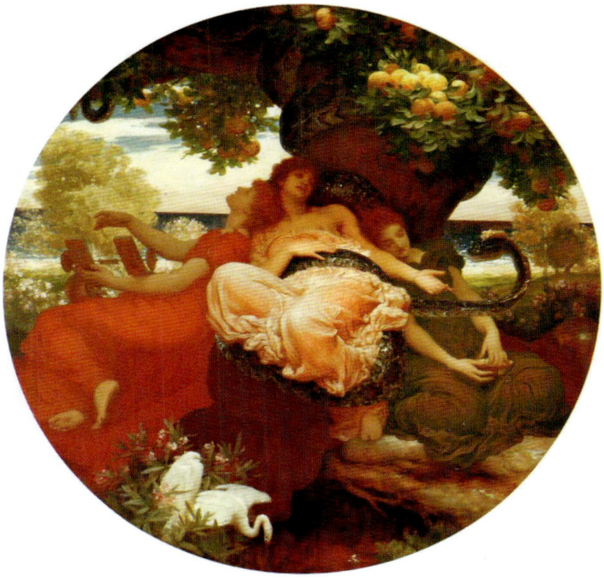

Hetty, Dorothy and Lena in the Garden of Hesperides, 1892

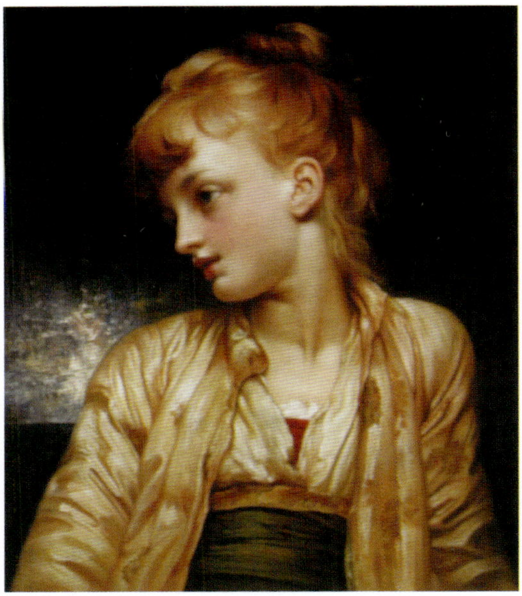

Lena Dene in Gulnihal, 1886

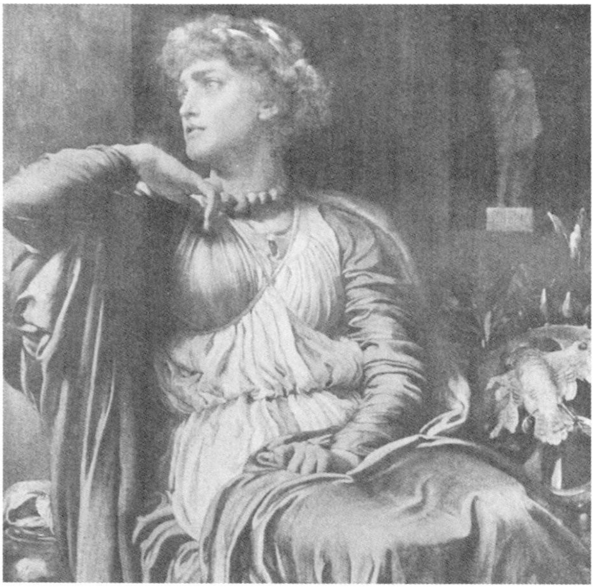
Hetty Dene as Simoetha the Sorceress, 1887

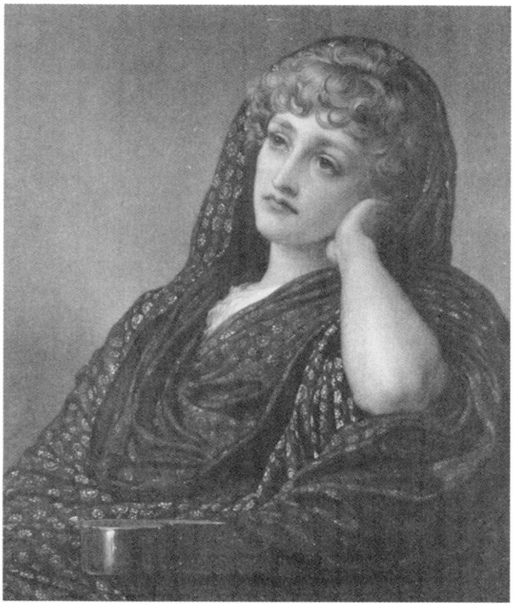
Edith Dene in Memories, 1883

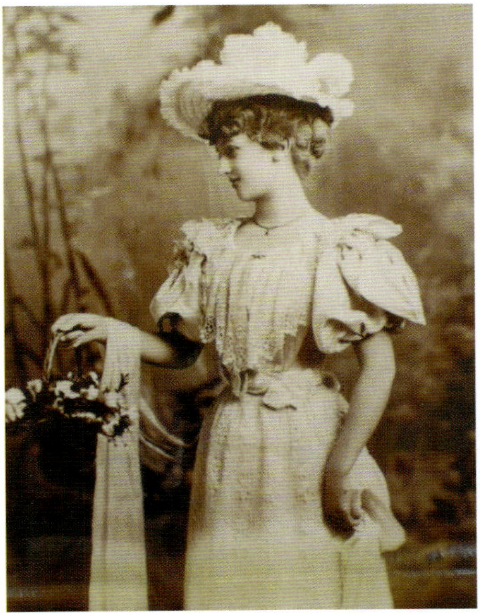

Kathleen, photo by James Lafayette, Dublin, 1895

No. 713.

Name and alias—**Kathleen Marvin.**

Residence—Uxbridge-road, Shepherd's Bush.

Place of business or where employed—none.

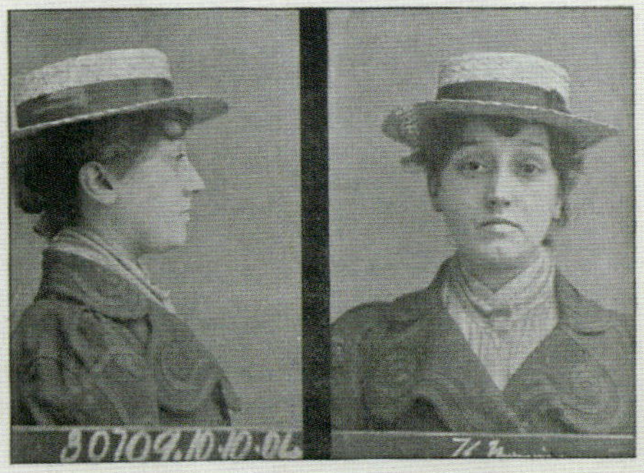

Age—28.

Height—5ft. 4in.

Build—slight.

Complexion—pale.

Hair—dark brown.

Eyes—hazel.

Shape of nose—straight.

Shape of face—long.

Peculiarities or marks—mole on right side of neck.

Profession or occupation—nil; married.

Date and nature of conviction—22nd December, 1904. Committed to a certified inebriate reformatory for 3 years.

Court at which convicted—Marylebone.

Remarks—frequents Edgware-road.

Police photo, 1904

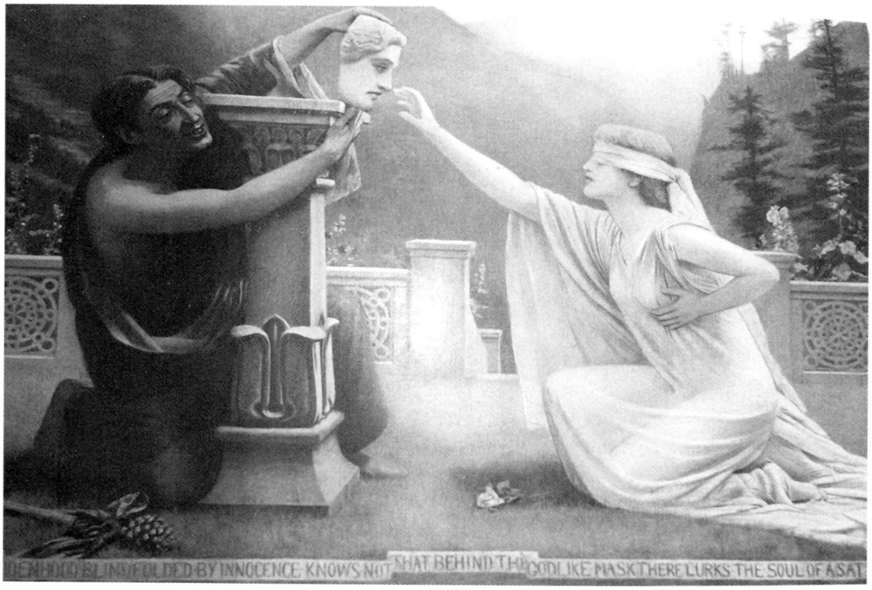

Love is Blind, by Herbert Schmalz, 1898

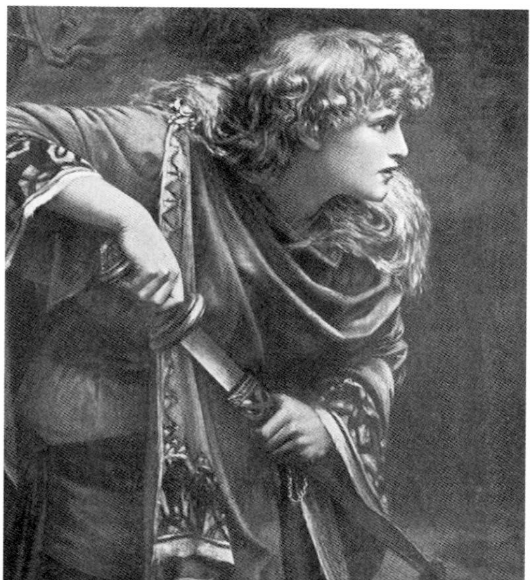

Edith Dene as *Imogen*, by Herbert Schmalz

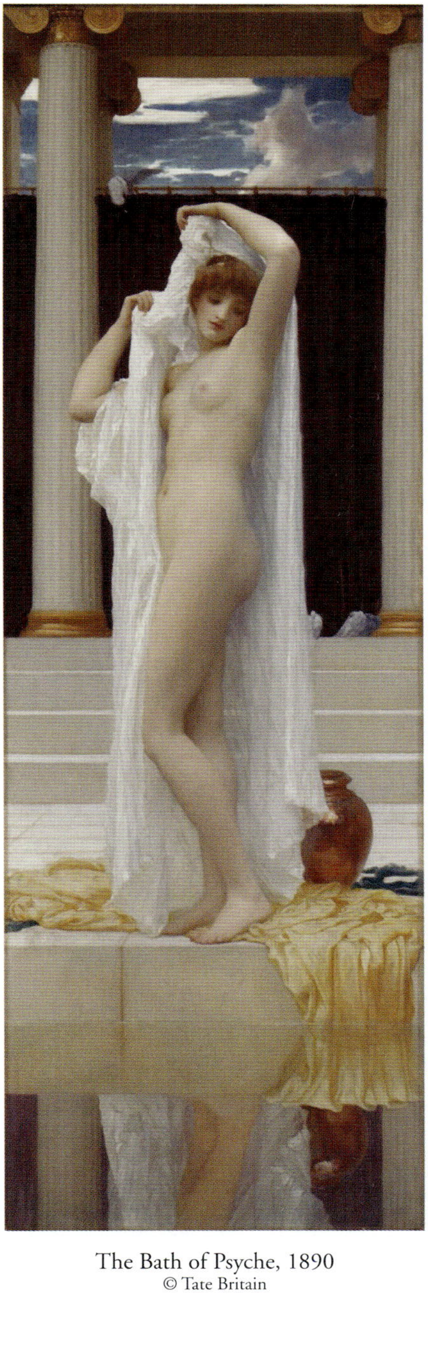

The Bath of Psyche, 1890

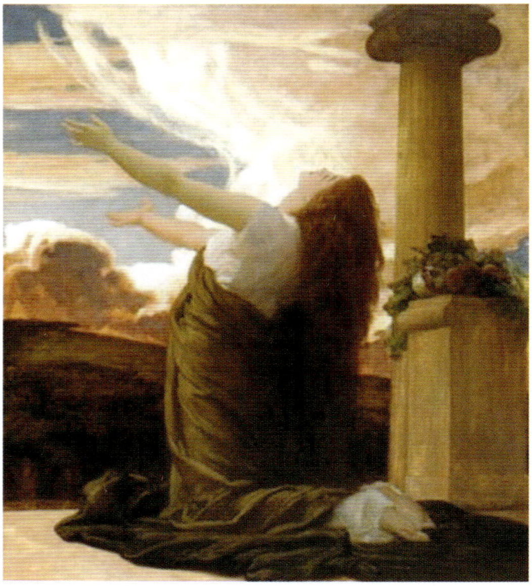

Clytie, 1895

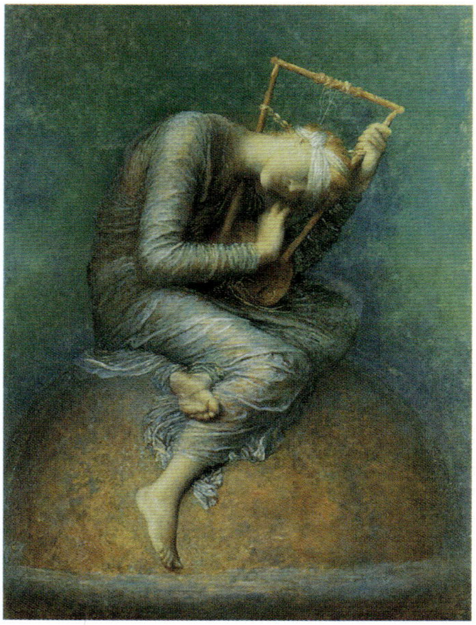

Hope, by G.F. Watts, 1886

warned that a photograph of an actress or of a professional beauty "will attract crowds who would fail to see any quality to be desired in a portrait by Millais." But having your photo taken was a sign that you have "arrived."

Most actresses had to pay to have their photo taken, others were given a bunch of prints in exchange for their sitting, but Dorothy was one the very few who received royalties from sales. Then as now, negatives were touched-up before printing, and wrinkles, puffiness and blemishes were erased. The *Graphic* warned that the public was often not seeing a true likeness. Reviews of her theatrical roles were now accompanied by photos, or by drawings based on the photos. When the *Court and Society Review* prepared an article about Dorothy, Leighton supplied an exquisite portrait of her in black and white chalk on brown paper, accentuating, as ever, her shiny, short curls, neck and soft, timid smile. The full-page drawing carried Leighton's flamboyant signature. Just a year earlier, he could not title a painting with Dorothy's name, but now he happily made her his explicit subject. Even the Princess of Wales wanted a piece of Dorothy, and Leighton gave her a study he had recently made of Dorothy in a Greek robe, holding an amphora. Leighton had just begun *Captive Andromache*, considered one of his greatest masterpieces, and he rarely gave out a study in such an early stage.

A popularity poll conducted by a penny weekly found that Nellie Farren – who excelled in comic male roles, was the most admired actress in Britain. She was followed by Ellen Terry and Mrs Kendall, and not far behind was Dorothy Dene, overtaking Mary Anderson. Dorothy was everywhere – on the stage, on the Royal Academy walls, and Victorians could decorate their homes with her photos and engravings of the paintings that she modelled; they could also visit dance halls and waltz to "Dorothy Dene" by Hermann Rosa. They could put their money on a "pretty little filly" named after her. Well into the mid-20th century, generations of race horses would carry her name.

The Dene household benefitted. Dorothy was paid handsomely by Leighton, made considerable money from the sale of her photographs, and was among the highest paid women in the theatre – a weekly salary of £30, twenty times as much as a model. *The Pall Mall Gazette*, however, thought that "success and prosperity are making Miss Dene plump, but she still poses with effect in the attitudes which Sir Frederic has immortalized in *Wedded* and other compositions." She was so linked with Leighton that she was even credited for pictures that she did not sit for, like *Wedded*.

***

Dorothy happily cooperated with the gossip press. The *Star* made a comprehensive survey of actresses' waistlines, concluding that third rate actresses "pinch and screw their waists to the smallest degree," while the prominent ones can afford to show a well-rounded figure. Ellen Terry had one of the widest waists – 28 inches, while Dorothy had a medium-range waistline of 24 inches. The press hailed her complexion as "the most beautiful of any woman in Europe" and asked her to share her secrets. She said that she never used cosmetics, hair bleachers, or anything that would be "likely to injure the freshness and charm of her loveliness. Of course, at times she must use a little red paint and sometimes white – one's parts require it you know – but she always goes to a Russian bath next day and has the last trace of it steamed out. She is very fond of going about in the rain, too, and lets it beat on her face." Returning home after a performance, she said that she never took anything but a cup of bouillon and a biscuit; on other evenings she would often sit up in bed until one o'clock in the morning "with a novel in her hand and a big plate of cake on her lap, she reads the novel and eats the cake; and the most astonishing part of it is, not that she doesn't have indigestion, but that she doesn't die, for with the cake she drinks quantities of chocolate. And now, out goes the light and down goes the curtain. The scene is done."

All the attention did not turn Dorothy's head. "Miss Dene is no mechanically trained puppet. She experiences to the full that absorption in her craft which every true artist must feel," wrote the *Court and Society Review*, who found her "agreeable and sweet-tempered as she's charming, and without the slightest self-consciousness of vanity." She was known to study assiduously for her stage roles.

In June 1886, a month after she had the audience at her feet as

Cassandra, she played a girl in a bizarre Bohemian household, sharing a flat with her male cousin and with a struggling musician whom she loves, as well as with a dog who gets shot. *Jack* adapted from the French, was the old mixture of love and money, which showed not very originally that "riches do not always bring content." She was again the star of the show, "over and over again she hit the right note, and stirred her audience," and was cheered to the echo. The Royalty Theatre, where *Jack* ran, was on Dean Street, and the *Fun* predicted that it will "be known as Dorothy Deane Street in the future."

But *Punch* rained on her parade: "Dorothy Dene is too good to be wasted on dog comedies and dog burlesques"; an actress like her, who has heart, voice and power, does unwisely to participate in "any entertainment initiated on frivolity, and based on bad taste." She was advised that if she avoided comedy, then in ten years' time all will bow to her as Priestess of the graver Muse.

The Illustrated London News blamed theatre managers and writers who overlooked her for better parts: "I cannot help thinking that with the actress will come the plays. *Phaedra, Hernani* and *Adrienne* were not considered 'revolting' when there was a Sarah Bernhardt to play in them. Our dramatists will be very unwise if they neglect to see the material that is blossoming, and that one day will illuminate their work." But the *Stage* threw the ball into Dorothy's court and raised the critical question: "whether she possesses that indisputable gift, *le temperament.*" This elusive quality – the artistic temperament – will indeed determine her future.

Her celebrity status and association with Leighton became an integral part of her theatrical reviews: "She is, I fancy, a friend of Sir Frederic Leighton. At least the president of the Royal Academy was there on Monday night, and evinced great interest in her," wrote the *Sheffield Daily Telegraph.* He was "much enamoured of her," hinted the *Country Gentleman,* and another concluded that "he makes no disguise that he positively worships the ground she treads on." The *Sporting Times* reporter noticed that Leighton "came to gaze at the fair face he has repeatedly immortalized." *Jack* was part of a double-bill, and Dorothy was much better received than Leighton's former model, Connie Gilchrist, who played rather badly in the other piece, *Mephisto.*

Connie would leave the stage in 1892, after marrying the Seventh Earl of Orkney.

The American Eben Plympton, co-star in *Jack*, was so keen on the play and on Dorothy, that he bought the American rights and invited her to join him. Crossing the Atlantic and touring the USA was every actor's dream. More money, more fame. Soon there was another, even more tempting offer, of a 30 weeks' coast-to-coast tour, including Canada, in Robert Louis Stevenson's thriller, *Deacon Brodie*. Leighton had always been interested in America and hoped to visit the country, and he took an active part in every plan of Dorothy's. When he received a letter from an American actor who came for a visit and asked to be introduced to Dorothy, Leighton consulted Robert Browning: "Would you very kindly tell me what you know of him? Has he any talent?" Dorothy was offered the leading female role in Thomas Talfourd's Greek tragedy *Ion*. Leighton had read the play years earlier but could not remember whether it was fine or "whether the woman's part is a good one, – perhaps if both are fine it might be worthwhile to act even with a bad actor."

But Dorothy turned everything down. She would not go to America until after she had fixed herself "still more firmly on her pedestal in England and added experience to that she has already gained." New York seemed to her more judgmental than London, and she did not "propose to risk making a failure on one side of the water."

***

Dorothy was the hottest name in the summer of 1886 and applauded even before opening her mouth. "Dorothy Dene rose superior to anything she has yet done and gave a powerful and emotional bit of acting that has rarely been surpassed," wrote *Reynold's Newspaper* about her next role, in *Love's Martyrdom* by Alfred Calmour. The play was based on an ancient legend; the hero, Lord Marston, was a desperately wounded warrior, returning home after fighting on the wrong side of a conflict. Afraid of being called a traitor, he makes his young wife swear that she would kill him rather than let him fall into the hands of his enemies. As he sleeps, exhausted, she hears soldiers approaching. She tries to wake him up, but when she cannot, she stabs him in his heart, as she promised. But then she finds out the footsteps she heard were not enemies but friends.

"She played with much dignity ... and the trying lullaby to her wounded husband was charmingly sung," wrote the *Pall Mall Gazette.* The review also praised her for showing remarkable tragic power when she was still so young. The play ends when she understands her mistake and turns the dagger on herself. Melodrama at its finest! One evening, at the crucial moment, Dorothy, groping on the floor for the dagger, failed to find it and had to "kill" herself with her two hands clenched one above the other. "Still, it says much for the genuine power of the young lady that nobody laughed," wrote *Funny Folks.*

Comedy was the more lucrative theatrical genre and Dorothy had to comply. She was first in *Cousin Dick* – a role that she had played already as a student – and then in a new play, *Noah's Ark* by Harry Paulton. She was the beautiful and gentle niece who is about to inherit a colliery. The critics loved her funny side but the part was "hardly worthy of her." Once again, she put effort into a play which did not survive beyond the opening night.

Later that year, just before Christmas, finally came a lead role which was to be one of her career peaks – Maud Deveson, a dutiful, loving daughter who is supposed to save her father from bankruptcy by marrying his enemy's son. When the son suddenly dies, she is suspected of murdering him. *The Noble Vagabond* was written by the prolific Henry Arthur Jones, and boasted a mad woman in the cellar, money, violence, love and mistaken identities. The critics could not agree on the merits of the work, but they were united in their praise of her – "I shall tell all my friends to go and see this piece for the sake of Miss Dorothy Dene's performance," wrote *Punch,* "I much doubt whether there is anybody of her youthful standing on the stage who could have played this part half as well." One critic predicted that "perhaps the day will come when she will become famous as Lady Macbeth."

The Noble Vagabond was the longest running play that she ever took part in – over a hundred performances, and London audiences adored her. She told William Archer, the theatre critic and writer, that she continued elaborating and improving the part night after night, until about the fiftieth performance, and then could do no more. He asked her whether playing such a long run has made the part nauseating: "If I once liked a part, I always like it," she said. She loved playing Maud so much that on her last night, "I had the great difficulty in restraining my tears through the performance; so grieved was I at relinquishing it."

Archer, who stressed that "I am an amateur psychologist," set out to bring psychological realism to British theatre and composed a very detailed questionnaire about the psychology of acting. He sent it to scores of actors in England and France, "not only 'actors of the highest order', but every intelligent artist who studies himself and others." Dorothy's questionnaire, in self-assured handwriting, had survived. She had left blank most questions about comedy, as if she had no knowledge or experience of the genre, and no desire to explore it. Archer asked if in scenes of emotion in real life, like standing at the death bed of a relative, she memorized her feelings for subsequent use on stage. "Yes – but quite against my will," Dorothy answered candidly.

"In moving situations, do tears come into your eyes?"–"yes, precisely," she answered. She wrote that in order to portray an emotional state exactly on time, she stands in the wings "several minutes before I am mounted and mentally going through the scene I am about to do!"

Archer wanted to know if a "part of your mind is intent on the character, while another part is watching the audience," and Dorothy's answer was, "I never see the audience when I am acting." She comes across as a totally absorbed actress, turning pale in scenes of terror and of anger and physically exhausted after an emotional scene. Archer used his findings for his book, *Masks or Faces*, which inspired Stanislavski and Lee Strasberg's Method.

Chapter Twelve

"Those well-formed maidens"

One evening, as Dorothy was preparing to play Maud in *The Noble Vagabond*, the 17-year-old theatre's call-boy, Alfred Edward Matthews was sent to fetch her. "I realized that he [Leighton] had made an excellent choice when I called her for the overture one night and, receiving no reply, opened the dressing-room door and looked in. She was posing naked in front of her long mirror! I started to apologize, but she cut me short with, 'That's all right – but get out!' then, as I kept on apologizing (for I'd never seen anything quite so pleasant), she had to push me out," wrote Matthews, who became a well-known stage and

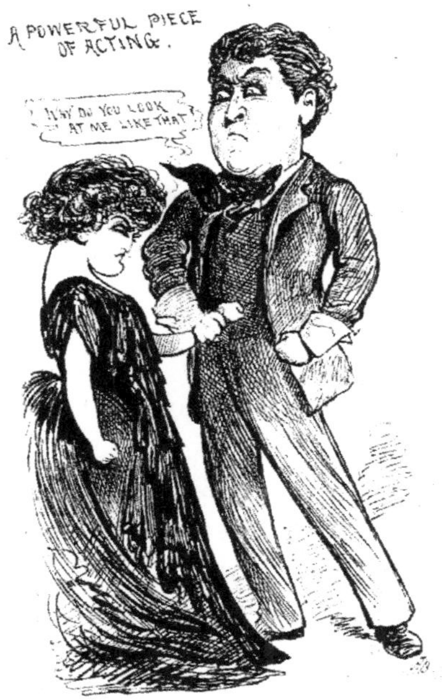

Caricature of the Noble Vagabond, *The Illustrated London News*, January 1887

film actor whose credits include *Carry On Admiral*, *Doctor at Large*, and *Around the World in 80 Days*.

Three years into her acting career, Dorothy was still unable to shake off her model's mannerisms and the pathos learned at her drama school. Why does she continually throw up her head and draw attention to her neck, "though as a neck nothing can be said against it," jabbed a critic. The studio was seen as an unhealthy contrast to the theatre as it put her centre-stage with no competitors, a still life with one frozen expression. Most models who gravitated to the stage left the artist's studio and only rarely did they return, primarily to have their portraits in their new profession.

Reviewing *The Noble Vagabond*, the *Fun* thought that Dorothy would be a better actress "when she has almost forgotten that she ever sat as a model to Sir Frederic Leighton and ceases to 'drape' herself as if she might be called upon to do so again at any moment."

But Dorothy owed so much to Leighton that leaving his studio was unthinkable although working with him took much of her time and energy. She clearly enjoyed modelling for him, seeing herself on canvas and then being watched by multitudes, more than any actress could expect in the theatre. Leighton must have known that in order to succeed, she would have to immerse herself entirely in the theatre, but he was selfish enough not to release her for a full stage career. Now that she was on the rise, they both looked forward to strengthening their partnership even further.

***

In her first stage roles, Dorothy had been fidgety and nervous, but experience made her stronger, more tender and passionate. She brought it all back to his studio. Leighton gave her the roles that, after her triumph as Cassandra, no theatre manager offered her yet. He cast her as Hero, a virgin priestess of Venus who lived in a tower. Tempted by the sweet words of the brave Leander, she would wait for him every night as he swam across the strait, guided by the torch she lit for him. They spent a secret blissful summer, until one stormy winter night the wind blew out Hero's light. Leighton chose to portray the tragic climax: Hero standing at the window until dawn, worn and weary as she scans the tempestuous sea, with fearful and tearful eyes open wide. All her hopes have drowned with her lover. The drama was projected not only in her face – her entire body expressed the weariness that comes from standing motionless for hours on end. Leighton added a small panel beneath the painting with the sequel to the story, showing the drowned Leander at the foot of the turret. When she sees his body, Hero jumps to her death.

In a letter to Charles Pooley of the Manchester Art Gallery, Leighton revealed that he owed Hero's expression "entirely to the kindness of that very gifted young actress, Miss Dorothy Dene." He did not miss the opportunity to champion his protégée and added that he has a very high regard for her and that she and her sisters "are great friends of mine and of many of my friends and I have known them since she was well back in her teens." Not that Leighton was weak on dates, he simply saw her as much younger than her years and felt that they have been together for ages.

The *Manchester Guardian* marvelled at the painting: "It is years since the President has done anything so good as this; in one respect – that is, in expression – we doubt whether he has ever equalled it before. In this, no doubt, he was helped to some extent by his model. She is understood to have been Miss Dorothy Dene, who is gifted with a power to fix her features into any required look that is quite unusual."

In 1887, The *Pall Mall Gazette* held a competition, asking readers to choose the best pictures of the year. In the category "the picture you would best like to live with," *The Last Watch of Hero* came fourth. The Manchester Art Gallery bought the painting even before it was shown in London. 26 years later, in April 1913, it was damaged by three Suffragettes, who attacked works in the gallery in protest against the sentencing of Emmeline Pankhurst to three years.

Leighton's next tragic subject came from a little-known text by the Greek poet Theocritus; Simoetha the Sorceress had lost her virginity and was then deserted by her lover. She sits by the window, and at her side her witchcraft tools – a wheel with a bird fastened to it, and the image of her lover stuck through and through with pins. A cruel expression is in her light blue eyes, her right hand clutching angrily at the beads around her neck. Reviewing Leighton's fresco for the South

Kensington Museum, George Bernard Shaw branded him as superficial for having chosen to portray, as the quintessential Arts of Peace, rich ladies beautifying themselves.

Now, six month later, facing *Hero* and *Simoetha*, Shaw changed his opinion saying that: "perhaps widening wisdom and disillusion are making another man of Sir Frederic. Pretty ladies who wish to be portrayed with waxen cheeks and jellied ear tips" should go to other artists. "For the presidential touch with women grows stern: they come from his hand terrible and sibylline." At last, Leighton seemed to infuse passion into faces and figures, and "he seems to have gone back to the best period of his youthful promise."

Leighton was in unusually good spirits at the private view at the Royal Academy. He was standing with Robert Browning who was "looking well, and parleying with endless persons of importance, and Miss Dorothy Dene was the beauty of the afternoon and threw a sympathetic glance at the President's 'Simoetha' as she passed it." Leighton's model now had a name and identity, and it influenced the way his pictures were seen. The interest shifted from the fresh works of Leighton to the new look of his model. Visitors to Burlington House played some kind of charade as they tried to guess in which of the president's paintings Dorothy Dene was hiding. Even art critics found it hard to disentangle the living woman from the painted one. *The Jealousy of Simoetha*, for example, was seen by Shaw as "Miss Dorothy Dene in one of her tragic moments," and the *Art Journal* described it as "a successful half-length portrait of Miss Dene in a fury." The knuckles of her right hand would inflict "terrible punishment on any giddy masher rash enough to sauce her," mocked the *Fun*. For the special supplement of the finest pictures of 1887, the *Gazette* persuaded Leighton "to lend his original studies for Simoetha (alias Dorothy Dene) and for Hero, which was sketched first from the nude and then clothed upon."

As it happens Shaw and all the others credited the wrong woman. The model for Simoetha was not Dorothy, but her sister Hetty who was eight years younger. "The face of Simoetha is that of the third of those well-formed maidens" wrote Leighton to Robert Browning, who knew all the Dene sisters. It was another case of mistaken identity, caused by the exceptional similarity between the girls, and by the predominance of Dorothy in Leighton's work.

That year, the youngest sister Lena also featured on the Royal Academy walls: in *Yasmeenah*, (Jasmine), the 12-year-old wore a white silk oriental dress, holding peacock feathers. *Profile of a Fair-haired Girl*, which was very similar to *Gulnihal*, showed her from the back, probably to avoid signs of her puberty. Robert Browning, who saw the work at Leighton's studio just before it was sent to the Academy, was so enchanted with the young model that he wrote these lines:

> "Yellow and pale as ripened corn
> Which Autumn's kiss frees, – grain from sheath,
> Such was her hair, while her eyes beneath
> Showed Spring's faint violets freshly born."

Naively, Browning sent the poem anonymously, but Leighton recognized his crest on the envelope and thanked him "warmly for sending me such a beautiful 'epigram', the little girl with 'faint violets' for eyes is the younger sister of the Miss Dene to whom you have been so kind." The epigram was added to the exhibition catalogue and the title of the painting was changed to *Yellow and pale as ripened corn.*

Yet another sister Edith was also represented on the Royal Academy walls, in Herbert Schmaltz's painting, *Widowed.* The 22-year-old was introduced to him by Dorothy. Schmalz was notorious for his schmaltzy, melodramatic historical paintings, and Edith had been sitting for him since 1883, when she was the broken-hearted Elaine, watching Sir Lancelot disappear. Now she was the fair-haired Queen of the Vikings, standing on the seashore with her young children beside her, welcoming the warriors returning from battle, led by her son, and asking, "Where is my Lord, the King?"

Schmalz was entranced and painted Edith also in a contemporary dress of moss green, set to bring out the delicate tones of her skin and the copper-gold of her magnificent, wavy long hair, her mouth finely curved and disdainful. But *Dreams of Yesterday*, at the rival Grosvenor Gallery, was jeered at. "We object to work of this kind," wrote *The Spectator*, "not only because of its fashionable and trivial character, but for its affected, morbid sentiment, and its utter absence of all genuine human emotion."

In February 1888, the sisters and their painters were present at the Graphic Gallery in Brook Street. The *Graphic* magazine invited 21 prominent artists to paint their favourite Shakespearean heroines. Leighton dressed Dorothy as Desdemona listening to the unseen Othello as he spells out his fascinating adventures. Her chin rests in her hand, her brow slightly knit and her eyes wide open. Schmalz chose a scene from *Cymbeline*, and painted Edith as Imogen, drawing her sword as she cautiously enters the cave of Belarius: "Maidenly timidity is well expressed in action of the figure, as well as the finely formed face," praised the *Graphic*. Schmalz's painting was considered the finest in the exhibition, while Leighton was criticized for his shallowness: "the canvas is full of prettiness and purity and dainty girlish grace, but why 'Desdemona'? Why not simply 'a lady listening'?"

Keen on being seen as an actress, Dorothy only modelled for Leighton with one exception. She remained loyal to the woman who gave her the first chance, Louisa Starr-Canziani. *Love in her eyes sits dreaming* was soon known as "a bust portrait of Dorothy Dene." The downcast eyes did not reflect Dorothy's personality; it was rather, the favourite pose of Starr-Canziani for her sitters.

***

Four hundred distinguished guests were invited in July 1887 to Pope's Villa, in Twickenham, the home of the MP and journalist Henry Labouchere and his actress-director wife Henrietta. The magnificent gardens were the perfect backdrop for the woodland scenes from *A Midsummer Night's Dream*. The stage was set under an old tree with gnarled roots, and electric lights were hidden in the branches so it looked like a monster umbrella. An artificial moon was prepared, in case the real one "should hide her silver face behind a cloud." Open air performances of Shakespeare usually took place in the afternoon, but the show was scheduled for 9 pm, to create a magical, mystic atmosphere, appropriate for Oberon and Titania. The audience sat in almost complete darkness, until the lights suddenly came on. A murmur of admiration arose. Dorothy emerged as the love-sick Helena, in a Greek dress designed by Leighton, and her flattering white draperies were embroidered in silver thread. At last, she had a Shakespearian role, but to her dismay she was not reviewed for her acting but for her looks: "Her graceful throat, and head well-poised, perfectly symmetrical, having already appeared and reappeared, and appeared again in our most famous contemporary pictures," wrote the *Northern Echo.*

After the performance, a select group, including Leighton and Dorothy, were invited inside for supper. Everyone was under the spell of fairyland still, and Leighton enjoyed watching Dorothy mingle so naturally, pleased that "she is adding, as she deserves, to the number of her friends, several of whom treat her with really maternal kindness." The success encouraged the Laboucheres to repeat the performance the next year when rain nearly ruined it. Dorothy declared her love misery on the soaking grass; the leaves of the trees were loaded with water, "each dew drop being turned into a flashing diamond of light." The play eventually reached the Albert Hall, and Dorothy's "statuesque figure and earnest acting were valuable to her excellent performance as Helena," wrote the *Era.*

In her next play, *A Secret Foe*, by the American actor-dramatist John A. Stevens, Dorothy played Olga Demidof, a Russian beauty who is pursued by two suitors; she marries one and makes the other an enemy for life. The play gurgled with sex, gambling and attempted rape, "such an absurd piece of bombastic work from beginning to end that it is difficult to be serious when discussing it," slaughtered *The Stage.* The audience laughed at the tragedy and sneered at the humour. Most critics were angry that a New Yorker thought that he could export such trash to London; Americans were warned that if they brought one more such piece, the relations between the two countries would be severed. And indeed, though Dorothy did her best, her acting was strained and unnatural. Leighton looked on gravely from the centre of the stalls, growing greyer and gloomier every minute. Dorothy – "a maiden of whom we are all proud" – was perceived as victim of shoddy theatre: "they must not make her ridiculous, or the Royal Academy will know the reason why," threatened the *Country Gentleman.* The critics were happy to notice, though, that she was beginning to forget the artist's studio, posed less and seemed less conscious of wearing pretty gowns.

Shaking off the model's mannerisms did not shake off the image of Dorothy which stuck in people's minds. The radiant face and shapely figure Leighton painted was constantly compared to her stage presence, not always in her favour: she was plump, wrote one reviewer, and another was sorry that her beauties were "threatened by premature adiposity."

Gossip was always twirling: she is a friend of Sir Frederic Leighton, he has great interest in her, he is enamoured, and he positively worships the ground she treads on. Like others at the time, *The Pall Mall Gazette* critic who wrongly identified Dorothy as Simoetha, hinted of the relationship between her and Leighton: "the President has clearly been fortunate in persuading his old model Miss Dorothy Dene to sit for the character." The reviewer added, cunningly, that unlike Simoetha, Dorothy did not bring out her desire strongly enough, since she "has none of the weird faith of the sorceress who turned her magic wheel to draw her lover home." All of this did not make Leighton less enthused about Dorothy.

Was it just a coincidence that at that time, Spielmann, the editor of the *Magazine of Art* and a friend of Leighton, published an article on the relationship between artists and their models? He wrote: "more than one member of the Academy, at the present day, can boast of a wife whom he has drawn from the ranks of models, and who has become in point of fact, a model wife."

Chapter Thirteen

Matchmaking

"Why doesn't Leighton marry? was constantly asked," the painter and socialite Henriette Corkran recalled. After all, he was extremely popular with the ladies. Many well-meaning acquaintances dabbled in matchmaking and Dorothy was a likely contender.

For some time, the press refrained from turning the accumulating bits of information into news; but when rumours became persistent, they could resist no longer. "Society has an alarm, and that a serious one. Miss Dorothy Dene – sweet Spirituelle Dorothy Dene – is – well, inclining to *embonpoint*, in other words, becoming stout," sniped the

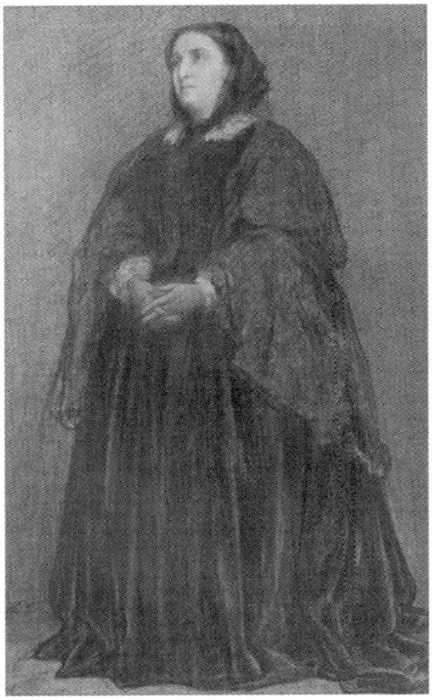

Adelaide Sartoris, a drawing by Leighton, 1867

Salisbury Times on April 14th, 1888, with mock concern. "She is losing her graceful outline in a developed beauty which is not so artistic. Rumour has it that Sir Frederick Leighton has wooed and won her, and the hope is universal that she may become Lady Leighton and the Academy have a Presidentess before the Dorothy Dene we had all admired has disappeared." The news travelled as far as Australia, where it was stated that she was engaged to be married to the President and "will probably retire into private life, appearing only on canvas at the Academy."

Dorothy was not the only candidate. The marriage bourse gambled on another possible. Louise Jopling was a thriving Royal Academician thirteen years Leighton's junior, and fellow artists admired her talent and beauty. She often visited Leighton's home, and flirted with the married Frith and Millais. After another unhappy marriage and the death of her second husband, Louise insisted that "I should, by marrying again, be simply cutting my own throat as far as my profession goes." Yet Louisa Starr-Canzianni remembered that Mrs Jopling "gave out she was engaged to Leighton." Her friends were surprised and delighted, and Lady Rothschild quickly sent her a note, "Let me know if, and when, I may congratulate." Leighton was quick to squash the gossip and ordered the secretary of the Royal Academy to "tell all my fellow members there's nothing in it." Louise Jopling had to do her share of sorting out the mess, especially to her most determined suitor, the lawyer George Rowe who was forgiving. Soon after that the couple got married.

Leighton took great care of his appearance and turning grey seems only to have enhanced his appeal. Men and women alike were struck by his charms: "Not only was he glorious to look upon, whether in the Apollo stage of youth, the Zeus-like phase of middle age, or the shaggier Poseidon presentment of later years, but he was so variously gifted as to be not one but all the arts' epitome," enthused the diplomat James Renell Rodd. With his looks, talents and the success which always appeals to women, he might have been irresistible, remarked another. Leighton was aware of his magnetism, but was not flirtatious. "A hero of romance in aspect and bearing," described the novelist Julian Hawthorne. Such perfection was obviously irritating, and his rival painter Whistler had a fine snipe when a woman exclaimed, enthusiastically, "what an accomplished man Sir Frederic is! He can speak Italian, German, French and lots of other languages. He is fond of music and makes such eloquent speeches.

'Yes, replied Whistler. 'And he paints, too, sometimes'".

At parties Leighton was always surrounded by the young and beautiful who enjoyed his attention and entertaining company. He seemed at ease, flourishing in their presence. But a caricature from 1872 by James Tissot for *Vanity Fair* is more telling: dandily dressed with white-gloved hands and an orchid in his lapel, Leighton reclines against an open door, turning his back on three shadowy female admirers. It was incisively and cunningly titled *A sacrifice to the Graces.* He was not just taking a break from the soiree; for the French Tissot, a new-arrival to London, Leighton, too, was an outsider.

***

Nothing is known about Leighton's love life before he arrived at Rome in late 1852, "very good looking, suggestive of the young Raphael style," remembered a female friend. People who met him thought that he was gay, light-hearted and radiated happiness; he was the life of the ball, "the best waltzer in Rome."

He was 22 when introduced to Isabel Laing, the daughter of family friends. His mother was pleased to read that her son had "lionized Isabel all over Rome and devoted to her all my afternoons ... It is the luckiest thing in the world, her coming here at a time that I'm not able to paint." Isabel sat for him for a portrait commissioned by her father, and Leighton gave her one of his early self-portraits that he had painted as a student, where he sported a wavy, bohemian hairstyle. But the budding romance never matured, because by the time he was courting Isabel, he had already met Adelaide Sartoris, and was completely won over. For her part, two years later, Isabel married arctic explorer Joseph Nias, who was 35 years her senior.

Adelaide came from the famous Kemble theatrical family. She was an acclaimed soprano who sparkled as Bellini's tragic Norma, but cut her career short when she married and had three children. Her husband turned a blind eye to his wife's entourage of admirers, who followed her into their home. Adelaide ran a literary and musical salon for a select group of English expatriates in Rome: diplomats, artists and writers including Thackeray and Robert and Elizabeth Browning. The group often spent sunny days together, picnicking in the countryside. "I am warmly attached to both, and her I dearly love," wrote Leighton, who was there almost every day – "for it would be a blank day to me in which I did not see her." He called her "my great resource" and shared his enthusiasm with his mother: "her conversation is most agreeable to me, not from any knowledge she displays, but from her great refinement of feeling and taste." When he was with her, he felt that "I am rich for life," but aware of the 16-year age gap, he reassured his mother about the harmless nature of their relationship: "I warm my very soul in the glow of her sisterly affection and kindness."

Adelaide Sartoris advised him how to "strengthen his character" and became not just his muse and mentor, but his ideal of a woman. He often stayed with her and her children for long periods when her husband was away on business. The ten days that he and Adelaide spent on their own in Florence, were so significant that every year she would write reminding him of their anniversary.

To his father Leighton admitted that "I look upon her as an angel, *ni plus ni moins,* and I feel terrified at the idea of how much more exacting she has made me for the future choice of a wife, by showing one what opposite excellencies a woman may unite in herself." Almost young enough to be her son, Adelaide called Frederic "Fay," in tune with the nicknames she gave her children – "Gay" and "May." In his company she often called herself "Sister Adelaide" or "Sister Ad."

Leighton's mother wanted him to marry, but he deflected her pressure. On his thirtieth birthday, he wrote to her: "about marrying, dear Mamma, you must not forget it requires two to play at that game. I would not insult a girl I did not love by asking her to tie her existence to mine, and I have not yet found one that I felt the slightest wish to marry: it is no doubt ludicrous to place this ideal so high, but it is not my fault – theoretically I should like to be married very soon." He vowed that he would never marry just for the sake of doing so. His family was worried however, and his exasperated mother complained to his younger sister Augusta that Frederic "is unreasonably fastidious."

In the summer of 1855 he followed the Sartoris family when they moved to Paris. He lived on his own far from the Latin Quarter and distanced himself from his bohemian friends. When Adelaide Sartoris settled back in London, Leighton also ended his European travels and was again a frequent guest at her salon.

"A desperate love affair that had gone ill," was socialite Mrs Phoebe Smalley's verdict on the Leighton-Sartoris relationship. The great politician Benjamin Disraeli made Leighton a character in his 1870 novel *Lothair*: he named him Mr Phoebus, "the most eminent painter of the age" who believed that "great artists should lead a princely life"; a small prick at the extravagance of Leighton, who, as Disraeli himself saw at Leighton's parties, fed his guests with delicacies purchased at Fortnum and Mason and served them champagne "in golden glass of Venice." Phoebus/Leighton was God-like and too good to be true, arrogant and haughty. Disraeli paired him with a rich, talented opera singer "of voluptuous symmetry," a replica of Adelaide Sartoris, "and the alliance is of the happiest. Never was there such mutual devotion."

Voluptuous flattered Adelaide; she was no beauty, though. She was dubbed "Sartoria the fat," a repulsive "mountain of rolling fat," and George du Maurier was struck by the great disparity between the two. "Mrs S. no longer fit for Norma; fat red face; Leighton looks so pretty & fresh by the side of her, and the contrast naturally suggests itself when one has heard all about them," he wrote to a friend. Other friends were less vitriolic. Viscount Fordwich stressed that Leighton was "inseparable from Mrs Sartoris (without scandal)." Without scandal meant, of course, without sex.

In fact, Leighton was too infatuated to see the real Adelaide; she often sat for him, grumbling to a friend: "I suppose he will go on painting me until one day it will flash upon him that I haven't got a hair on my head or a tooth in my head." He contributed illustrations to her roman a clef *A Week in a French Country-House*, inspired by one of their vacations. She cast him as a Monsieur Kiowski, a young and passionate Polish painter, a great linguist and a gifted singer. The Leighton-look-alike was a puppy at the service of his mistress, and Sartoris satirized his desire to appease and serve: "[He] was anxious to be of use to her, and fidgeted round her with a Lucifer-match, which he had rushed to get from the hall; but she ignored him completely." Not what one would expect from such intimate friends, unless Adelaide wanted to divert gossip.

In 1864 Adelaide contracted a life-threatening illness, and Leighton channelled his anxiety into a painting, The Angels of Life and Death fighting for the soul of Mrs Sartoris, while her family pray off stage. When she recovered, he turned the composition into the mythological *Hercules wrestling with Death for the body of Alcestis* and exhibited it at the Royal Academy in 1871. He accompanied Adelaide on her recovery trips to spas in France and Italy: "He is an angel and no mistake," she wrote to her daughter May. "Neither one's father – nor one's mother – and certainly not one's husband or one's brother could take half the tender care of one as he does of me."

Adelaide appreciated Leighton's talents, enjoyed his ardour and was flattered by his devotion, but had no intention of jeopardizing her comfortable marriage. "She had tied him so firmly to her platonic apron, that he was powerless to seek a wife," writes Ann Blainey, her biographer. Phoebe Smalley, wife of an American correspondent in London, accused Mrs Sartoris for she "burned poor Fred's heart to ashes, and then said "No"! She had not permitted the relationship to go too far – or far enough. Since then he had been a social butterfly, but the honey of all other flowers had been bitter in his mouth." As much as he was successful, rich and petted by society, "domestically he was a man manqué," concluded Mrs Smalley.

Leighton's long experience of love and female companionship without sex would influence him for the rest of his life. Adelaide tried to find Leighton a wife but her attempts at matchmaking were futile. A suitable bride was under her own roof: her daughter May, young and beautiful. The thought must have crossed the minds of all three involved, but it might have been too much of a tangle.

Adelaide's final years were tragic – with failing health, and devastation following the death of her son in a riding accident. A month before her death in August 1879, she wrote to Leighton, "do see if you can simplify your life somehow." By then, Dorothy Dene had appeared in Leighton's life.

Chapter Fourteen

"Half-hidden from himself"

But it was not just Leighton's unattainable love for Adelaide Sartoris, and the high bar that she set, that hindered him from marriage.

Three out of the eight artists who preceded Leighton as presidents of the Royal Academy, and two others who were offered the post and declined were bachelors who "lived and died free from the thraldom of Hymen." When the bright student John Flaxman announced that he had just got married, the president, Sir Joshua Reynolds, warned him that it would stunt his painting, for "Art should be the artist's only bride." However, Flaxman went on to enjoy a brilliant career and

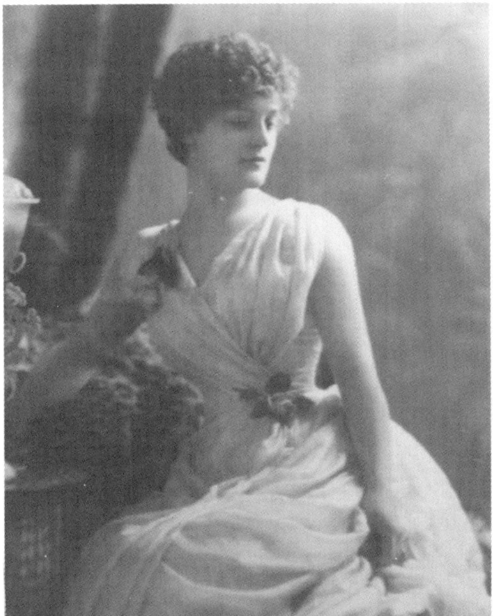

Photo: Henry Van der Weyde, 1886

a very happy marriage. Avoiding marriage for the sake of art was just a pretext for Reynolds. Frederick W. Hilles, professor of English Literature at Yale, concluded that Reynolds "was somewhat lacking in a capacity for love." Celibacy suited his lukewarm temperament, and his sister lived with him as housekeeper and made up for the absence of a wife.

"Should artists marry" was a much-debated subject. One who identified himself as "a London bachelor of longstanding" published an article, counting the blessings of staying single, quoting the17th century philosopher Sir Francis Bacon who said that the greatest works of art were produced by unmarried or childless men.

In Leighton's day, one of the most popular writers in France was Alphonse Daudet who wrote a collection of stories on the wives of artists. He argued that the influence of a wife upon an artist is always negative. Even in a happy marriage, "the bent of his genius is almost certain to be turned ... her influence is always perilous; and, in case of incompatibility of any sort, disastrous." When the issue came up at Mrs Sartoris' salon, she remained silent "until a great friend of hers – an old bachelor – stuck up stoutly for the freedom of the unmarried. Then, very softly she said: 'poor fellow! With nothing better to go home to than a flat candlestick!'"

Already in his twenties, Leighton imagined his dream house, and to sculptor Harriet Hosmer, whom he met at the Sartoris salon and became a life-long friend, he "sketched his intended plan, in every respect, as it was afterwards executed." The spacious house was built a decade later, with only one bedroom, and no rooms for children. He enlarged the house several times – with the help of his architect George Aitchison, also a bachelor – but never added any family rooms. As much as he adored women and children, he could not see himself living with a woman and raising a family. To Alexandra, the Princess of Wales he said that he cannot "find sufficient leisure to devote to a wife."

It is telling that Leighton's bedroom was ascetic, a single iron bed in a sparsely furnished room. Over 40 photographs of early Italian masterpieces hung on the dark-blue wallpaper, rather like posters in a student's dormitory. This monastic like bedroom was in sharp contrast to the majestic house, and to the rest of his pampered life: gourmet food, expensive champagne, a regal wardrobe and long vacations abroad. The bedroom reflected a man who wanted discipline and control over his private life. He created a monk's cell that would discourage him from inviting anyone in. To safeguard his privacy even further, there was no place for guests to stay overnight.

A riddle today, Leighton was unfathomable even to his closest friends. The very force of his courtesy kept many of them at arm's length. "You could never get over the idea that his kindnesses were mechanical, that it was the man's voice that was speaking to you, not his heart," wrote the *St. James' Budget.* His colleague Frith said that he had known Leighton "from a boy – and a very cheeky boy, too, – and I don't know him yet." He should not have been surprised, since at times, Leighton was even "half-hidden from himself," as Emily Barrington diagnosed him.

Even as a young man, Leighton stayed aloof from others, "as he passed them hurriedly, as if afraid to linger – on some high errand," remembered writer Frances Minto Elliot who had known him in Rome. He never drank or smoked in public and his friends never saw him with his arm linked in another's. His biographers Leonée and Richard Ormond say that those who met Leighton regularly were conscious that his politeness and charm often concealed nervous tension: "his fits of depression, the psychosomatic disorders, the emotional insecurity, were aspects of his character of which few were aware. He learned to control and disguise these nervous symptoms, often, one suspects, by conscious effort of will. While he was invariably generous and outgoing in his relations with other people, he avoided intimacy of any kind."

"I'm enjoying unsociable solitude keenly, bear as I am," he wrote to Emily Barrington from one of his travels. He lived by himself but was not lonely and enjoyed travelling on his own which left him free to engage with strangers. He had the company of his sisters who lived nearby, widowed at a young age with no children, and they sometimes vacationed abroad together. Nearly every evening he dined at the *Athenaeum*, and the club offered something very familiar and a little domestic.

In *The Literary Character* – the history of men of genius – Isaac

Disraeli, the prime minister's father, quoted Michelangelo as saying, "I have espoused my art: and it occasions me sufficient domestic cares, for my works shall be my children." Echoing his icon, Leighton used to say, "I am married to my art," and the sharp-eyed Lord Redesdale agreed that indeed he was in love, "but it was with his art – she was his mistress, and to her he was faithful to the end." Evidently, not having found the right woman was a pretext – Leighton was not seeking one.

Despite his monkish privacy, some of Leighton's paintings suggest some ambivalence. As a young man he painted several tragic scenes of love and death: Romeo and Juliet, the Fisherman and the Siren, Samson and Delilah, Paolo and Francesca, Orpheus and Eurydice. Then, in his mid-thirties, he painted two warm portraits of a marriage: in *The Painter's Honeymoon*, a young artist and his newly-wedded wife are huddled together, his sketching board resting on their knees. Hands clasped, their heads touching, nestling like two doves side by side, she watches him draw. "The woman has resigned herself to a dreamy delight, and bows contentedly before the god of her idolatry," wrote *Bentley's Miscellany*, and went on to quote Robert Browning:

> "all, her body and soul,
> that complete his whole,
> all that women add to men
> is given up to him alone,
> and in the knowledge of that her happiness consists."

Leighton withheld *Painter's Honeymoon* from exhibition for two years, as he may have felt "that he had put too much of himself into it," according to the art historian Christopher Newall. When finally exhibited, women loved it and, "a possible result of it may be to increase the chances of painters in the matrimonial market." In a matching work, *Golden Hours*, the same effeminate male model is a sombre-looking musician, playing the harpsichord to his young wife, who is seen from behind as she leans forward towards him. In both paintings, the woman is the dominant presence, and the timid man the passive object of her desire.

"Whatever noble fire is in our hearts will burn also in our work,"

Leighton told his students at the Academy, "for as we are, so our work is, and what we saw in our lives, that beyond a doubt, we shall reap for good or for ill." His vision of marriage seemed to be of tender happiness and mutual interests: the man, self-absorbed in his work, and the woman, beautiful and gentle, his attentive audience. Dorothy could easily play the part.

The American novelist Henry James was part of Leighton's circle but never liked him. In his diary he outlined a story he wanted to write exposing "the private identity of a personage suggested by F. L." In *The Private Life*, published in 1892, he described the famous painter Lord Mellifont, "the handsomest man of his period," "the host, the patron, the moderator," who only thrives under the public glare, and evaporates in private. Lord Mellifont/Leighton was one whose "reputation was a kind of gilded obelisk, as if he had been buried beneath it." Mellifont was presumed to be having an affair with Blanche Adney, an actress, who "was beautiful without beauty and complete with a dozen deficiencies ... she was like the model off the pedestal. She was the picture walking about, which to the artless social mind was a perpetual surprise."

Henry James knew Dorothy, of course. In his story, Blanche/Dorothy, frustrated with not having done better as an actress and tired of Sheridan and other writers of comedy, "was haunted by the vision of a bigger chance." Her relationship with Lord Mellifont is illicit, since they are both married, though unhappily. She dreams of a brilliant role written for her by their friend Vawdrey, a thinly-disguised Robert Browning. Henry James even wrote himself into the story, as a writer in love with Blanche.

As they are all on holiday in a Swiss ski resort, Blanche returns alone from a stroll in the mountains with Lord Mellifont, and the writer asks her bluntly: "Did he make love to you on a glacier?" Blanche bursts out laughing: "Lord Mellifont, poor dear? What a funny place! It would be indeed the place for *our* love!"

***

Burying his private life made for speculations: Leighton was said to be passionless since the naked women that he painted seemed lifeless, more wax than flesh. His contemporaries complained that as an artist, his heart is "dead or dormant," and his paintings "do not sway our hearts." The art historian Dr. Stephen Jones believes that Leighton "was temperamentally averse to intimate human relationships of any kind." The Ormonds suspect that he had a weak sexual drive and was "too fastidious ever to have contemplated an active sexual life." He was described as "effeminate" in several memoirs by his contemporaries: "he was as sensitive as a woman and had quite a feminine sense of yielding" wrote his early biographer, Edgcumbe Staley. All of it led to speculations that Leighton may have been homosexual.

Adelaide Sartoris introduced him to Henry Greville, a very wealthy English aristocrat. The elderly homosexual – the same age as Leighton's father – was much taken with the handsome young man; his letters to Leighton are full of erotic hints. He nicknamed him "Bimbo" and "my little boy" and placed his photograph by his bed so that he could see his face "the first thing upon waking." He tried to control and channel Leighton's artistic and romantic life ("you know my opinion of the young ladies who 'adore you'") and dissuaded him from going to parties without him; he suggested instead to "go to bed early." Greville even invited Leighton to live with him, saying that he could not wait "till the pleasant moment of having you under my roof arrives."

Worried for Leighton's sake, Adelaide raised the issue of depravity. "I am *very* glad you are trying to help yourself in real earnest ... once you choose to look honestly at the subject instead of going blindly on, the ugliness of vice would repel you," she wrote to him in 1865. It's unlikely that she meant associating with prostitutes, which was acceptable among Victorian gentlemen. The ugly vice that she referred to was more likely homosexuality, which was a punishable crime. 20th century critics, analysing Leighton's work from a queer perspective, find in his women a "massive scale and masculinity," his naked young men lovingly painted, and homoerotic elements in works like *Hit*, where a young man teaches a boy to hold a bow. Professor Christopher Reed suggests that Leighton's huge sculpture of an athlete wrestling with a phallic snake is a form of "resistance to or escape from homoerotic desire." There were several homosexuals in Sartoris' circle, and Leighton was evidently attracted to the physical beauty of young models of both sexes, and he "fulfilled some part of himself in the company of young men," wrote the Ormonds, although "The label of homosexual, however, is too crude an umbrella for someone as ambivalent as Leighton."

In Leighton's diary of 1852, he writes that just before arriving at Rome, his "day-dream of long years," he suddenly got cold feet. "How is it that my pleasure is not unalloyed? That I involuntarily shrink from grasping the highest of my wishes?" He compared himself to a lover who had an image in his heart and teetered on the edge of physical love. "I cannot help thinking that an imaginative man must feel something similar when on the point of changing courtship for marriage," he wrote. The art historian Sir Michael Levey, former director of the National Gallery in London, interprets Leighton's confessional words as evidence that he was afraid of sex, heterosexual or homosexual.

The truth may be more complex as Caroline Dakers has discovered. The 27-year-old Lily Mason was married to a commercial traveller and a mother of two young daughters, when she came to Leighton's studio in 1872. At first, her seven year-old daughter Jenny interested Leighton, later Lily herself also modelled; she took part in the fresco *The Arts of Industry as applied to Peace* and also posed for the *Daphnephoria*, as one in a procession of singing women.

In 1874 Leighton drew a series of three head-and shoulder portraits of young women: Lucia, Teresa and Lily. Lily Mason was paid for modelling in February of that year, but the only surviving photograph of her is from later years, so it's impossible to tell if she is indeed *Lily*, the lovely redhead painted from the back.

In October 1875, Lily gave birth to a son whom she named Frederick, which was also her husband's name. The birth was not registered as it should have been by law. Checking the statements from Leighton's bank account at Coutts, Professor Dakers noticed that eight months before the boy's birth, and then regularly until Leighton's death, the Masons received massive payments amounting to £9000, although Lily or her daughters were no longer modelling for him.

Leighton and his sisters remained on very friendly terms with Lily and her son. "Dear Lil, Thank you vy [sic] much for the pretty little locket & your good wishes on my 54th birthday," Leighton wrote back, asking Lily to give little Fred a "kiss from his old godpa." When Fred was 19, Leighton paid for his scientific education in Germany.

When Leighton died, Lily, by then widowed, received £1450 from his sisters, who were the executors of his estate. When Leighton's sister Augusta died in 1919, she left Fred Mason £4400, as well as a watch and a gold ring mounted with diamonds. Fred Mason worked as a company secretary of a successful manufacturing firm in London. He died in 1953. Among his books were Leighton's set of Shakespeare's plays and some of his drawings. In the absence of written evidence and scientific proof, Professor Dakers cautiously states that "Leighton was, or believed himself to be, the father of Lily's son Fred."

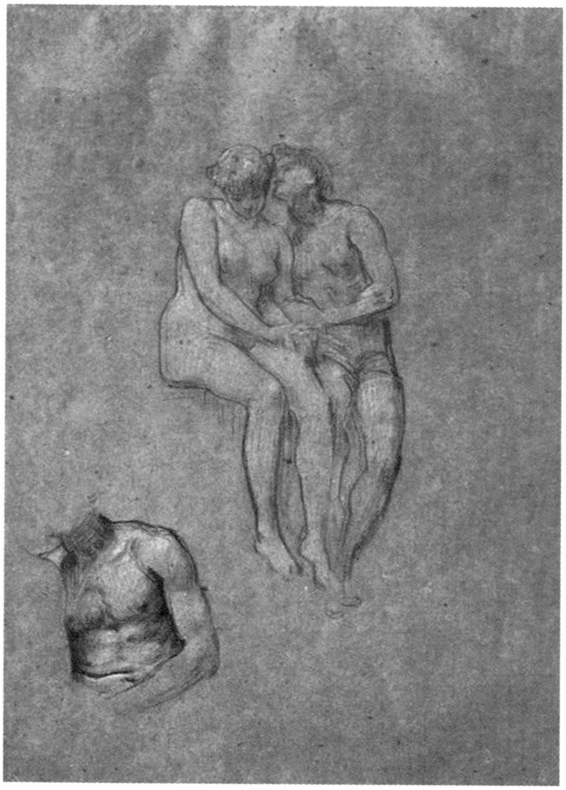

Study for *Whispers*, Dorothy and Gaetano Valvona, 1881

Chapter Fifteen

His Wife

Leighton had two muses: Adelaide Sartoris ruled his formative years, Dorothy Dene graced his prime. Two entirely different women, two entirely different relationships. Elderly and physically unattractive, Adelaide Sartoris was Leighton's ideal woman in life but not on canvas. He was captivated, she stirred him and enriched his mind, tastes and emotions, but she never posed for him as a model. Dorothy Dene was the face and figure which cast her spell and ruled his canvas to his last day.

The muse is "the feminine part of the male artist, with which he must have intercourse if he is to bring into being a new work," suggests Professor Germaine Greer. "She is the anima to his animus, the yin to his yang, except that, in a reversal of gender roles, she penetrates or inspires him, and he gestates and brings forth, from the womb of the mind."

The great masters were usually Leighton's major source of inspiration. In *Flaming June,* he was influenced by Michelangelo's *Night* but gave the credit to Dorothy as he did in many of his works, reinforcing her status as his muse. There was no muse-worship in their relationship, for to be dependent on anyone was against his nature. In their lives, he was the sustaining sun, and she the admiring, revolving star.

Dorothy Dene was a "notable 'Hetaira" who benefited from Leighton's efforts to educate her, says curator Alison Smith. In ancient Greece, the Hetaerae were beautiful, cultivated and independent courtesans, who earned wealth and respect in exchange for their long-term companionship. But Dorothy was neither a classy prostitute, nor a guttersnipe Eliza Doolittle, but rather Leighton's Galatea. She brought a new degree of warmth and sensuality into his paintings, and succeeded in making him more human. The relationship between artist and muse is often passionate, dramatic, intensified by separation or death, but Leighton's and Dorothy Dene's bond was steadfast, devoid of crisis, and they became closer with the passing years. In his maturity, no woman was ever closer to him than she was.

***

Men who delayed tying the knot were likely to get into the habit of celibacy, wrote Reverend Edward James Hardy, the author of the very popular handbook, *How to be Happy though married* (1885). This "agony uncle" introduced himself as a graduate in the University of Matrimony and warned that like all other bad habits, it was difficult to break away from. Hardy then declared that near the age of sixty, men will suddenly want to marry "and they will propose right and left to everything in petticoats, until at last they are picked up, not for themselves, but for their money or their position."

Age may have mellowed Leighton; but in a class conscious society, Dorothy's humble background was an obstacle to marriage so much up the social ladder.

"I don't know whether you would like him, very blasé and finikin, and quite spoilt–one of the world's little darlings, who won't make themselves agreeable to anything under a duchess," George du Maurier wrote of Leighton to his future wife Emma. Even before being created a baronet in 1886, Leighton had close ties with royalty, being a friend of the Prince of Wales and his family, and he counted many Viscounts and Marques among his friends. The *Cosmopolitan* reminded its readers that "Dorothy Dene is a type of the wild flower beauty that springs from no one knows where on the roadside, and in her way attracts as much admiration and gives as much delight as the hot-house lily that has had generations of nurture."

In the circles that Leighton moved in, it was just not done, says curator and art historian Philippa Martin. "Other artists could marry their models, but they were not invited to the Prince of Wales. Leighton's position as the president of the Academy meant that he was required to converse with the aristocracy and members of the royal family on a regular basis, and social invitations to him would naturally have to include his wife if he had one. Dorothy could make it very problematic and awkward for him if she became his wife. He must have realized it."

A few aristocrats did marry below their class, choosing actresses and models for wives: the music hall singer Dolly Tester married the 4th Marquis of Ailesbury, actress and singer Jane Louisa Reynolds married Baron Brampton, and the famous skirt-dancer Kate Vaughan, Dorothy's idol, married Colonel Frederick Arthur Wellesley, son of the first Earl Cowley. Some of Leighton's peers married their models: Dante Gabriel Rossetti, William Morris, Ford Madox Brown, Frederic Shields, and Frederic Sandys. Oscar Wilde was cynically cautious about such matches: "For an artist to marry his model is as fatal as for a *gourmet* to marry his cook, the one gets no sittings, and the other gets no dinners".

Dorothy pondered the paradoxes of love. On stage, she was always the coveted one, often courted by two men. Asked if she would play Juliet better if the Romeo was in love with her, she answered that "I think I should play Juliet better with a Romeo who was indifferent to me." A celebrity and professional beauty was constantly pursued by men of rank and wealth. A past as an actress was just about acceptable, but a past as a nude model might just be too outré. Katherine Fitzpatrick, who also modelled for Leighton, was dumped at the last moment by her fiancé, on the pretext that she had modelled in the nude. The jury accepted her claims that she only sat for the head, ears and hair and awarded her £150 in damages. Similar disaster struck Dorothy, argue the Ormonds, Leighton's biographers, when her engagement to Anthony Crane was "broken off by his parents, who did not consider her suitable. Leighton could do nothing to protect her in such a situation."

The story seems plausible; Mrs Crane was a known prude and forbade her husband from using naked female models. For his *Reminiscences of Venus*, he had to engage an Italian male and make the necessary anatomical alterations. All his colleagues including Leighton easily identified Alessandro Di Marco. Such a woman would certainly have vetoed any of her sons from marrying a nude model like Dorothy. The story has a flaw however. Walter and Mary Crane never had a son named Anthony, and their son Lionel, born in 1876 would have been twelve when he was supposed to marry Dorothy.

Recently discovered correspondence in Italian between Giovanni Costa and George Howard, the 9th Earl of Carlisle, who was Costa's art student and Leighton's long standing friend, offers intriguing hints. In a letter dated July 1886, Costa tells Howard that he received a letter from Leighton saying "that he has been to the Grosvenor again, calmly (which means 'without his wife')." Further on in the letter, Costa writes that "I and my daughters will be able to enter his studio-house, albeit his Wife keeps the reception room's door barred to us. Poor Wife! For all her husband's preoccupations, she seems to me to be destined to certain death!"

In another letter to Howard, dated November that year, Costa is infuriated and describes his last meeting with Leighton in Perugia: "I said to him… 'I am not going to send one of my sons to your house, since we do not find favour with your wife'."

According to curator and researcher Philippa Martin, the mysterious "wife" seems to be no other than Dorothy. Costa knew her well – she was his guest in Italy a few years earlier, and he painted a glorious portrait of her. In his visits to London, he enjoyed meeting her and her sisters – "In the morning, lunch with the Dorotheas," he wrote to his wife. Did Dorothy assume such authority in Leighton's house, in Leighton's life, as much as to distance him from one of his closest friends, whom she herself was very friendly with? And for what reason? Just a decade earlier, Leighton went out of his way to arrange for Costa's wife and daughter to stay the night in his bedroom "and you will have your usual one upstairs; and I shall put up in the new little room on the ground floor," he wrote to Costa. The family visit never happened, but Costa is the only known person to ever stay the night at Leighton's house.

Having read the letters in their context, and bearing in mind that Costa only had daughters, and no sons to send to Leighton's house, we believe that the "Wife" is not Dorothy or any other woman, but the Royal Academy. When Leighton went to the Grosvenor Gallery to see Costa's paintings, he visited as a friend, without his formal baggage as President of the Royal Academy: this is what Costa meant when he wrote that Leighton came "calmly, without his wife." Costa's resentment against the Wife, and his decision not to send any of his sons to London, stands for his annoyance with the selection committee of the Royal

Academy which did not accept his works; he was disappointed that Leighton has not tried hard enough to get him in. Costa regarded his paintings as his beloved children and was indignant they were rejected. His prediction that the Wife is "destined to certain death" refers not to any tragic fate of Dorothy's, but to the old-fashioned policies of the Royal Academy which, if not changed, is bound to perish.

***

Her parents' failed marriage had shaken Dorothy Dene. Leighton, who entered her life just a few months after her father's desertion, became the paterfamilias, and she felt safe and taken care of. She appealed to his benevolent nature: "Once the tender spot of pity touched, a self-ignoring energy of helpfulness and desire to benefit arose," wrote Emily Barrington. "Pity with Leighton was ever allied with profound respect. He gave as one indulging himself in a privilege rather than as one conferring a benefit." Patron and protégée were the foundation of their relationship. A journalist who spotted them together at a party noted that Leighton looked at Dorothy "in a paternal and proprietary manner."

More than ever before, men and women in late Victorian London could afford to stay single and their number was rising. The trend intrigued the press: "Often, men do not marry because they are too busy. They want to make the most of life, and marriage does not seem to them essential to that result," wrote the "London bachelor of long standing," in the religious magazine *The Leisure Hour*. Statistics in the 1880s showed that 30% of women between the ages of 20 and 40 were unmarried compared to 25% of men. The Dene family unit was not a rarity: one quarter of the lower middle-class households were headed by single women, and nearly 10% of adults lived together with a sibling.

At this stage, being single suited Dorothy. Like Leighton, she wanted to devote herself to her art, and when the rumours of marriage frothed, her career had not yet taken off. If she married, she would have to give up acting, and she had not yet fulfilled her theatrical ambitions. The gossip columns reported her either with Leighton or sometimes with Browning. No other man was ever paired with her, for Leighton's presence kept all others at bay. Journalist-editor T.P. O'Connor added another possible reason for her celibacy: "With all her beauty, she had none of the charm and not one little touch of the 'devil' that turns the heads of men."

The age difference of 30 years does not seem to have been an issue. In a rare interview Dorothy said, "although Sir Frederic is over 60 years old, he is the youngest man I know, and I might add, the kindest, most generous." She had some form of conjugality to enjoy with him: he took care of her material needs, and they spent hours at his home and in the studio, chatting and dining together. She was there at his soirees and concerts, and took part in London's cultural life next to him. The dream-like attraction, he to her bewitching beauty, she to his charismatic artistic persona, became an intimate attachment. Each became the other's "significant other."

The waspish Mrs Barrington used biographical details for her 1892 novel, "Lena's Picture: a story of love." The young heroine, Lena Provost resembles Dorothy Dene: the pearl-like tints of her complexion, her long beautiful lashes and her statuesque form, which "the sculptor himself has chiselled and finished to the furthest point of finish." Her character, too, is like Dorothy's: "her grave, reposeful quietness in attitude and movement, a grace also echoing that of the early masters' ideals." The words which Barrington the novelist used, are almost identical to those Barrington the biographer used to describe Dorothy. It was no coincidence that of all possible names that she could choose for her heroine, it was not Dorothy – that would have been too obvious – but Lena, the other most painted of the Dene sisters.

Lena, a born musician, played the piano and admired Wagner's operas. She was overjoyed when a wealthy titled couple asked her to go with them to Bayreuth. For Leighton, his sisters, the Barringtons and many of the London intelligenzia, the annual Wagner Festival was one of the outings of the year. In Bayreuth, Lena/Dorothy met a music-loving painter, Gustave Allbretcht, an elderly bachelor, slim and distinguished looking, who immediately saw his artistic ideal in her. "All about her fascinated him and inspired in him an admiration far beyond that of the eye only. He was entranced. No personality he had ever before encountered had given him the same satisfying delight and contentment. He had never before seen, he thought, such dignity and simplicity." They speak of art, music, religion, fall in love, and then enraptured, listen to Wagner's tragic *Tristan and Isolde.*

Allbretcht/Leighton proposes to Lena and does not understand why she refuses. "I can never marry," she says finally and tells him a terrible family secret. It is the madwoman in the attic of *Jane Eyre* with a twist. Lena's disturbed mother and little sister have both been put away in an asylum. She and her older brother have agreed that they must not marry not to pass the hereditary illness on. "Her 21 years of life had added reasons for unusual self-control, restraint and reserve. It was not exactly a sad face, but a very silent face – there was a depression as well as a strength indicated, strange in the expression of a simple-natured girl". Allbretcht asks Lena to share her weight of sorrow, to heal the wound, if possible. Even if she does not marry him, he says, he will always wait for her and there will never be another love for him. But although Lena loves him dearly, she is adamant in her refusal, not wishing to burden him with her troubles: "you owe your life to your art," she says. "I have heard you say that an artist should keep his life as simple as possible." She returns home, alone, and dies soon after.

Mrs Barrington knew all the people involved. As much as she appreciated Dorothy, she never thought that she was a good-enough match for Leighton; when she wrote his biography, she stressed their relationship was that of a benevolent patron and a lovely young woman in need. Her novel allowed her to mix many elements from the real characters' relationship, and strudel it into an actual love story. Even in fiction, however, Barrington could not let them overcome all obstacles and live together happily ever.

Unlike previous occasions, Leighton did not issue a statement denying the rumours, nor did he get cold feet. The marriage speculations would continue and would have no effect on his closeness with Dorothy.

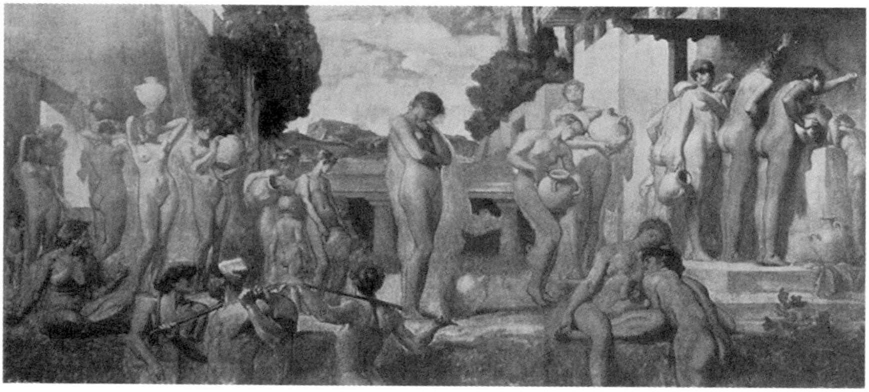

Nude sketch of *Captive Andromache*, with Dorothy, Hetty and Lena

Chapter Sixteen

Faithful unto Death

Dorothy's sisters enjoyed a carefree existence, not having to sweat for their living. They modelled a bit, socialized a lot, and one sister after another followed Dorothy onto the stage. They relied on their beauty, her coaching and the experience they gained at the artist's studio. In July 1887 Edith made her debut in the nondescript detective drama *Obed Snow's Philantropy*, but it was her role as a love-stricken maiden in W.S. Gilbert's *Broken Hearts*, that earned her compliments for carrying the audience completely away with her.

Next it was the 21-year-old Hetty's turn. She debuted in 1888 in Margate, where the actress Sarah Thorne ran a school of acting which offered three and six-months crash courses. Hetty joined Mrs Thorne's company, appearing in *Midsummer Night's Dream* and *Hamlet*, and in March 1889, she scored success in *Alone,* – a loose adaptation of *King Lear* – playing a devoted daughter whose blind father rejects her, thinking she had lost her honour. Bizarrely this was a comedy, which was her forte, and she was commended for her emotional expression and "pleasant and effective speaking voice."

Dorothy joined the company of Genevieve Ward, a well-known classical actress, but the comedies and melodramas that she acted in made little impact and received mixed reviews. In *Forget Me Not*, a play written for Miss Ward and so favoured by the Prince of Wales that he came to see it twice in a fortnight, Dorothy was pretty and earnest as the suffering, young virtuous bride but "while there are real tears in her eyes, her tone is monotonous, and her emphasis wrong. Study will conquer this, and my remarks are not intended to discourage the young actress," concluded the *Theatre* in May 1888. Simultaneously, she was in *The Loadstone*, a soufflé whipped up with two murders and a sudden death. The play was ridiculed, but Dorothy was sufficiently miserable as the "sadly-serious, though not unlovable girl." The critics perceived her as a talented novice rather than a finished performer. "Miss Dene is still a studied rather than a natural actress, and has a bad habit of attitudinizing; nevertheless, she is making good progress, and may yet accomplish great things," wrote *The Stage*.

Cassandra became her touchstone, but roles like that were rare, and for better or for worse, she was always compared to that monumental triumph. She had good looks, intelligence and earnestness, but her problem remained the poor choice of plays. She knew that many of them were mediocre, with thin plots and hackneyed writing, but if her role was appealing and challenging, she took it, and "my opinion of the play does not in the least affect my acting if I like my own part," she told William Archer.

***

For most of his artistic life Leighton was haunted by a scene in the *Iliad*: Hector, the Trojan leader, who predicted the humiliation of his wife Andromache if he died in battle. Leighton had the picture in his mind's eye, and returned to it again and again, positioning various models holding pitchers in their hands. He was thinking of a processional work with several distinct figures, like his first masterpiece, *Cimabue's celebrated Madonna* which gave him public recognition and was instantly bought by Queen Victoria 30 years earlier. Now though, he could not move forward beyond the preliminary sketches.

Seeing Dorothy as a Greek tragic heroine in Professor Warr's play may have helped motivate Leighton and he began to work intensively on *Captive Andromache*. It was massive – four meters by two – and he chose to portray the part in Hector's prediction that Andromache will be "a trembling, weeping captive," a slave to his enemy, "to bear the victor's hard commands or bring the weight of waters from Hyperia's spring." He made many nude studies – more than ever before – of the sad and disconsolate Dorothy. Finally, he chose one pose, standing in profile, sorrow-laden and queenly, all alone in the world. Dressed in black from head to toe and holding a jar, she waits her turn by the fountain to draw water for her captors. All around her are free women in colourful robes, laughing, gossiping, getting on with their lives, while she is enslaved and bereaved. She glances at a young couple blissfully fondling their baby, a reminder of what she has lost. Three of the sisters were in the picture. Hetty portrayed the fortunate wife and mother while Lena was a joyful teenager with her golden hair up in a bun, standing just behind Dorothy and surrounded by other children.

Leighton only hinted at the more gory details of the Greek tragedy, where Andromache's baby is thrown from the walls of the city and she becomes the sexual-slave of the murderer's son. The loss and despair which the picture conveys so strongly "may reflect Leighton's own sense of what he had sacrificed in devoting himself so single-mindedly to his art," wrote the art experts Louise d'Argencourt and Douglas Druick in *The other nineteenth century*.

The price tag that Leighton put on it – £8000 – was supposed to reflect twenty-five years' thought and preparations, and two years of hard work. He was quite disappointed that although received warmly by the public and the critics when exhibited in 1888 – "probably the greatest picture that has been produced during the century" wrote the *Manchester Courier*, it failed to find a buyer. It was too big and too expensive. Several buyers opted out and only the newly established *Walker Gallery* in Liverpool remained, at a cut price of £6000. But the Liverpool council refused to ratify the sale and finally *Manchester City Art Gallery* picked it up, at the even lower price of £4000. The embarrassing details of the price-haggling were reported in detail. Still even £4000 was as much as sum a working man might earn in his entire life.

***

Just as Leighton came often to Herbert Schmalz's studio to view his work, the young artist was a welcome visitor at his patron's house. He could not have missed *Captive Andromache*, Leighton's pride and joy. Schmaltz was taken with the theme of a woman falling from the heights into the darkest pit and developed it into his *Zenobia's Last Look on Palmyra*. The third-century warrior-queen created an empire in the Middle East, which included her native Syria and some of Turkey, Palestine and Egypt. But her victories were short lived. In Schmalz's painting, the captured Zenobia stands with golden manacles on her wrists, her dagger confiscated and its scabbard empty. She takes a last look at her beloved and defeated city before being exiled to Rome. "Even in that moment of humiliation, her face wears an expression of mingled grief and pride, and her clenched hands and the tension of the muscles of her right arm help to indicate the determination of her character, as well as the resentment of her proud spirit at the indignities to which she is being exposed," wrote the *South Australian Register* when the painting arrived at Adelaide, where it is still held.

Of all the Dene sisters, Schmalz picked Hetty to model for this work. Dorothy belonged to Leighton, and in any case, was better suited to resigned and submissive roles. Edith was too delicate and sweet to portray the fierce queen. But Hetty, with her robust physique and muscular arms, so powerful and vengeful in Leighton's *The Jealousy of Simoetha* of the previous year, made a perfect Zenobia. "It is one of his best pictures of late," wrote the *Pall Mall Gazette* when it was exhibited at the New Gallery in Regent Street.

But it was another, sensational and controversial work that year that shot Schmalz into fame. More than 350,000 visitors paid a shilling to view the Royal Academy summer exhibition of 1888. It was one of Leighton's finest vintages, as it was for the 32 year-old Schmalz. He concocted suspense, cruelty, sadism and sexual violence into his *Faithful unto Death*. It became the talk of the town and Queen Victoria was so intrigued, that she asked for the painting to be brought to her for a private viewing. Unlike many painters who drew inspiration from the classics, Schmalz, influenced by his brother Ernest who was a vicar, was turning more and more to the New Testament for subjects. "As a Christian who is a member of the Church of England," he said, "I must confess sacred subjects appeal to me."

Faithful unto Death was set during the reign of Nero Caesar. Early Christians who refused to renounce their faith were taken to the Roman Coliseum – as treats for the hungry lions. On the back of the painting, sold in 2018 for $68,750, there was a caption in Schmalz's handwriting: "Waiting, under the pitiless eyes of blood thirsty multitude, from Senator and Patrician dame, to low baffoone parasite. Waiting, till fear becomes hope, and shame grows shameless before the promise of death!"

Public torture was entertainment. The herald shouted *"Christianae ad leones!"* and all eyes turned to the maidens who awaited their doom in the corner of the arena. It was the feast day of Bacchus, and statues of the god were mounted on poles; on each one a naked young girl was bound. In the painting, one girl has fallen "with nameless horror in her dead face; another nearest the lion's den shrinks as if she hears the growling of the impatient brutes," detailed the *Dundee Evening Telegraph*. "The chief power of the picture lies in its suggestions of horror rather than in any grim and gruesome details. The lions are half in shadow; there is no blood yet on the sand; but a passing chariot wheel has turned up a bare human bone, a mute witness of former carnivals of slaughter." The torture and execution of young Christian women highlighted the moral superiority of Christianity over the cruel pagans.

Schmalz worked for three years on the painting, which had 2000 faces of Roman spectators, each one distinctly individual. Among the seven naked martyrs were two Dene sisters. 14-year-old Lena, with her golden locks hid her face in fear and shame. Schmalz told the *Strand* that Lena gave him the inspiration, without speaking a single word; she was resting, just about to resume the modelling session, when unconsciously she stood in a position with such dramatic force that it deeply affected him. "Keep that position," Schmalz cried out, picked up a block of paper and made a rapid sketch of her. The bonds which bound Lena to the post, cutting into the soft flesh of her arms, were "realized absolutely by the model, for Mr Schmalz had a post erected in his studio and bound the girl to it exactly as represented," thrilled the *Strand*. Only one martyr was standing defiantly, her marble-white body "bearing on her delicate limbs manifest evidences of struggling against the brutal roughness of the attendants": Schmalz gave this heroic role to his girlfriend, the 23-year-old Edith Dene.

For months, *Faithful unto Death* toured the provinces, attracting thousands of paying customers. "I have recently stood before a painting by Herbert Schmalz, which has done more to stamp upon my soul the faith of the early saints and the cruel inhumanity of Rome than anything that I hitherto read about these sad times," wrote the Reverend Robert Munro in *Quiver*, a religious magazine. Devout Christians were encouraged to go and see those unfortunate sufferers, and Munro and others may have overlooked the heavy sado-eroticism; but many more came exactly for that: to have a legitimate peep at beautiful naked girls in bondage. Lawrence Alma-Tadema admired the painting so much, that he asked Schmalz to single out Lena of all seven martyrs and make her the subject of a painting for his newly renovated house.

Not everyone liked the painting, though. Many critics found it distasteful and reproached Schmalz for displaying beautiful nudes who "look as if they had been fattened for the occasion and even as if they did not particularly care about it," wrote the *Manchester Courier*. He could not sell it to any museum in Britain or overseas, but the public loved it and Schmalz enjoyed hefty profits from prints and exhibition fees.

Throughout his career, Schmalz was falsely identified as a German, and when he painted another version of *Faithful unto Death* thirty years later, he signed it as Herbert Carmichael, using his Scottish mother's maiden name. It was the end of the First World War, and he adopted the name because Britain was charged with anti-German sentiments. Dr Allison Smith believes that his work had an influence on Hollywood films like Cecil B. De Mille's 1932 *The Sign of the Cross* "which includes a similar scene in which a nude female martyr is shown bound by garlands to a herm in the arena, awaiting her fate."

That year, four of the Dene sisters – Dorothy, Edith, Hetty and Lena graced gallery walls all around Britain. The only one left out was 17-year-old Kathleen. She was as beautiful as her sisters, and not shy of public glare – she would soon become an actress – but there was some wildness about her that made her less suitable for the artists' studios. Cracks in the sisters' bond were forming.

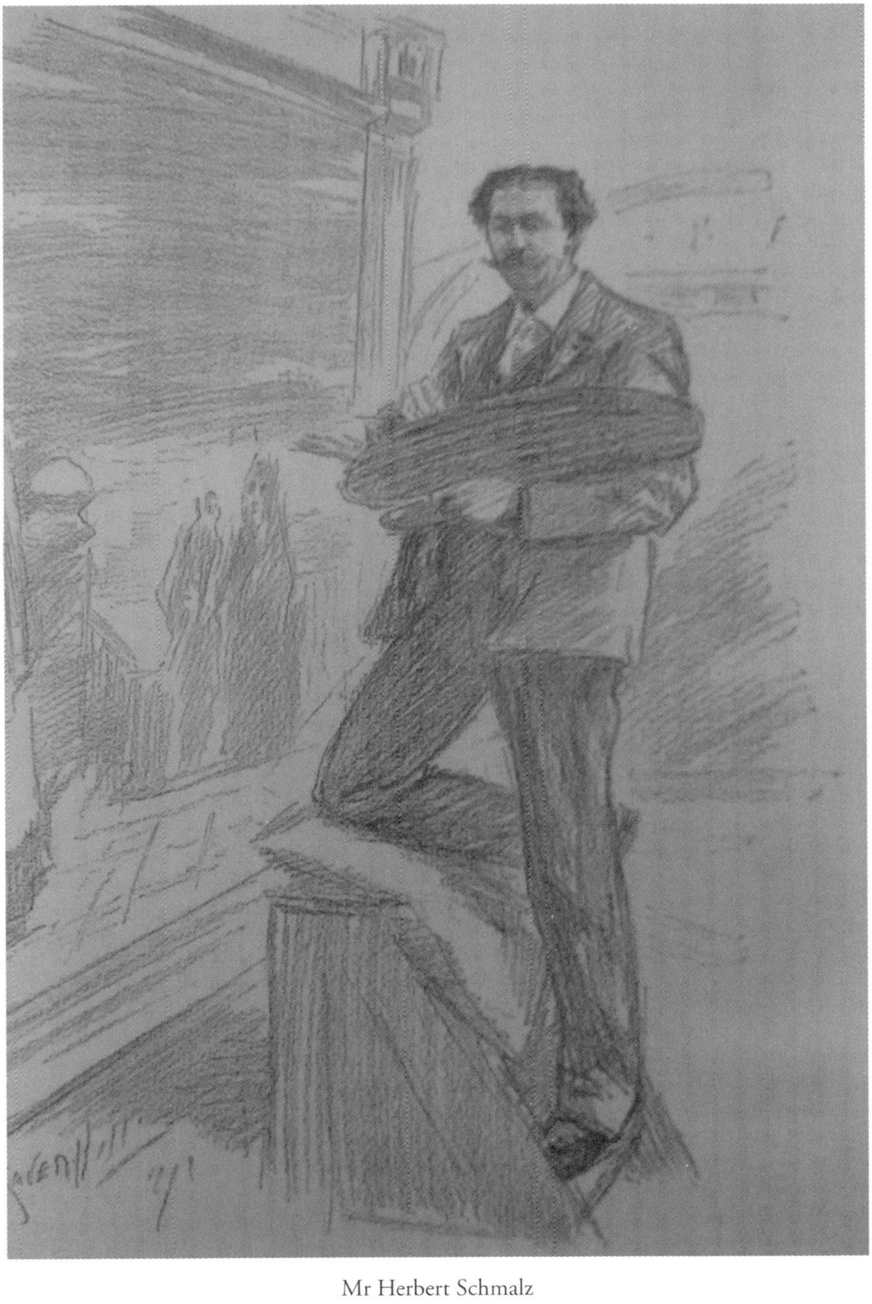

Mr Herbert Schmalz

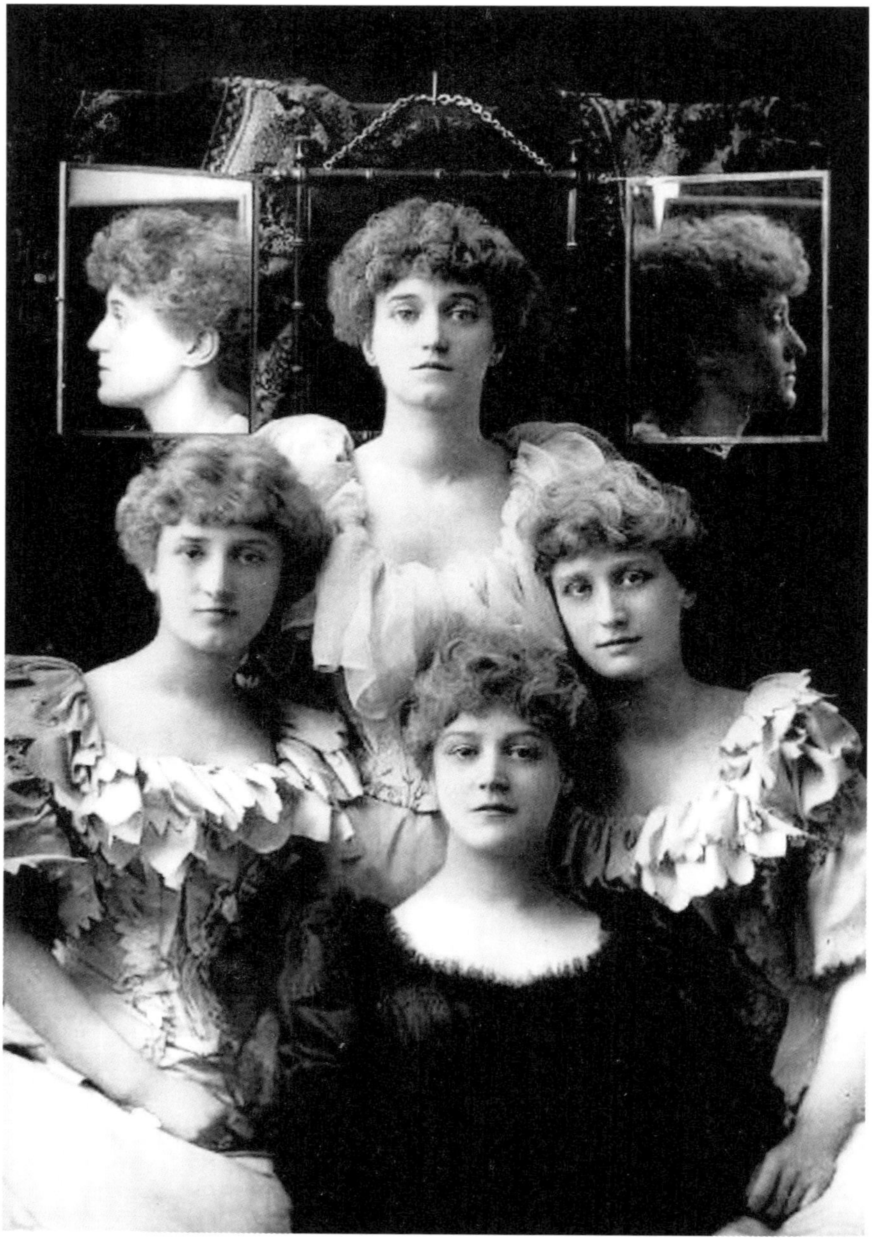

The Misses Dene. Standing: Hetty, left; Kathleen, right; Lena, sitting; Dorothy, by W. & D. Downey, in Cabinet Portrait Gallery 1893.

Chapter Seventeen

Nocturnal visits

In the summer of 1888, Dorothy realized that her diary was totally empty for the coming season. She decided to test the water and advertised in the *New York Dramatic Mirror*: "Miss Dorothy Dene, of the leading London theatres, invites offers for America." She gave her address, and promised to answer at once by cable, but only to "leading businesses."

When nothing materialized, she kept on job-seeking in London, but the only offer was to replace the leading lady in the successful *Union Jack*. It was a well-written melodrama combining high and low comedy; she played yet another dishonoured girl and again was criticized for her "too frequent habit of turning a fixed gaze upwards" with tear-filled eyes. She used this pose much more effectively on Leighton's canvas, in *Invocation,* for which she was posing at that very time. She was a priestess in a white muslin veil, who had just placed an offering of flowers on the altar. Standing still with her arms raised above her head while Leighton was arranging and rearranging the folds of the cloth on her body was so stressful that he commissioned a young sculptor, to model a life size statue in clay of Dorothy. Usually only small clay models were made.

Dorothy's next role was a Greek prophetess, sitting brooding "with a far-away look, as if she would pierce the mysteries she is about to reveal." *Sybil* received first-rate publicity when the *Magazine of Art* devoted an entire article to it; for the first time, there was a recognizable drawing of Dorothy in the nude, which was quite sensational. The aim was to demonstrate Leighton's methods, and the first drawing showed Dorothy with her elbow on her knee, her legs crossed, and her midriff and left breast exposed. The other three drawings showed her in various stages of getting dressed. Leighton explained that "the nude model, no matter how practiced he or she may be, never moves or stands or sits, in these degenerate days, with exactly the same freedom as when draped." So after making a small sketch of her in the nude, he enlarged it to life-size on the canvas – "every muscle, every joint, every crease is there, although all this careful painting is soon to be hidden with the draperies." Without using the word "muse" he gave Dorothy full credit for inspiring the work. He said that she moved her hand and wrist in a gesture that was "anatomically beautiful and desirable," reminding him of the Sybils of Michelangelo on the Sistine Chapel ceiling that he had long admired; so he decided to build an entire scene around Dorothy's pose.

"I have no special models, and there is no model who sits for me alone. Models are constantly ringing at my side door, anxious to become engaged," Leighton told Harry How of the *Strand*. It was an odd attempt at denial from an artist who must have known everyone knew he did have a chosen and recognisable special model. "His pictures were known to everyone, not as Hermione or Helen or Andromache, but as Dorothy Dene," wrote the *Pall Mall Gazette*. Her contemplative pose in *Sybil*, surrounded by scrolls of her prophesies was ridiculed by the press. *Punch* portrayed her as a vain hussy, Leighton's puppet on a string, who was not thinking about prophesies but about which wall paper to buy. "Can't get any of these wall-papers to suit," Sybil/Dorothy is complaining in the caricature. "Want something new and unclassical but must be governed by President." The *Pall Mall Gazette* suggested that *Liberty* department store which specialized in free-flowing dresses could use the painting as an advertisement.

In the third work, *Greek Girls Playing at Ball*, Dorothy was the ball-catcher. Leighton was trying to give a classical interpretation to modern life, argued his contemporary E.E. Minton. "If he lived with Phidias and Praxiteles in his dreams and in his studio, in his waking life he was with the men and women of the Victorian era." His nymphs were rather girls of the tennis lawn than of ancient Greece, and it was easy to see them as undergraduates of Girton or Newnham College. Everyone looked at Dorothy when she attended the Royal Academy opening. A reporter for an Australian newspaper was standing by *Invocation* and admiring the "idealized and magnified edition of Dorothy Dene, draped in dazzling white robes and throwing up a pair of plump arms to heaven." The journalist had "the oddest sensation" watching "the little pearl powdery model who happened to be in the room as I passed through on Friday. It also showed what trifling inspiration is needed to a really great artist."

***

On April 11th, 1889, Dorothy celebrated her thirtieth birthday. With her humble background and string of family tragedies, just staying afloat would have been a success. But in ten years, she had leaped from obscurity to prominence, able to afford luxuries that she could only have dreamed of once. She had bypassed the class system, befriended the cultural elite and was a welcome guest in Mayfair and Belgravia. As an actress, however, she was still plodding behind. She did not find a theatrical patron that could equal Leighton in the art world.

As a result and always hopeful, Dorothy welcomed any theatrical experiment. In the winter of 1889 she made regular trips to the village of Bushey, at the outskirts of London, to rehearse at the recently established theatre set up by the painter Herbert Herkomer. The play that he wrote, composed and directed, *An Idyl,* was a musical drama influenced by Richard Wagner. Most of the players were amateurs, but for the lead roles he chose professionals. Dorothy got the part of Edith, the beautiful daughter of a blacksmith, played by Herkomer himself. It was a simple romantic plot about young love, love almost lost, and finally the celebration of that love in marriage in 14th century England. Edith is betrothed to honest Dick, a workman, whom she loves, but her head is turned by a high-born lord who attempts to seduce her. The moral was simple. Don't try for love outside your social class.

Herkomer used his plays to try out scenes for his large-scale paintings. His ingenious theatrical experiments were a breakthrough in three-dimensional scenery, and naturalistic lighting, which in *Idyl* ranged from golden sunlight to a silvery moon. The two-hour play ran without a word of dialogue, as it used movement, mime, song, dance and music. It was a non-commercial enterprise, and the number of participants – 100, including the orchestra, conducted by the famous Dr. Hans

Richter who came especially from Vienna – almost equalled that of the audience.

Dorothy "was admirable in the emotional character of his daughter," acted with "feelings and natural pathos," sang softly, and was "a picturesque figure in blue," described Alice Corkran. It ran for 13 performances; the audience arrived in a special train from London and was then driven in carriages to the theatre. It was all financed by Herkomer and the proceeds were given to charity. After the show, Leighton walked back with Dorothy and some guests, and young novelist-poet Katharine Tynan remembered his "ruddily handsome face and grizzling beard. Going up to town in the train we had for travelling companion Miss Dorothy Dene." Miss Tynan admired Dorothy's looks and clothes but was critical of her bearing: she thought that Dorothy "bellied her beauty by talking a great deal of nonsense in the fashionable slang of the day." In the eyes of the *London Evening Standard* critic, though, Dorothy was far from vulgar: he found her both in appearance and manner "too delicate and refined for a rustic belle".

***

Edith was the first of the Dene sisters to wed: on April 30th, 1889, she married Schmalz. As expected, she stopped acting and modelling for others, remaining her husband's chief model and inspiration. A week after the wedding, Schmalz exhibited a rather puzzling choice for a newlywed: *On the Banks of Allan Water* showed Edith, sitting on the grass, a letter having just fallen from her hand, "the sweet face, with closed eyes and lifted head is eloquent of the despair and sickness of heart which betrayal has brought with it." The press knew enough to comment that it was "not complimentary to his bride." As Mrs Herbert Schmalz, Edith became a socialite in her own right, and her presence and elegant wardrobe at various social events was widely reported. For most of their marriage, Edith had to accommodate the presence of her brother in law and his family, who lived with them.

Oblivious to the wagging tongues, Leighton brought Dorothy closer to him. At the beginning of August 1889, he wrote her a cheque for £203. It was the down payment for the lease of flat 10 in Avonmore

Mansions, a six-storey red-brick house, in a pretty pocket of West Kensington. It was a smaller flat than that in Clapham, but a marked upgrade, and the trump card was the address: only minutes' walk from Leighton's house. The Dene sisters – Dorothy, Hetty, Kathleen and Lena, and their brother Samuel, divided the three double bedrooms between them. There was a luxurious bathroom with hot water and a large kitchen, scullery and pantry. The flat boasted high ceilings with picture windows and terra cotta walls as well as a balcony. Though the building was new, Dorothy insisted on renovations; she chose the trendiest, yellow William Morris wallpaper from Liberty's for the drawing room and added blue Morris carpet and white wood chairs. She had great fun describing her struggle with the workman to paint the doors and the mantelpiece in black lacquer, copied from Leighton's house. She loved to imitate the man's Cockney accent, "I will do it if you like, Miss, but it will look like a 'earse!"

Visitors were overwhelmed by the large array of works of the most eminent painters, presents from artists that the girls sat for. Looming over it all was a portrait of Dorothy by Leighton, and "a curious profile portrait of her (painted in Italy) which has somewhat the effect of a cameo." From the surviving photograph, it seems to be the swan-neck portrait of Dorothy, by Giovanni Costa.

The celebrity interviewer Helen C. Black was curious about the well-filled bookcases: they contained many of the best works in prose and poetry, travels, history, biography and various editions of Marlowe, Browning and Shakespeare, which Dorothy and Hetty "nearly know by heart." The splendid reception room had full length mirrors. Dorothy was a splendid conversationalist, and the sisters' twice-monthly Sundays at home were very popular among artists, actors, musicians and men of letters.

Leighton made his own nocturnal visits, which he did not hide from the compulsive gossip Emily Barrington. "I go to see them," he told her, "when I want to let my back hair down and get off the stilts." She understood his need: "As he felt vitality waning and mental effort a greater strain, the little family of Pullens [sic] had to Leighton somewhat the same resting charm that Italy had in early days, when he turned from the German austerity in study to the relaxation of the *dolce far niente* [delightful idleness] of Italian national life." Inviting the girls to his house was out of the question since he was surrounded by peeping neighbours but the short walk in the dark, on his own, transported him to another world. The Dene sisters could pamper him and return some of his immense generosity. They were probably the only ones who saw Leighton without his presidential gown and persona.

When Mary Watts was compiling her husband's biography she received from Augusta Matthews, Leighton's sister, a bundle of letters, with a covering note: "I've not read them, and if they should contain any reference to Lord Leighton's affaire, I'm sure you would not publish without allowing me to see them." What "affaire" was Leighton's sister referring to? What did she want to protect his posthumous reputation against?

It seems that the answer lies in Mrs Barrington's authorized biography of Leighton, published in 1906, where she devoted a chapter to Dorothy and her sisters: "It is almost unnecessary, as it is distasteful, to mention that this beautiful paternal attitude Leighton displayed towards these orphans was made the subject of ugly gossip," she wrote. "For are there not always the *misérables* of the world who seek the ugly rather than the beautiful? misinterpreting the beautiful so that it should come within the range of their scandalous arrows, more especially when the darts attack a man in the high position Leighton held."

Some "kind souls" made sure that the "ugly gossip" reached Leighton's sisters, and they were so alarmed that they decided to alert him. He replied in a lengthy answer, ending with the following sentence: "But let me turn away from the whole thing, it has pained me more than enough. I implore you not to reopen it. On the only thing that matters, you are *absolutely assured, if you believe in my honour*. If you hear these rumours again, meet them with a flat, ungarnished denial. Let that suffice – it does for me."

To a lady friend Leighton wrote still more explicitly, in order, as he said, that there should exist in his own handwriting an explicit and unmitigated denial of the malicious falsehood. This letter was lost or destroyed sadly.

Ten years after Leighton's death, when his biography was about to be published, his sister Augusta still felt that the "ugly gossip" about

Leighton's "affaire" was too strong to be ignored. Mrs Barrington had to refute it in an oblique way. To judge by her hints, it was not about Leighton and Dorothy's closeness, which was common knowledge, but rather, about his association with all the Dene girls, "these orphans," in the plural, as she wrote. His visits to the Dene home, and spending time alone with four beautiful young women, launched these "scandalous arrows."

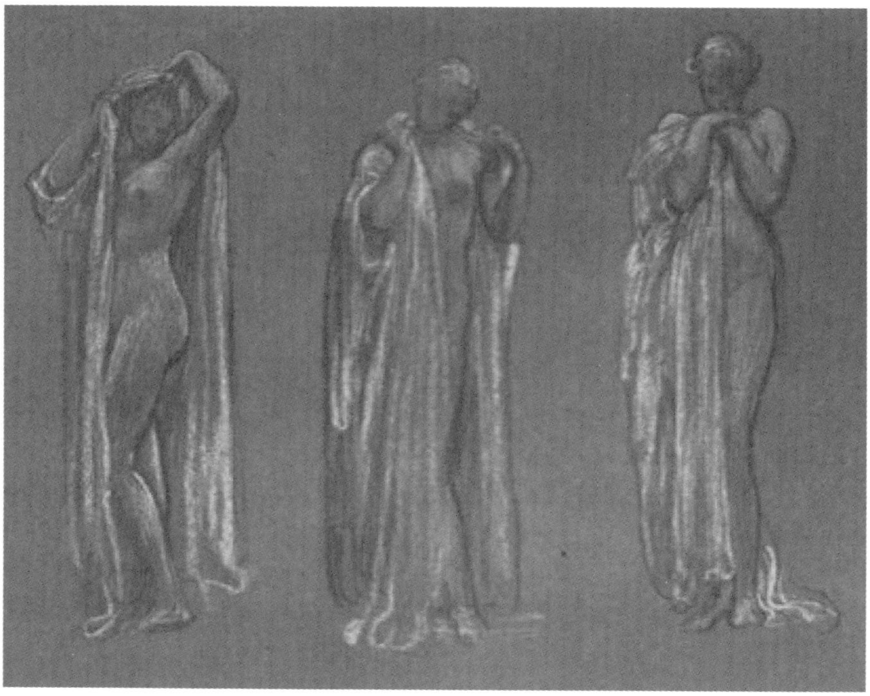

Figure studies for the *Bath of Psyche*, 1889

Chapter Eighteen

"Not fit for public inspection"

Young actresses were advised to avoid hiring themselves out as nude models. Dorothy Dene was the only Victorian actress who was also a full-time artist's model; but although she flaunted very revealing poses, modelling in the nude did not damage her reputation on stage and in society. Only once, in Liverpool, the authorities refused to allow her to perform because of that. But one picture was indeed scandalous, and the police had to intervene.

In 1886 Lawrence Alma-Tadema moved into his new house in Grove End Road, St. John's Wood, and asked his friends to contribute works for the entrance hall. He left the choice of subject to them, and 45 painters rose to the challenge. Leighton was troubled by the confined space – just 16.5 cm wide, 81 cm tall. At dinner, as they sat directly opposite one another, he lifted up a long, narrow-bladed desert knife and said: "what sort of subject do you expect me to paint on this?"

Only four of the artists painted nudes, among them Herbert Schmalz with Lena Dene as a Christian martyr. Leighton's gift was Dorothy as a Greek goddess taking her bath which pleased his host; "No man could have filled the panel better: it is the best thing on the screen." But Leighton felt he was hampered by the small size of the panel and asked Alma-Tadema to allow him to work it "out again in another way." He had already painted a Venus disrobing for the bath twenty years earlier, using an Italian model, but he had stopped painting nudes altogether until he met Dorothy. Alma-Tadema agreed.

Leighton and Dorothy started the modelling sessions by recreating her bashful pose in *Crenaia* (1880), with her head down. Gradually she straightened up and opened her robe, revealing more of her body. Leighton then asked her to turn sideways, lift her left arm, hold the robe above her head, and look down with half-dreamy eyes at the imaginary pool, admiring her reflected curves. Behind her he painted a pair of doves, birds which were associated with Venus, the goddess of love and beauty. Just before submitting the life-size painting to the Royal Academy in May 1890, he changed her name to Psyche, most probably because a year earlier, Edward Burne-Jones exhibited his own *Bath of Venus.*

The mythological Psyche could not find a husband since her overwhelming beauty deterred her suitors. Zeus transported her to the Golden Palace of his son Cupid, and each night she slept with the god of love but was not allowed to see him. Leighton focused on her preparations for the night of love, as she dropped her last garment before getting into the bath. "A personification of fascinating womanhood," hailed the *Lloyd's.* Gloating reports that Dorothy was gaining weight with her addiction to cakes and hot chocolate were apparently exaggerated. Her photographs from the time show her as stunning as ever. None of the photos, though, carry that hedonistic expression that Dorothy gave Leighton. Some critics found the figure lifeless, and *Punch* caricaturized her as a determined bather despite the below-zero temperatures: "Ice is Cheap Today," was the title of the cartoon. Leighton admitted the painting was incomplete and that he intended to make the flesh rosier; he would not make her sensuous, though, since "the great test in looking at nude presentments is that there should be no suggestion except that of elevation and of beauty; if otherwise, the picture is a degrading one," he said.

The press did not see any degradation. One paper praised Leighton, saying that "even Mr Horsley and the British Matron may gaze upon it without green spectacles or a blush." The image of sexual awakening was seen as harmless and was immediately purchased by the Chantrey Bequest for £1000 and given to the South Kensington Museum. But a mere three weeks after it was shown at the Royal Academy, it became part of the ongoing moral debate. The Royal Aquarium hung a poster of Zaeo, --Miss Adelaide Weiland--, a young aerialist, lifting her arms and smiling, wearing only a tight bodice. The National Vigilance Association took the organizers to court for displaying an indecent image, and Judge John Breech ordered it to be removed from the billboards. The fact that only one mile separated Zaeo from Psyche arose some questions; "what would Sir John Breech say is if that picture [the *Bath of Psyche*] were brought before him? Where is the line to be drawn?" asked the *Hampshire Advertiser*.

The annual summer exhibition which toured the provinces in the autumn of 1890 was dubbed "the blushing season." When the *Bath of Psyche* arrived at Liverpool, it was suggested that it should be exhibited in a separate room with other nudes. But "what would be thought of those ladies, young or otherwise, who should venture into that apartment," asked a reader who signed himself "Adonis." "The fact of their presence there, surrounded by no other picture upon which to bestow their glances, would point them out as indelicate, if not bold young ladies." Others were frustrated by Dorothy's too-perfect body which encouraged the "senseless custom of women screwing in their waists with stays so as to have 'spindle waists' – entailing endless suffering in afterlife – and motherhood."

The emotions and motivations of young women who stripped for money in front of a man were also discussed: "would any of the ardent supporters of paintings from the nude like to see their own sisters standing before an artist as a model?" As to the sexual tension in the studio, it was thought that the "artist is no more affected than a surgeon would be," although there were warnings that young men seeing these naked beauties on canvas might be tempted to use the service of prostitutes, since "the flesh is frail, and the 'social evil' a terrible scourge in our midst."

As the debate went on, the *Walker Art Gallery* organized a vote among visitors, to choose the best figure painting. The *Bath of Psyche* got the highest number of votes, and "ladies voted equally with the stronger sex," reported the *Liverpool Mercury*. "Neither religious bigotry nor the fantasies of crotchet-mongers had any effect on the decision of the public." Twenty years earlier, a reproduction of such a painting would have had a very limited sale. But all the engravings of the *Bath of Psyche* were ordered long before the day of publication, and the prints sold like hot cakes. It was Leighton's most popular reproduction and when G. F. Watts asked for a copy, Leighton apologized to his wife Mary that he had run out of certified ones, and offered to send an ordinary one, as well as a print of *Solitude*, to hang the two side by side: "I'm delighted Signor likes the daubs this year," he told Mary.

The National Vigilance Association launched a counter-attack. "Is Sir Frederick Leighton to be prosecuted for his *Bath of Psyche*," challenged one reporter. They managed to force a Liverpool gallery owner to remove the prints from his shop, and in Dublin, it was taken down on police orders.

In 1894, it was one of six nude posters by prominent British artists that were displayed in the window of a Glasgow gallery. Large crowds gawped from the pavement, and the Chief Constable asked the owner to remove the posters, since they were "not fit for public inspection," and caused the street to be obstructed. Leighton was furious that his work was marked as obscene, and felt that it was not the artist but the public who had to fight censorship: "Time alone, and the increasing influence of the more enlightened among your citizens, who are no doubt many, can be looked to bring about a more wholesome, let me add, cleaner frame of mind," he complained to the gallery owner.

In May 1899, the police raided a Dublin gallery which held an exhibition called *Life in Paris*. The gallery was packed with men and women, inserting coins in stereoscopes to see nude photos and paintings. The vice squad of the police scrutinized hundreds of images and confiscated sixteen. In the trial, a minister of the Presbyterian Church testified to the inevitable immoral and evil effect on the minds of onlookers. Cross-examining him, the defence counsel used the *Bath of Psyche* as a yard stick: would that be obscene too? The Reverend said that he had seen it but did not find it indecent. As in previous cases, the police agreed not to destroy the works, and to drop charges on condition that the proprietors will "clear out of Ireland at once and take the pictures with them." In March 1905, in Richmond, Virginia, a gallery owner who exhibited a reproduction of the *Bath of Psyche* was not so lucky; he was fined and sentenced to one day's imprisonment.

By the turn of the century, British producers felt safe enough to put on stage Living Pictures based on famous paintings. One of the stars of the 1907 show was a young woman calling herself "Venus", who claimed that she was the original model for the *Bath of Psyche*. She posed on the Empire Theatre stage, inside a huge golden frame, her nude body covered in pink enamel.

The pose inspired a 1916 film called *Purity*. Audrey Munson, who was an artist's model in New York and was dubbed The American Venus, was the first woman to appear naked on cinema. Just as Victorian artists used mythology to justify painting nudes, so did film producers: the pretext for Miss Munson's full-frontal nudity was that her poses recreated important artworks such as the *Bath of Psyche*. The 70-minutes silent film was a box office success with around the clock screenings and escaped the censors' scissors, since it was treated as homage to art.

With her perfect contours, Dorothy "displays her charms for the admiration of mankind," revelled James Harlaw, Leighton's early biographer. The 'indecent' postcard of Psyche enjoyed popularity all over Europe well into the 1920's. Lord Leighton's name made what otherwise could have been classified as a soft-porn photo artistically respectable. In 1936, Selfridge's sold bath towels with jacquard weave, showing Leighton's Psyche.

In 2011, the picture took centre stage in the *Cult of Beauty*, an exhibition curated by the Victoria and Albert Museum, and also crossed the Atlantic. The *Bath of Psyche* lived up to the prophecy of Edgecumbe Staley, who wrote in 1906 that in years to come, the painting "will be looked upon as one of the most splendid pictures in the world."

***

Posing in the nude and being a celebrity put Dorothy under much scrutiny: her complexion was suddenly "seen to be a little faded, probably the result of using pigment and powders for make up on the stage." In fact, this was the pallor of anaemia, as throughout Dorothy's career delicate health was an issue. In November 1889, she was due to play the lead in *Her Father*, a tragedy adapted from the Spanish. At the last moment, she "was prevented by indisposition," and announcements about her sudden illness were hung outside the theatre. It must have been painful for her to read in the following day's papers that "her place was admirably filled at very short notice by Miss Maud Milton, who gave every satisfaction." Dorothy also had to skip a number of performances in Oxford and Cambridge, but she did manage to step back on stage at the end of the month. She was still unwell and "had to struggle against obvious hoarseness and was therefore severely handicapped."

Dorothy was lucky not to lose her next engagement, the lead in a new historical play by Brandon and Boas. *The Favourite of the King* premiered on March 11th, 1890. Dorothy played Helen Aston, who was engaged to be married to the man she loved. An astrologer warns that if he marries Helen, his career at the King's court will be wrecked: Helen is a Roman Catholic, while her lover is an Anglican. He uses this pretext to break off the match. Then to silence Helen, he has her thrown into prison. Her love turns to bitter hate and she vows revenge, especially when she learns that afterwards, he had married a rich Catholic.

Dorothy was at her best. The role demanded tempestuous emotions, on the brink of hysteria. "Miss Dene gave great intensity to Helen's hate and remarkable fierceness to Helen's fury," applauded the *Era*. She took the bouquets of flowers that she received on the gala night, and distributed them to patients at the next-door Charing Cross Hospital.

Again she played Helena in *Midsummer Night's Dream*, her favourite role. Looking as if she had stepped from one of the picture-frames of Leighton doubled her triumph. She had played it every summer in the last three years in private mansions, and now, at the London Globe, with Frank Benson's company. She was commended for the natural intelligence with which she invested poetical spirit into her character; "no actress we have seen could look the Athenian maiden better," wrote the *Era*.

If one sees Leighton and Dorothy as a double act, 1890 was one of their best years. It was not only the *Bath of Psyche*: Dorothy was the star of all of Leighton's submissions to the Royal Academy. Together they swaggered through different moods, from an amorous young woman to a gloomy and heartbroken one. In *Solitude*, she is deep in thought, fully covered from head to toe, seated with her shoulders slumped and bowed head resting on her hand. In another work, she is on a terrace by the dark sea, with scrolls of poetry and a golden lyre, a picture of tragic intensity. "The Muse is of an olive complexion, melancholy and beautiful, fine contrast to frivolous little Psyche," wrote the *Daily News*. Leighton named it *The Tragic Muse* – one of his nicknames for Dorothy – but at the last moment changed the title to *The Tragic Poetess*. He was keen to make it known that Dorothy was not just the model for the painting but a respected working actress as well. When *Midsummer Night's Dream* reached Manchester in August 1890, he wrote to Charles Pooley who had chosen his works for the City Art Gallery that he should go to see her play. Pooley did, but apparently mistook Dorothy for an amateur. Leighton was quick to correct him, with a polite reproach: "young as she is, she is not a novice (as you no doubt perceived) – she is not, indeed, at present in an engagement here but she is well known as a "leading lady" & very highly thought of by those who appreciate poetic work."

While Psyche was waiting for her lover, the heroines of Solitude and Poetess were deserted and alone. As he got older Leighton's melancholy and loneliness became more acute; these two paintings exuded his sadness– "but it is also a commentary on the transience and frailty of human beauty, bounded by darkness," explain Leonée and Richard Ormond, Leighton's biographers.

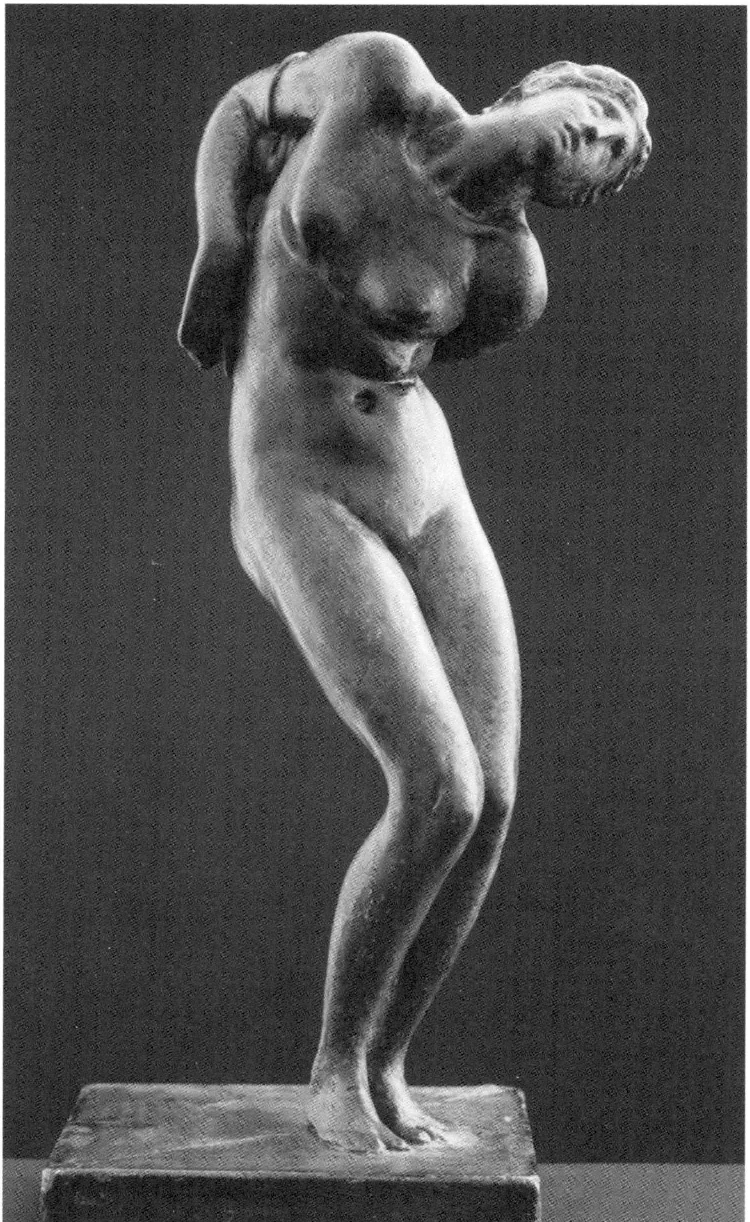

Model for the figure of Andromeda in Perseus and Andromeda, 1890
In The Royal Academy

Chapter Nineteen

"To fit or not to fit"

For years Hebert Schmalz was obsessed with the image of the Virgin Mary, supported by Mary Magdalene and St. John the Baptist, as they returned from "the awful event [that] contained in it more human interest of a pathetic character than any other one scene of the World tragedy," he wrote. Broken, they walk away with still "a certain peaceful trust. All was as God had willed it to be."

To make his reputation and be admitted as a Royal Academician, Schmalz placed all his hopes on this one painting of the return from the Calvary. He worked for months on end, but was disappointed with the result. He used sketches that he made during his trips to Morocco some years earlier and read reports of travellers to the Holy Land. He studied landscape drawings and illustrations of costumes, but they seemed to him "very lifeless and unconvincing." Anxious for advice, he turned to Leighton, who had visited the area in 1873. Leighton strongly recommended a trip to Palestine, which would improve his work "and be remembered in value all his life." He gave him tips how to minimize the journey's hardships and traps and mapped out a route of the places of special interest and how long to allot to each of them-- "four or five days quite sufficient for Jerusalem." All this excited Schmalz. Absorbing the local atmosphere would make him more sensitive to the subject.

It was soon after their wedding, so he suggested it to Edith as a honeymoon trip, and she happily agreed. They left London in February 1890, and Edith was always at his side when he went out to sketch, and very often sat for him. In Hebron, the couple had a narrow escape from being stoned to death. Schmalz was very much impressed by the story of the Hebrew patriarchs and wanted to paint at the site of their burial. He knew that "the descendants of Ishmael have now possession of this," and the place was off limits to anyone but a Moslem. He crept in with Edith, closed the door behind them and started sketching hurriedly. It was not long before they were discovered, the door was pushed open and angry Moslems besieged the blasphemous Christians. Schmalz packed his tools hastily "and we pushed our way through the howling crowd, and hurried on not knowing whither we went, being followed by sundry stones from the hands of our tormentors."

Estelle Blyth, the daughter of the Anglican Bishop of Jerusalem who hosted the Schmalzs, remembered how she walked round and round Edith, carefully studying her beauty from every possible angle. With her deep blue eyes and masses of bright golden hair, fastened with large-turquoise-headed pins, Edith seemed to the girl "as fascinating a lady as ever lived out of Fairyland." The old Sheikh of the Mosque of Omar in Jerusalem, "grew somewhat troublesome in his admiration for my wife," wrote Herbert Schmalz in his memoir, *A Painter's Pilgrimage*. "One day, he was there as we were leaving, and when she put on her veil, he was much upset and begged of her not to do so."

The delicate Edith stood up well to all the difficulties of the voyage, including their twenty-three days' ride from Jerusalem to Damascus by Nazareth and the Sea of Galilee, living in tents all along the route.

Leighton heard these adventures when the couple returned to London in the summer and was shown the many studies made on location. He was so impressed that he gave Schmalz a generous cheque of £150, to help him concentrate on his *Magnus opus*. Schmalz hoped to complete the *Return from Calvary* and present it at the next Royal Academy summer exhibition. But the darkness of winter worked against him. In the scarce daylight, Schmalz raced against the clock. He locked himself in and refused to see visitors. Nevertheless, he missed the deadline and it took him almost a year to finish it.

The *Return from Calvary* was finally exhibited at Dowdeswell Gallery in New Bond Street and brought to Windsor Castle for the Royal Family to view. For four years, the immense canvas, with life-size figures, toured the provinces and attracted a million viewers. It was exhibited in a room of its own and aroused religious fervour everywhere. In Blackburn, someone suddenly began to sing a hymn; others immediately joined in, "the picture being apparently all they needed to inaugurate a revival meeting." The engravings sold very well, and Queen Victoria bought one for herself.

Though the Anglican Bishop of Jerusalem gave Schmalz a statement testifying to the "faithfulness with which the features of the locality have been reproduced," it was clear that he had taken poetic license – like most artists who travelled to the Holy Land and recreated Jesus and his circle as Europeans. Realistic accuracy was the main purpose of the trip, so naturally Schmalz was alarmed when Mary Magdalene, with "luxuriant golden hair," was identified as Edith. He argued that he drew the head of the repentant prostitute from a peasant woman in the village of Cana in the Galilee but then came the admission that; "Although of the requisite type, she had not the requisite expression, and this was given me in a short sitting at home by Mrs Schmalz".

That "fiendish" winter at the end of 1890 did not slow down Leighton's creativity. He had a better-designed studio with larger windows which enabled him to finish two of his most dramatic works. Posing as Andromeda was probably Dorothy's most aching and distressing experience. As Leighton's clay model of Dorothy shows, her arms were tied behind, her torso twisted, her neck and head thrown backwards, her knees bent, as if she were about to collapse. She was, in Leighton's words, "in the very shadow of death," clutched by a nightmarish monster long and slimy as a serpent, with a crocodile head and the wings of a dragon.

Unlike Schmalz, who bound Edith and Lena to a pole in his studio as Christian martyrs, the terrorized naked Dorothy had to act as if she was bound to a rock. Her eyes are closed, and only we, the viewers, are aware that deliverance is at hand. Hovering in the sky, firmly seated on his flying horse is the radiant, handsome hero, Gaetano Valvona in the role of Perseus, who happened by at the very last moment. Most painters had Perseus dive from above and hit the fiend with a sword, but Leighton put him in a safe distance, darting arrows from his bow. One has just penetrated the monster, which belches flames of fire and smoke from its jaws and nostrils, and another arrow is about to follow. Soon Andromeda will stretch her arms to receive her saviour, "brimful of love she caressed him/ Answering lip with lip," wrote Charles Kingsley in a poem well-known to Leighton. Perseus receives his reward and makes her his bride.

Dorothy's other mythological role was less stressful; she was pale Persephone emerging from the underworld, again in the arms of Gaetano Valvona, this time as Hermes, the messenger of the gods. Persephone "is lovely, and fresh as a blush-rose washed in dew," and her return to her mother is the return of spring. Yet again another maiden in distress was saved, although every six months Persephone would return to the dark abyss of Hades.

"Why are you always so Greek, Sir Frederick?" he was asked by the *Pall Mall Gazette.*

"I don't know that I am," he answered. "I treat my subjects in a Grecian manner not from special or direct interest in the Greeks, but because they are the least trammelled art-subjects ... Greek art is the most modern because it is the most for all time and most entirely human and unaffected."

The Return of Persephone was optimistic showing the reunion of daughter and mother, the rescue from the dead, and "of beauty rescued from the ugliness of the industrial age," writes the art historian Malcolm Warner.

***

Rachel Beer was a London philanthropist, the wife of the *Observer*'s proprietor and editor, and soon to be herself the owner and editor of the *Sunday Times.* For three successive nights in February 1891, she held a special event of *tableaux vivants* at her Mayfair home in aid of nursing charities. It was the first time that all three Dene sisters – Dorothy, Kathleen and Lena performed together. Hetty was busy with her own gala night in the Princess Theatre.

Tableaux vivants had taken London by storm. This newly fashionable 'special effect' consisted of groups of actors posing without moving – a living freeze frame. The elaborate lighting effects at the Beer's mansion, with breath-taking costumes and props, and a cast of 30 players as well as musicians and singers, were worthy of a West-End production. The scenes all centred on well-known stories of beauty, romance and death and were devised and directed by the veteran actress Mrs Bancroft. Lena was the busiest and most popular of the sisters. In a white satin dress, she dazzled as Juliet opposite the handsome young Romeo, played by Gordon Craig, Ellen Terry's son. They made a perfect pair of lovers, and the scene reminded the audience of her recent modelling for Leighton's follower Charles Perugini, in his *First Words of Love.* She scored a triumph in another scene of *The Queen of Beauty,* being crowned with roses, and was very much applauded in four scenes of "a lovers' quarrel and reconciliation," which ended with the lover planting a kiss on Lena's coy cheek.

Dorothy had just one, but very powerful role, as Queen Katharine of Aragon in two tragic scenes, one of the trial when King Henry VIII forced her to divorce him and the second of her death in a nunnery. She changed her dresses for each scene – white, black and violet – and had to struggle with the heavy 16th century costume, looking "pale and grave and wistful in the unfamiliar Tudor coif and wimple surmounted by a jewelled coronet." Kathleen, who had never been painted and had never been on stage, had one role that night: Queen Henrietta Maria, the wife of King Charles I who was beheaded. In her yellow silk dress and side curls she "was a gracefully pathetic figure."

Imaginary queens and kings were on stage, but the audience was truly regal: a procession of princes and princesses, dukes and duchesses sat applauding in Mrs Beer's salon, and the sold-out cultural and social event was hailed by the press as one of the best ever given in London. That intoxicating experience inspired Dorothy. For a long time, she had been disappointed with the parts offered to her. If she were to form her own production company, she could avoid worn-out, mediocre plays and give a chance to new dramatists that theatres did not want to take risk with. She could even commission especially tailored plays. Her three younger sisters could join in and offer the public the novelty of four almost identical beauties on stage. A month later, she was sitting proudly in the audience watching Kathleen and Lena debut together in *Kissing Cup's Race,* a comedy in four acts by the Scottish dramatist Campbell Rae-Brown. It involved a horse race, a fraudster and a gold mine, and the young sisters gave excellent performances.

***

A few days later they all had another public appearance and got rather less praise. With Leighton's fees and many gifts of money, Dorothy could indulge in shopping sprees for herself and her sisters. They were always one step ahead of fashion. Like other actresses at the time, she had to provide her own stage costumes at her own expense. Being at Leighton's side, she needed many more for her public engagements.

In mid-April 1891, the press had a field day: apparently, the four Dene sisters had their dresses designed and made by Mrs Beatrice Manley of 490 Oxford Street; but although they had several times been tried on and altered, nothing seemed to make them fit. Dorothy's back seemed like the trunk of a tree, and Kathleen's sleeves were like trousers. Many of the other outfits were also less haute couture than botched couture. As a result, Dorothy declined to take them and refused to pay. The dressmaker sued the sisters, complaining that "every effort had been made to suit them, but without success. Nothing seemed to please them": in Mrs Manley's opinion, the dresses fitted perfectly, and she demanded her full fee of £44.

Bloomsbury County Court was rather empty when the case began, and the plaintiff displayed the costumes in dispute. Judge Francis Henry Bacon ordered each of the four Dene girls to retire to an adjoining room and try them on. The rumour that a fashion show was about to begin spread and the sisters returned to a packed hall. His Honour, like a seasoned *haute-couturist*, tested the length of each skirt, the position of the seams and the length and fit of the bodices. He suggested several small alterations and adjourned the case until these were made. Ten days later, Dorothy, who spoke on her sisters' behalf, reported that they have tried them all but instead of making them fit, the dressmaker had "utterly spoiled them."

Few judges are specialists in fashion but the bachelor Judge Bacon was famous for his sartorial expertise. Once, when a defendant claimed to be desolate, he remarked that her hat indicated the opposite. The woman objected, saying that the hat was five years old, but the judge denounced it as a lie, since "women did not wear such great flowers in their hats five years ago. I observe, and I know," he boasted.

Dorothy came back to the room, turning the court into a catwalk, walking around in her brown and gold dress so that His Honour might examine her outfit from all angles. Mrs Manley jumped to her feet and said that Miss Dene was standing as awkwardly as she could.

"I am standing as I always do," Dorothy insisted indignantly.

The judge asked her to hold her head up and lift her arms, and she modified her positions according to his orders. He looked closely and agreed that it did not fit.

"Of course, if she puts it on awkwardly, and stands awkwardly, it will not look right!" the dressmaker protested.

Next it was Hetty's turn – she complained that her dress collar was too tight. The judge beckoned her to the bench. He always had a tape measure at hand, to resolve such disputes, but this time, he tested the collar with his finger and agreed. Judge Bacon usually found in favour of dressmakers and tailors, knowing clients often tried not to pay by padding their underclothes to prove that the clothes did not fit; however, his judgment in the Manley versus Dene case was balanced. Dorothy was exempted from paying £8 for her dress, and £5 more for the matching cloak and accessories, and £5 were taken off Hetty's bill. Kathleen and Lena's outfits had to be paid in full, however.

"To fit or not to fit," punned the *Punch*, and the judge was congratulated upon the diligence that he showed to his duties, and the fact that he did not "cause a jury of matrons to be empanelled to try the delicate question as to the 'fit' of the garments but undertook this pleasing duty himself." It was seen as "another proof of the superiority of the masculine mind over the feminine," as the judge needed no training to be an arbiter of fashion. The *Funny Folks* suggested courses on fashion as part of the legal training – "You may fail in Latin or in Roman law, but you must take care your dressmaking's all right."

Dorothy, however, was furious: she expected to be refunded in full. She was not impressed by the judge's fashion acumen, and complained that he "could not understand that it was impossible to wear a bustle when it had gone out of fashion." From the transcript of the trial, she comes across as vain and capricious.

When Dorothy and Hetty went to the private view at the *New Gallery*, their black and pink dresses "were viewed with a double interest by many present as being probably the dresses on the fit of which Judge Bacon gave an opinion the other day." Dorothy's fussiness at the trial was not forgotten. A year later, as she attended the Royal Academy opening, the fashion critic of the *Newcastle Courant* pointed out that her gown did not look clean and fresh enough – and was possibly too tight – since it showed signs of "past gastronomic delights in the shape of dinner parties or other evening entertainments."

Van der Weyde, who took Dorothy's photos in the past, was intrigued by the trial and invited all four sisters to his studio. Their portrait in their frilly, ruffled dresses, "on bromide, but without retouching" won him a special gold medal in the Leeds Photographic Exhibition in December 1891.

Chapter Twenty

The Misses Dene

Piccadilly was blocked with carriages for the Royal Academy summer exhibition opening. The President, "the handsomest host in London," stood at the top of the flower-lined staircase of Burlington House. For four hours Leighton welcomed the dignitaries. Some found him "profoundly pompous, and fairly beams with satisfaction in himself and his environments."

The British excel at pageant; the head porter would announce names and titles, and Leighton would receive each one with a smile, a handshake or a bow, and just the right words. Dorothy was a most welcome guest and never missed the annual event. She was there in

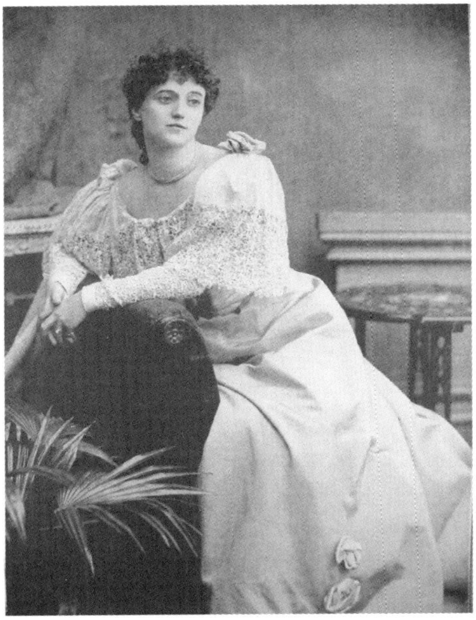

Hetty Dene, press photo by Alexander Bassano

triplicate one might say – as Leighton's intimate, as a model that no year's exhibition was complete without – that year she was both Andromeda and Persephone – and finally, as a celebrated actress.

There were over 2000 guests in the gala night of 1891, but only 38 men and women made it to Grenville Manton's group painting, among them actresses Ellen Terry and Mary Anderson. Leighton is at the focal point, greeting a slim and tall young woman. Grenville Manton painted the elegant guest only from the back, making it hard to identify her, leaving room for speculation.

All four Dene sisters were thriving in the theatre, so they could compare roles and reviews, but it had no bearing on their bond. In fact, Hetty, Kathleen and Lena had more engagements than Dorothy, but they were playing minor parts – and there were plenty of those – while she was looking only for leading roles. They all tried to perform at least in pairs, and theatre managers liked the publicity stunt. The physical similarity between the sisters made it easy for them to replace one another in case of illness.

In May Dorothy and Hetty were in Oxford with the Arthur Bourchier's company, playing in a double bill. The titles of plays were not exactly nuanced: Hetty played an actress whose husband detests her profession, in the comedy *That Dreadful Doctor*. Dorothy was a wife who rescued her husband from financial ruin by cheating at cards, in Arthur Wing Pinero's *The Money Spinner*.

Dorothy's acting was emotional and sincere, giving the impression "of *feeling* not *posing*, which is singularly rare in a very pretty woman on the stage," wrote the *Oxford Journal*. In September, Kathleen and Lena were in a comedy named *School*, at the Garrick Theatre. It became a long-runner – 90 performances – and the critic Cecil Howard, who thought that the play was brilliantly-written but a bit childish, wondered "how many of those who appeared as the pretty school girls will by-and-by make their mark." Kathleen's next role was in the comedy *Fourteen Days,* but she was so nervous that the critic, who praised her beauty, thought that it would be unkind to pass any judgment on her capabilities: she had 36 more performances to overcome her stage fright.

Hetty was the busiest sister with the longest running plays: she had true comic talent, good timing, perseverance and some luck. She was noted among the emerging actresses of her time for her "so strong feeling for character."

Hetty's pictures were also in shop windows, and she made it to the cover of the *Illustrated Sporting and Dramatic News*, wearing a large feathered hat in her older sister's style. The celebrity photographer Alexander Bassano published his full-page portrait of her for a special 1894 Christmas edition of the *Sketch*. Hetty looked like a confident, high-born society lady. She continued to be at Dorothy's side in all her sister's social engagements and was never seen with a male companion. Lillie Langtry took Hetty under her management. She cast her in the successful one-act curtain raiser, *Rachel's Messenger*, as a pretty daughter who is about to sacrifice herself for the sake of her parents and marry a man she does not love.

In October, Hetty acted a small part in one of Pinero's satires of the failures of English society, a four-act play titled *The Times*. She had to wear spectacles to play a Newnham college girl and did it "with a simple but pathetic force which gives good promise for her artistic future." Pinero, soon to be hailed as the promoter of English Ibsenism, was enthusiastically cheered, and the play was a box-office hit running for five and a half months

Henrik Ibsen's work was unlike most of the fluff on the London stage. The Norwegian playwright arrived in London in June 1889 when *A Doll's House* was first staged at the *Novelty Theatre* and caused fierce controversy. Did Nora, the heroine, have the right to abandon her children? Many thought the play abominable. *Ghosts*, in 1891, shocked with its treatment of religion, venereal disease, incest and euthanasia, topics that were not expected to feature in the theatre then. Compared to plays about wicked lord and girls fluttering about their virtue, Ibsen was grimly realistic. He had become "the theme of many pens and tongues ... a barometer of the intellectual weather," observed Henry James. Just as Leighton was criticized for being out-dated, so was Dorothy. She was never offered a part in any of Ibsen's dramas, and for that matter, in any other modern one. She was gradually losing ground, appearing in genres which were going out of fashion.

In October, Hetty acted a small part in one of Pinero's satires of the failures of English society, a four-act play titled *The Times*. She had to wear spectacles to play a Newnham college girl and did it "with a simple but pathetic force which gives good promise for her artistic future." Pinero, soon to be hailed as the promoter of English Ibsenism, was enthusiastically cheered, and the play was a box-office hit running for five and a half months.

***

"The tendency seems to be to keep the actor in one groove – a tendency that the public is perhaps as responsible for as the manager," Dorothy complained to a journalist. "If one makes a hit in a couple of parts of the same nature at once there is born the belief that one cannot succeed in another direction." Feeling that she was not valued enough, she decided to take the initiative. She would have her own show, with a scope of roles to demonstrate her versatile abilities. Hetty was her trusted ally and was willing to halt a promising solo career in order to play side by side with her: "I read your little play and think it's quite charming," Dorothy wrote to D. Stewart, one of several writers that she approached. "My sister Hetty has also read it and likes it extremely. I wish you had a three or four-act play that would suit me."

Like many young women of her time, Dorothy read *Moths*, the best-selling novel by Ouida, the pen name of the English novelist Maria Louise Ramé. Melodrama hardly does justice to this brew of adultery, domestic violence and divorce. *Moths* aimed to shock and show marriage as it was for many: a form of slavery and legalized prostitution. Several successful stage adaptations were made, and Dorothy put together her own choice of the key scenes. She cast herself in the lead as the beautiful, serious, innocent teenager Vere Herbert. Her corrupt mother forces her to marry an elderly, lecherous Russian prince, in order to pay her debts. Vere – meaning "truth" – is abused by her husband, who rapes her in their marital bed, and beats her viciously when she refuses to share a house with his mistress.

Dorothy also commissioned a special one-act play for all her sisters, and as a publicity stunt, they came to the Downey studio in Ebury Street. They lagged behind her "at a respectful distance in point of beauty, but [were] very like her in hair and clothes," wrote the *New*

York Times. Dorothy, in black, sat regally surrounded by her sisters: Hetty, in white, stood behind, her profile reflected in the side mirrors. The younger ones, very serious and sombre, stood on both sides, Lena on her left, and Kathleen on her right. William Downey called it *The Misses Dene* and valued it so much that he included it in his book of famous portraits and sent an enlarged print to the Chicago World Fair.

On Thursday, February 25th, 1892, the curtain rose at the *Prince of Wales Theatre* for the *Dorothy Dene Matinee*; apparently, her high hopes were abandoned, and instead of the daring *Moths*, the program was rather conventional. It began with *Cousin Dick*, a short comedy by Leighton's neighbour, Val Prinsep. Dorothy played an over-romantic teenager, a role she had already done twice. The next was a replay from her days at the School of Dramatic Art: two scenes from Shakespeare's *King John.* As the bereaved Queen Constance, she was electrifying, and "surprised even her previous admirers by the gravity and depth" of her acting. Hetty trans-ed for the show and played the Queen's son, Arthur, brutally murdered so that his uncle John could grab the throne. Hetty was commended for her "considerable tragic power" as the doomed prince.

The only original piece in the show was *Sixteen Not Out,* especially commissioned from the Scottish journalist James Blair. It was a modern adaptation of the Cinderella story; the mistreated heroine is a boarding school girl, Kitty. Her two cruel sisters refuse to take her to a fancy ball, since she has not yet been "out" in society. Her mischievous girlfriend plays a practical joke on the older sisters: she dresses up as a millionaire Russian prince, dances with them at the costume ball and proposes to each one of them. Kathleen played Kitty, Hetty donned the trousers and Dorothy and Lena were the evil sisters. For the scene at the fancy dress ball, Dorothy dressed as Georgiana, the Duchess of Devonshire, while Lena was Portia, from the *Merchant of Venice.* The audience loved it and laughter rocked the theatre. "Quite lost my virgin heart to dear little Cinderella," wrote the *Sporting Times* critic.

In Manchester, *Sixteen Not Out* was a curtain-raiser to *Hero and Leander*, a poetic musical play. Leighton's picture of Dorothy as Hero was hanging in the Manchester Art Gallery, but she did not get the part. Hetty, Kathleen and Lena had minor roles as virgins in the temple of Aphrodite. They danced the *can-can* in Greek togas in a provocative way which was a sensational success. "Four very pretty young maidens/ Which nobody can Dene-eye," the *Clarion* punned on their names and physical appearance: "Dorothy, the portly; Lena, who is leaner; Kathleen, who is rather lean; and Hetty, the Pretty."

Dorothy was not so pleased though. She had spent a great deal of money putting on the production and hoped to start a new chapter in her life as an actor-producer, but she only received offers to stage her *Sixteen Not Out* yet again as a curtain raiser. She turned them down, and theatre critic Jacob Grein was surprised;

"If I were you," he told her, "instead of announcing in the *Era* that I was 'resting' – a placid participle often hiding a tale of misery – I should seek an engagement in a theatre where a curtain-raiser is on the programme."

Dorothy was horrified. "No, no, no, not that! You might as well ask me to get buried alive! And as she spoke, she shuddered as if an east wind of despair were chilling her to the bone."

She explained to Grein that the pay for a curtain raiser was wretched, while the producers of the main play of the evening were paid generously, getting a large percentage of the gross receipts. The critics hardly took notice, and the audience also underrated the curtain-raiser. They did not take their seats until the main show began, so during the front-piece "the stalls and the dress circle yawn in emptiness." She felt that "To play in a front-piece is to come down in one's profession; it is evidence that one is not wanted in the 'show' of the evening, that one is on the shelf, as it were."

Grein listened sadly, "for it was an experienced woman who spoke – an actress who possessed brains and other gifts that gave weight to her opinion".

Dorothy still hoped to play Juliet and Desdemona and did not think she was too old to do so.

Chapter Twenty-One

America

Leighton celebrated the Dene sisters' joint debut in his own way. He invited three of them – once more Kathleen was left out – to pose for one of his most important paintings.

Three nymphs guarded the tree of life with its golden fruits. In the Greek myth, a hundred–headed dragon watched over them, to stop them eating the fruit themselves. Leighton changed the dragon into a benign serpent, eating from the girls' hands. Under a Mediterranean orange tree, the three sisters were lazing, languid, almost as if they had been drugged. Dorothy, on the left, was singing and plucking gently on the lyre, Hetty, in the centre, was humming herself to sleep, while

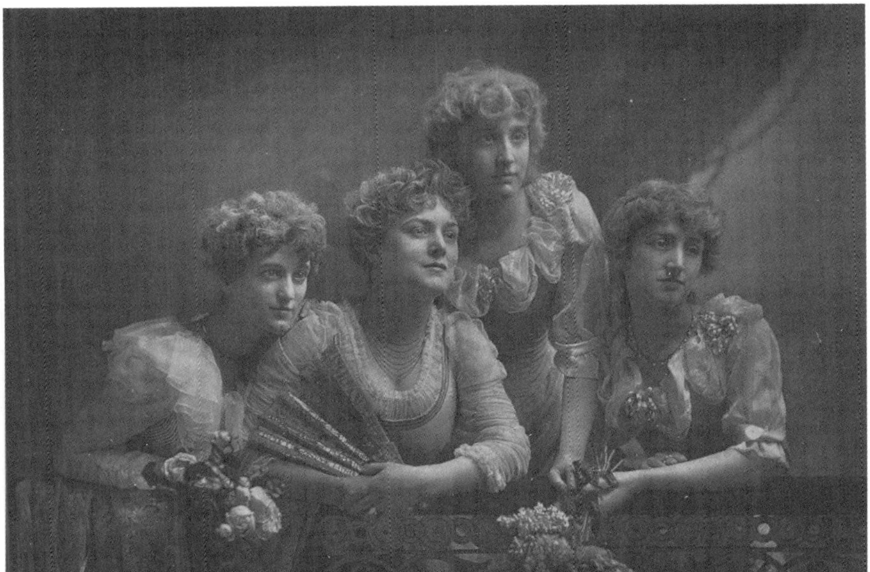

From left to right: Hetty, Dorothy, Lena, Kathleen, 1891, by Van der Weyde

Lena, on the right, was feeding the serpent. Tranquil and joyous, nothing suggested the imminent danger of Hercules bursting in to slay the serpent and steal the golden fruits. For the modelling sessions, Dorothy wore for the first time her Flaming June diaphanous dress. Bewitched, Leighton would paint Dorothy like that in three more works.

On the Sunday before the summer exhibition, journalists and art lovers went round the Holland Park studios to inspect the new harvest. A woman journalist for *Hearth and Home* bumped into Dorothy, "looking unusually handsome in a long cloak." Standing in front of the *Garden of the Hesperides,* the reporter was moved by the strange enchanted atmosphere of the "marvellous picture, so beautiful, so far away from this life of ours," and decided to see no more pictures that afternoon, not to break the magic spell. The *Clarion* commented that the picture, with its abundant greenery and its fountain with goldfish, a swan and a dove, is "better known in the seat of the scoffer as 'the Sisters Dene at the Zoo'."

Like *Captive Andromache,* which took Leighton years to execute, his next painting for the 1892 summer exhibition also was a labour of time. "I have myself a weakness for this picture, which I brewed for some 15 years," he wrote to Charles Pooley of the Manchester Art Gallery. He asked Dorothy to recreate her pose of Persephone – stretching her arms up to embrace her mother – but this time, he made her into Clytie, the nymph loved and abandoned by the sun god Apollo. Dorothy was on her knees, arms raised in supplication, begging him to return, "night and day, under the open sky, she sat dishevelled, bareheaded, on the bare earth," wrote Ovid in his *Metamorphoses.* "Without food and water, fasting, for nine days, she lived only on dew and tears, and did not stir from the ground, she only gazed at the god's aspect as he passed, and turned her face towards him."

Leighton put all his energy into the Turner-like setting, full of clouds and a burst of light, with Clytie/Dorothy a diminutive figure at the lower right corner of the canvas. It is tempting to interpret the scene as autobiographical: female submission and unrequited love, the enamoured Dorothy worshipping Leighton, who would not return her affection.

But if Clytie is symbolic, she is not necessarily Dorothy, but Leighton himself, begging the sun, the source of his vitality, not to desert him at this stage in his life, in his 62nd year. He always sought the sun, spending several months every year in warm climates. "Sunlight can never be accessory – its glory is paramount where it appears, everything except water is tributary to its song of splendour," he wrote. He did not sell the painting and returned to the scene three years later.

Dorothy's third representation that year was *At the Fountain*, standing in semi-transparent classical attire, leaning against a white marble fountain in Mediterranean scenery. The Milwaukee Art Museum snatched it quickly. There was a fourth painting. Leighton wished to explore the theme of a woman parting from her beloved, but so as not to overuse Dorothy, he used Hetty. In *Farewell*, Hetty stands crying on the porch of a mansion; her lips tremble as she takes one last glimpse at her lover's disappearing ship. The dark, angry-looking cloud over the horizon predicts disaster. "The surroundings of the woman are distinctly Greek; but the passionate regret which looks out from the eyes gives the figure a universally human interest," wrote the *Graphic*.

***

These were hard times for actors in London. Theatres were going bankrupt; bailiffs were at the stage doors, emptying the cashier's drawers, and confiscating the scenery, props and costumes, everything that could be sold to cover debts. There was less work for actors, and even the lucky ones who did work, suffered a severe drop of income. Earlier a fortnight was the shortest run of a play, now many ended after just three or four nights. Given that actors were not paid for rehearsals, which could last between two weeks up to a month, it was a total loss when a show was taken off stage after a few days. Running her own company was now too risky for Dorothy.

Every aspiring British actor dreamt of crossing the ocean and conquering America. The theatre managers there offered contracts that could not be matched in London (on her first American tour, Lillie Langtry received $2000 a week: more than five times her London salary). Good press reception and box-office figures would boost one's career back home. The Americans were paradoxical; they welcomed actors from Shakespeare's homeland, but more often than not, they frowned on their guests' stale genre and style. Most of the British repertoire was almost unknown across the Atlantic. Aware of that and anxious about leaving her sisters alone, Dorothy put the American dream on hold. But now, she badly needed an overseas success to rescue her career.

In the summer of 1891 Nat Goodwin invited Dorothy to play opposite him in New York. Though it was no perfect match – he was a vaudeville star, and the role offered was in a farce, she accepted, and turned down two productions in the coming London season. She was all set to sail, but a fortnight before her departure, the deal fell through because of "some misunderstanding." It was too late to make new arrangements, and she lost out on all sides; out of work in England for several months. She was deeply disappointed, but the rejection only fuelled her determination. A year later she decided to take the plunge and go, even without a contract, and try her luck.

To ease stress and to give her sister the prospect of success, she asked Hetty to join her. Three young Denes remained in 10, Avonmore mansions: Kathleen, Lena, and the school-boy Sam. When the sisters disembarked from the *Servia* at Ellis Island on 26 September 1892, Dorothy elegantly deducted nine years from her age in her statement to the immigration authorities. To the *New York Times* she went even further and declared that she was "about twenty-one." The press, all over the USA, was in love, even in cities and states she was not planning to visit. "She is sunshine incarnated," gushed the *Morning Call* of San Francisco. "Her bright smile and cordial manner are as suggestive of sunlight as in her hair of sunbeams." She never gave so many interviews in her life and was praised for her "high-bred manners of a gentlewoman."

Before leaving for the USA, Dorothy furnished herself with letters of introduction from London's top socialites to their counterparts in New York. She was surprised when her American hostess told her that it would be best for her not to speak too much of her profession, as actresses in America had no social position.

"Why! The actresses that are ladies are sought after in London," Dorothy exclaimed, "and they have the entree to the best circles of society." She had met American actress Mary Anderson at a Royal

Academy soiree, and there was no reason that it should be any different in the USA, Dorothy said. The reporter concluded that "if the idea needed revolutionizing [in America], none could do it better than beautiful Miss Dorothy Dene."

Given the bad experiences of British actors in America –one actress, Miss Eastlake, was left penniless and had to borrow money from England to cover her debts – Dorothy tried to lower mutual expectations. She presented herself as a tourist, visiting friends in New York, and said that she simply came "to take a look around at American life and manners." The *New York Tribune* thought otherwise: "the reason is that there was a great famine in her land. That is to say, there was a long theatrical season in which anybody connected with the theatre who did not starve, was lucky; and the more acting was done, the less was gained by it. So Miss Dene, being in danger of actual starvation, and thinking she foresaw another season like the last," decided to try America. Striving to present herself as a serious actress, she played down her modelling. In interviews, she detailed her sisters' acting careers, flaunted the photographs of the four of them together, and was duly presented as a member of a theatrical family. She would stay a few months and perhaps much longer if engaged to play, and "she wants her sisters to come over here, too."

Dorothy was energetic as ever. She and Hetty were staying at a friend's opulent home in Manhattan, and from there, she pulled every string, met agents and fellow actors. Producer and manager Daniel Frohman, who gave a party in her honour at the New York *Lyceum*, declared that Dorothy Dene was "one of the cleverest actresses on the English stage." Only one paper dared to spoil her visit and question her abilities, the *Pittsburgh Dispatch*, that bitched under the headline that Her Face is Her Fortune, that her chief qualification has always been her beauty, which "seems to have palled on the British public, else why should she be put to such straights as to enter this easily gulled country, unheralded and practically begging a job?"

It was a very wet November in New York, and both Dorothy and Hetty fell ill. It took about six nail-biting weeks until Dorothy's first theatrical appearance. It was a one-off performance in the newly-established Theatre of Arts and Letters before an invited audience. She played the title role in *Mary Maberly* opposite American actor Eben Plympton, with whom she worked on the London stage. The playwright Frederic Jesup Stimson remembered that they had hardly any rehearsals, and that he "sat up till two the last night in Dorothy Dene's apartments, going over the fine points and I know she did her best." Fine points there were few. Dorothy played a woman torn between two men and marrying a third, who proves to be a drunkard; she was hampered because the play was so poor. *Town Topics – the Journal of Society* wondered why Dorothy was paid an incredible sum of $400, since "there was certainly nothing in her position or her achievements to warrant such an expenditure" of importing an English actress for the role.

Her first commercial show took place on January 9th, 1893, in the comedy *Captain Herne USA*, with the company of Edward John Henley – a British actor who moved to New York. She played a mysterious, beautiful adventuress during the American Civil War and was "passionate and vengeful." It ran for just a week until Henley decided to replace it with a double-bill comprising of the comedy *Our Club* by F.C. Burnand, editor of *Punch*, and a psycho-drama by Stanislaus Stange, called *Yesterday*. The latter suited Dorothy, who always did well with insane characters. She was a woman driven to madness because her lover had been murdered. Even better, the role required her to sing, which she did very well. She kept Leighton informed of all the turns and twists and he shared it with their mutual friends. The ocean did not really separate them.

Dorothy played for three weeks in the Union Square Theatre, with some mishaps – once she missed a show because she slipped on the ice and suffered greatly from nervous shock. As the company began a tour of New York State, Dorothy was cheered as she turned from "a laughing maiden to an insane woman." But she could not enjoy her triumph for long; at the end of February, she fell ill again, this time more severely with pneumonia, which she caught when the train she was travelling on was stuck in the snow for 48 hours. Hetty replaced her. Having a sister in reserve was useful but Dorothy minded missing the show. She was bedridden for weeks and clearly lost her momentum.

Chapter Twenty-Two

The Queen was not dethroned

Leighton made a note in his diary to cable New York on April 11th. Dorothy turned 34 on that day. She was very much present in his studio.

His new picture of "a tall, graceful girl of the well-known Leightonian type ... in sentiment and design is a pendant to the beautiful 'Bath of Psyche'," wrote the *Evening Herald.* The recent uproar about nudity did not stop Leighton painting another pensive Dorothy undressing for a bath, looking at her reflection in the water. It was a full frontal nude, covered only with transparent drapery which "permits her fair form to be traced, and her skin to be seen beneath." Before she left for

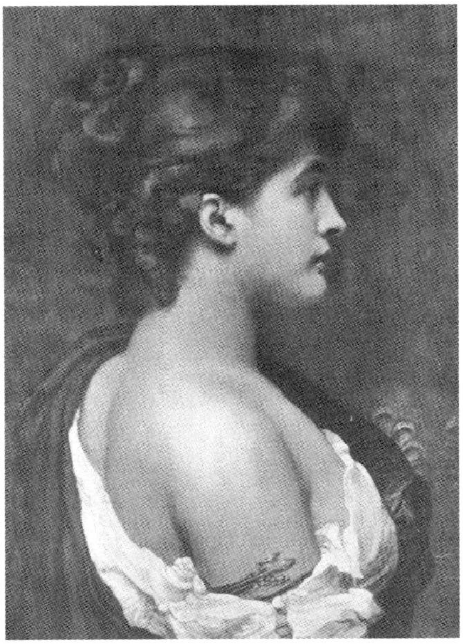

Mary Lloyd as Atalanta, 1893

the USA, he painted her "as a nude, as completely and thoroughly as if it were so to be left," and completed the *Frigidarium* in her absence.

No one knew how long Dorothy and Hetty would be away in the USA– success could make it a year. Obviously, Leighton could not wait for his chief model to return, and the sweet, childish Lena, unsuitable for dramatic roles, could not replace her. For the first time in more than a decade, he had to find a substitute.

Mary Lloyd, born in 1863, introduced herself as the daughter of a country squire in Shropshire. When her father went bankrupt, she had to fend for herself, and moved to London. No documents have been found to verify her account. Her past remains shrouded in mystery, and it is unclear what she did until she rented a room near Regent's Park. She was thirty, rather old to start modelling. She told the *Sunday Express* that she obtained an introduction to Millais, who was "captivated by her beauty." Her Greek profile, full lips, thick eyebrows and strong jaw, together with a mass of long dark hair were her main appeal. She remembered sitting by the fireplace in Leighton's studio "when he was painting the Corinna. How kind he was."

In the winter of 1893, with uncharacteristic speed, Leighton made three paintings with Mary Lloyd. *Corinna of Tangara* was a character made for Dorothy, but Mary Lloyd, with no previous modelling or theatrical experience fulfilled it superbly. Corinna was said to have won a poetry contest against Pindar, the greatest Greek lyrical poet. She triumphed "not so much on account of the excellence of her verse (it has been said), as on account of her beauty," wrote the *Pall Mall Gazette.* Leighton dressed Mary in rich sumptuous draperies, crowned her with a wreath of golden laurel, and gave her the golden lyre that Dorothy used not long before. Mary Lloyd claimed that she never posed in the nude. If she told the truth, Leighton must have used another model for the body.

The *Sunday Express* article from 1933, "The Story of Mary Lloyd who had the face of an angel but outlived her luck," carried a photo of the 70-year-old woman looking up to the youthful portrait of herself as *Atalanta*, another victorious mythological woman. The virgin princess, a fearless hunter and athlete, refused to give up her freedom to a husband. She challenged each of her suitors to a race, gave them head start, but always won, and had them killed. Mary Lloyd was in profile, looking to the right, her shoulder exposed by a falling sleeve. Emily Barrington welcomed her and thought that *Atalanta* was Leighton's strongest work; she was impressed by the enormous power and the "noble beauty of the Pheidian type, in the grand simple pose and the modelling of the throat and shoulder ... the worthy record of the beauty of an English girl."

Very proudly, Mary told the reporter that Leighton presented a portrait of her as a wedding gift to the future King George V and Queen Mary in June 1893. It was very similar to *Atalanta,* though in the gift portrait she was looking to the left, gold fillets in her hair, and decently covered in Greek dress. By then Dorothy was already back in England and was no doubt annoyed that it was not her portrait which was given to the Royal Family. It still hangs in Sandringham House.

All these years, another trio of sisters was going around artists' studios in London. Hetty, Lily and Rosie Pettigrew were born in Portsmouth and pushed to destitution when their father died. Unable to feed her children just by needlework and fearing that they would drift into prostitution, their mother was advised to take her pretty daughters to London and make them artist's models. Hetty was 15, Lily 11 and Rosie was 9 years-old when painted by Millais in *An Idyll,* in 1884. The "three little gypsies," as he called them, became an instant success with painters and sculptors, who agreed to pay much above the going rate for their lithe, slim bodies, pale, half-starved complexions and the variety of moods they could put on. They played one artist against the other, and when James McNeill Whistler neglected to pay Hetty for a whole month, she went on a strike in the middle of an important sitting and did not resume work until he settled the debt in full.

Like the Denes, the Pettigrew sisters lived together; in the 1891 census they stated their occupation proudly as "an artist's model." For the extra guinea, Hetty and Lily were willing to be photographed in the nude by Linley Sambourne, in saucy, risqué poses together and alone. It may have been the trail of gossip which discouraged Leighton from using them, but he finally did, in late 1892, when Dorothy and Hetty were away in New York. In a note to his neighbour Hamo Thorneycroft, he asked him if he could "spare Etty Pettigrew on Wednesday"; Thorneycroft was sculpting her and working against the clock, since she was often absent, but he couldn't refuse.

Leighton needed Hetty Pettigrew for his biblical *Rizpah*, a sombre, powerful tragic scene of the Hebrew mother, the mistress of King Saul, whose two sons were unjustly executed; for seven months Rizpah refused to have her sons buried and, a sickle in her hand, guarded their bodies against vultures and wild beasts. "It is a gruesome scene but wondrously painted," wrote a reviewer when it was shown at the Royal Academy. "Indeed, Sir Frederick seems to be passing into a gloomy vein ... the days of the lighter moods of *The Garden of the Hesperides*, of the Greek Maidens at play, of Cymon and Iphigenia ... are now but memories of this picturesque pencil." Apparently, the President of the Republic of Art, remarked the reviewer, "now finds his greater delights in the house of the dead."

In the 1893 Royal Academy summer exhibition, all four models were represented: Dorothy in the *Frigidarium,* Hetty in *Farewell*, Mary Lloyd in *Atalanta* and in *Corinna of Tangara,* and Lily Pettigrew in *Rizpah.* "How persistently and charmingly Sir Frederick always portrays the most beautiful women one ever sees anywhere, and he seems to add to their natural beauty a subtle charm by his own conception of what they might be," hailed the *Wrexham Advertiser.*

Some models became romantically involved with the artists they posed for: Hetty Pettigrew had an affair with the sculptor John Tweed to whom she became engaged; when he ditched her, she returned to be the long-term muse and mistress of the married painter Theodore Roussel and bore him a daughter. Hetty literally took matters in her own hand as she learned to sculpt and exhibited in several art galleries. Her sister Lily was the muse and lover of John William Godward and he painted her over and over again; pretty Rosie was the muse of Whistler, and engaged to Philip Wilson Steer, who painted her constantly and was heartbroken when she left him to marry a musician.

***

In New York, Dorothy was offered to play in *Midsummer Night's Dream* in the prestigious John Augustin Daly's theatre. She agreed to play either Helena or Hermia, and asked for a salary of $75 a week, in addition to her costumes. It was a modest request as the average salary for such a role ran between $100 to $300 a week. But the play was due only in three months' time, and eventually, Dorothy and Hetty decided not to wait idly in New York but to return immediately to London. They missed the grand opening of the Chicago World's Fair, where they were represented in several works by Leighton at the British Pavilion: *Bath of Psyche, Perseus and Andromeda,* and *The Garden of the Hesperides*, as well as in Downey's joint photograph. Going to Chicago could have got her work, but Dorothy was too frail and somewhat disappointed to make the effort.

Her short visit made Dorothy famous enough for several American tobacco firms to see her as a sales-booster and place her photos into their cigarette packs and chewing tobacco boxes. The cards were collected, exchanged and carefully pasted into special albums. Sweet Caporal Cigarettes distributed pin-back buttons with her image. Thomas Ogden of Liverpool also included her in his Guinea Gold cigarette series, but the similarity between the sisters led to a printing error, when Hetty's image carried the more famous Dorothy's name. it seems that the commercials were the main benefit of their visit.

The eight months Dorothy spent in America proved to be a disaster on all fronts. Daly's offer to join his company and perform in his new theatres in London and in New York never materialized. Other American impresarios did not make her offers, and she was left with the remote dream of trying her luck in Australia. London did not court her either. Her pneumonia developed into chronic rheumatic fever. She slipped into enforced idleness. It was a year and a half until she would get her next acting job.

But the queen was not dethroned. On her return to Holland Park, Dorothy immediately resumed sitting for Leighton, and Mary Lloyd was given a letter of introduction to the painter Herbert Draper. In less than five months – until he went on his annual European trip – Leighton produced four new paintings of Dorothy. He was replicating her most beautiful poses, mainly sitting or lying down, which now suited her delicate health. The variety of moods –melancholy, introspection, hedonism and sensuality – showcased her dramatic skills. Leighton, it seems, was trying to help her back into her theatrical career.

The Spirit of the Summit was a companion-picture to *Solitude*, which Leighton painted three years earlier. Once again, he dressed Dorothy in snow-white robes, and sat her in queenly solitude on a summit of the Zermatt glaciers at the dead of night. She was pressing her hand to the rock firmly, "her head thrown back and her face with parted lips, as though she were listening to the music of the spheres, lifted towards the zenith. The expression of the face is that of serene contemplation." Leighton might as well have called it "The Spirit of my Painting," wrote the French art critic Robert de la Sizeranne, and Edgcumbe Staley added that "she is, in short, the genius of Leighton personified." More than Dorothy's splendid isolation, the painting symbolized Leighton's striving for the highest ideal and the price of loneliness that he had to pay. It was said that not one in a hundred English painters could, "having attempted this theme in this way, have won so notable a success."

For her next role, the chaste prophetess *Fatidica*, Dorothy wore white again; half-seated, half-lying on a silver throne, brooding over the future. The pose – wistful eyes, face resting on her hand in deep meditation – was reminiscent of her *Tragic Poetess* and *Sybil*.

After two strong, cerebral, solitary women, Dorothy was cast in two softer domestic scenes. The *Bracelet* echoed *The Light of the Harem* and the *Arts of Peace* that Leighton painted when Dorothy began modelling for him. In the atrium of a Pompeian house, standing by a chair on which her outer garments have been thrown, a young beauty admires an expensive bracelet clasped around her forearm. Her shapely thigh and leg peeped from under her golden silk robe. She was not alone this time – the young woman had a family, a little girl sitting at her feet holding an open casket of jewels. It seemed that Dorothy was not one woman for Leighton, but all womanhood. He never got enough of her. A journalist later wrote that "conscious of his inability to put on any one canvas the sum total of her charms, Sir Frederick gave the world a hundred or more Dorothy Denes; each accentuating some particular feature or expression."

Summer Slumber was the most sensuous of the four. Wrapped in her Flaming June dress, Dorothy was a sleeping beauty, by a marble bath on which doves perched. Leighton amused the seven-year-old Estella, daughter of Louisa Starr-Canziani, by telling her how he fed the doves bread soaked with brandy and water, and, becoming tipsy, "finally they all went to sleep and he was able to paint them."

Everything in the picture suggested a lazy, hot Roman summer, and "the girl's light draperies veil without concealing the beautiful lines of her figure." Having the naked Dorothy lie on her back with her legs apart was evidently too scandalous, so Leighton hired an effeminate male model to pose in the nude. He sketched him and made the necessary anatomical modifications, and then brought in Dorothy to lie down covered with the draperies. In fact, three models posed for *Summer Slumber*: the body of a man, Dorothy's face and curves, and the long, wavy blond hair of another female model. The sensual pose got the attention of the ever randy Prince of Wales, who was given a final study.

George Moore, frustrated painter and prolific Irish writer was intrigued by *Summer Slumber*, and he wrote a poem in French: *De quoi rêvent-elles?*

> What do they dream of? Flowers
> Shadows, stars or tears?
> What do these sweet women dream?
> Of their lovers or their souls? Slaughtered white lilies
> they sleep the hushed dreams
> In the large oval window
> Open on the summer night.

A special program of *tableaux vivants* was organized at the *Lyric Theatre* in late June 1894, to raise funds for the Victoria Hospital for Children. The *Spirit of the Summit* and *Invocation* took a central place. Leighton supervised the posing of the models in the show, which was under royal patronage. Strangely enough, it was not Dorothy who reconstructed on stage the roles she performed in his studio, but two young actresses, and their "resemblance to the originals being noted with keen delight." The show got a standing ovation and was repeated around the provinces.

Only illness could keep Dorothy away from the stage and from Leighton's *tableaux vivants.* Apparently, she didn't have the energy to reciprocate him and enjoy the fruits of her triumphant modelling.

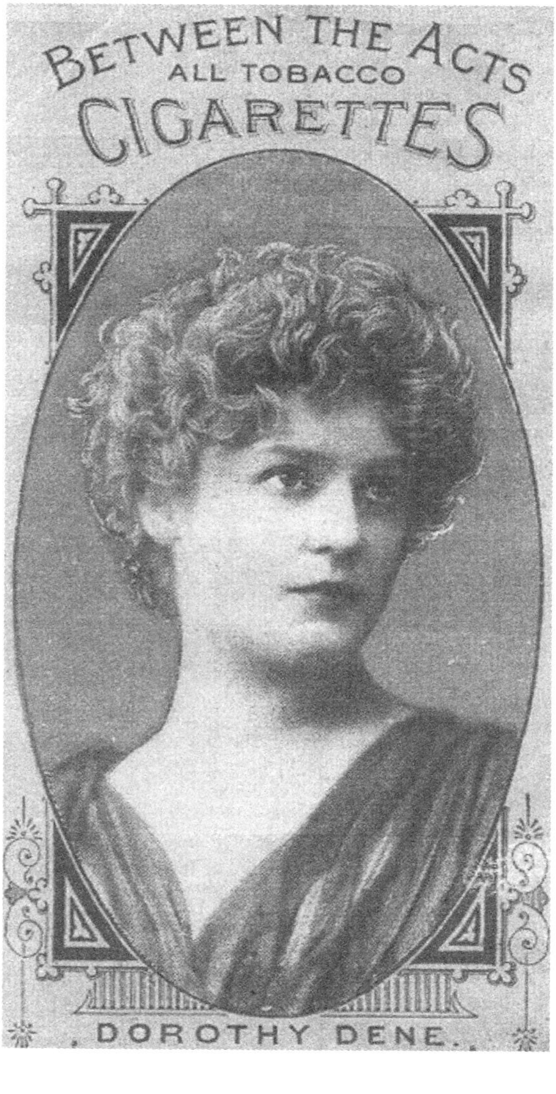

Chapter Twenty-Three

"The art of pushing"

In September 1894 Dorothy finally stepped back on stage in Wilde's *A Woman of No Importance.* It premiered a year earlier, and was so hugely successful, that three companies were doing it simultaneously. Dorothy was cast as Mrs Allonby, a flirtatious female fashionista. Lord Illingsworth is a handsome bachelor and a promising diplomat. Women lust after him, including Mrs Arbuthnot, an apparently respectable widow and regular churchgoer. But she has a dark secret: she had been Illingsworth's mistress, and bore him an illegitimate son.

Dorothy's character shared Illingworth's loose morals and philosophy; one of their sharpest lines was Wilde's witticism, "all women become like their mothers. That is their tragedy. No man does. That is his." The company opened in Birmingham, and in two months, proceeded to Edinburgh, Glasgow, Newcastle, Manchester, Liverpool and Sheffield.

Dorothy stood out as the audacious, cynical, brilliant woman-of-

MISS DOROTHY DENE.
Address,
10, Avonmore-mansions, Avonmore-road, Kensington, W.

MISS HETTIE DENE
Disengaged.
10, Avonmore-mansions, Kensington, W.

MISS KATHLEEN DENE,
Ingénues. Disengaged for Five Weeks. Re-engaged for Spring Tour with Mr and Mrs Kendal. 10, Avonmore-man., W.

MISS LENA DENE.
Address,
10, Avonmore-mansion, Kensington, W.

Job seeking ads in the *Era*

the-world and "greatly pleased the audience." To add intrigue, she switched roles with Florence West who played Mrs Arbuthnot, and on successive evenings they alternated between the two very different female characters. Dorothy excelled in both roles, and the *Era* critic was especially impressed by the painful scene with her former lover that she "played with care and finish, rising to a height of intense emotional power."

Dorothy's absence from the stage put on hold her sisters' careers as well. Now that she was back, all three followed. Hetty joined the Augustus Harris' Drury Lane Theatre in London. *The Derby Winner* was a long-running successful comedy that played nightly with real horses on stage, and enough gimmicks to entertain the audience for over four hours. It was a tale of aristocrats who always cheated in love and horse racing. Hetty played "the stereotyped injured girl of the nursery governess type," and William Archer, who, unlike most other critics, did not like the play, remarked that "even the pleasure of seeing Miss Hetty Dene in a governess-cart ... does not, in my case, amount to rapture." Kathleen was an innocent girl falsely accused of jewellery theft and sentenced to three years hard labour in *The Wife of Dives* at the Opera Comique. It was a prelude to a real and painful brush with the law that Kathleen would soon have.

Their sister, Edith, "exceedingly intense and cultured," was not doing much. About once a year her husband would paint her, and she was gradually missing out even on social events. She was drinking. Her husband at least had the Midas touch, and bought a four-storey house in 49, Addison Road, just around the corner from Leighton. His brother, with his wife and young daughter, moved in as well but there was room enough. The house had seven bedrooms, six bathrooms and a magnificent walled garden. Schmalz added a cathedral-style studio with a high glass ceiling and a wall of tall arched windows. On the top of the outer wall he placed a bas-relief of an angel holding a torch, with the dedication year – 1894 – and a motto in German "*strebe aufwärts*" –"struggle upward," from a prayer that Beethoven wrote when he learned that his deafness was incurable. Until the new studio was ready, Schmalz used his former one in Holland Park Road and locked himself up for days on end to work.

On Sunday, November 25th, 1894, close to midnight, Schmalz popped out from the studio to post a letter. Passing Leighton's house, he noticed a man and a woman walking towards him, "talking, but they did not seem to be on particularly good terms." On his return, he heard a thud, and saw them both fall to the ground, and the woman cried out, "you brute!" Schmalz hurried forward, banging his stick on the pavement to frighten off the attacker, and shouted, "what the devil are you up to, you brute?"

When Schmalz got closer "the man jumped up and ran away, and I pursued him. As I passed the woman on the pavement, she got up on her knees and exclaimed, "Oh, Christ!" I pursued the man into Addison Road, and saw him turn into High Street, but did not shout anything because I did not know what he had done." When he lost sight of the attacker, Schmalz, eager not to get involved, did not return to the victim to offer help, but went home to Edith. His nerves were so shattered that "though unaccustomed to spirits, he drank half a bottle of brandy" and went to sleep.

In the morning papers he read the gruesome details, that the young woman's throat was slashed from ear to ear with a knife. He meant to keep his terrible adventure to himself, but a friend urged him to go to the police. Which he did, but only later in the week.

The victim, 28-year-old Augusta Dawes, was said to be "of the unfortunate class," a single mother of two young children from two different men who refused to support them. She came of a respectable family but had been driven to destitution when her father deserted them and sailed for Canada. For a time she was a governess and a Sunday school teacher, "but took to drink and went wrong."

Three years earlier, London had been terrified by the Jack the Ripper murders, and the police thought he might have killed Augusta Dawes. Detectives who had been working on the Whitechapel murders were called in. Schmalz was an important witness since he had chased the murderer, and being an artist, had a good eye for faces and details. The detectives asked him to sketch what he saw, which was limited as "the man's face was in shadow, and he could not, therefore, well remember it."

A few days after the attack a letter arrived from Dublin, admitting to the murder and signed by "Jack the Ripper." The letter was traced to Reginald Saunderson, 21, the son of a judge and nephew of an MP; he had taken a morbid interest in Jack the Ripper. The jury found him insane and he was sent to Broadmoor Criminal Lunatic Asylum where he died fifty years later. The verdict carried a recommendation that lighting in Leighton's street should be improved "so that it might not be a harbour for questionable characters."

***

Dorothy tried to use the success of *A Woman of No Importance* to revive her career. She distributed her CV and citations from favourable reviews to journalists, to initiate interviews and profiles. She told the *Sporting Times*, known for its theatrical tittle-tattle, that some managers thought that she was suffering from "the disease known as 'swelled-head'," others imagined that she had no desire to act, and some that she did not need to earn a living. "On all these points she tells me people are quite wrong. She is most anxious to work, both on account of her love for acting, and because she has to earn her bread and butter by it. She has been far from well lately, owing to worry at her inability to get an opening on the stage of late, but is now, happily, much stronger and better, and dying to get into harness again."

Leighton did all he could to help. "I hardly give anybody a letter of introduction," he wrote in July 1895 to George Du Maurier, making an exception for "my friend Dorothy Dene," who asked to meet Du Maurier, probably to commission a play for her. "It is not a begging letter, but a serious one (?) – I have known Miss Dene (as I therein say) since she was back well in her teens, and her sisters since they were little children; I have seen much of them and of her, and have for all of them not only a true friendship but enormous respect (knowing only too well what a profession theirs is!)"

As the years went by, Leighton became convinced that Dorothy's personality hampered her. "Miss Dorothy is a true artist, caring intensely for art & work for its own sake," he added to Du Maurier, underlining the important words, "she is full of imagination and enthusiasm, as well as gift, and had she had the art of pushing, & been other in ways than she is, she would by this time have had more prominence than has fallen to her share." The veteran journalist and editor T.P. O'Connor, who had also known Dorothy for years, agreed: "She had not the robustness nor the push that are required in a profession where competition is fierce, keen, and perhaps not always very scrupulous."

George Bernard Shaw, however, saw Dorothy for all she was worth: "Her speech showed unusual signs of artistic cultivation; she had plastic grace; she took herself and her profession seriously," he wrote in the *Saturday Review*. He blamed the short-sightedness of theatre managers: "Were the managers obdurate in their belief that there is only one safe sort of actress – the woman who is all susceptibility and no brains? Far be it from me to deny that every deviation from this type involves a certain risk of unpopularity." The 1890s theatre preferred silly beauties on stage and Dorothy did not fit. Shaw, who had seen her on stage several times, never found in her any traces of rough, 'common' upbringing. Dorothy Dene was not his Eliza Doolittle.

The 19th century saw much popular interest in psychology. To spice up an article in the English edition of *Le Follet* – a journal of fashion, literature and art, Dorothy was asked to hand her photo to Annie Oppenheim for a character analysis. Oppenheim introduced herself as a professor specializing in physiognomic study based on what she called, scientific methods. On Dorothy, she said:

> *The size of her brain and its position as regards the ears indicates a vivid imagination, ambition and large ideality. The fullness of the centre of the forehead is due to the development of the organ of memory. The straightness of the bridge of the nose shows a love of refinement, with a lack of power to exert herself in opposition to her tastes. The eyebrows are straight, being indicative of a truthful and outspoken nature. The nostrils are dramatic and the eyes eloquent. The thinness of the bridge of the nose denotes generosity and a love of spending money. The lower lip is full and sympathetic. The small square chin suggests a desire for affection. The length of the throat indicates independence of spirit; but the small nostrils suggest a horror and distaste of scenes, quarrels, or anything of an emotional character.*

Oppenheim was indignant when classified as an entertainer, among mind-readers, fortune-tellers and palmists, though employers were encouraged to use her methods when interviewing job applicants, and her books on the subject were best-sellers.

An unexpected publicity stunt occurred with *The man on his flying machine* by the prolific songwriter Harry Dacre. In the winter of 1895 it became a hit performed "to unbounded applause in all the principal pantomimes." It was sung in pubs, played on barrel-organs and hummed all over the country. The printed sheet of music, sold for one guinea, had her surname as Dean, but everyone else spelled it Dene, and it was clear who it was about.

For years I've been courting a lady
Beautiful Dorothy Dean
But she has turn'd out rather shady
Although she was once all serene
Since Mister Alberto Mac Springer
Brought on his new flying machine
At Lover's Lane vainly I linger
Awaiting Miss Dorothy Dean

Chorus

Oh! Dorothy Dorothy Dean
Oh! Dorothy what can she mean
She's suddenly flown
To regions unknown
Along with a man on his flying machine
Quite early one bright Sunday morning
Beautiful Dorothy Dean
Arose from her bed without warning
To sample that flying machine.
With Mr Mac Springer to spoon O!
She rose till no speck could be seen
They may have reached Venus or Juno
Mac Springer and Dorothy Dean

Chorus

Ah! night after night I am dreaming
Dreaming of Dorothy Dean
I fancy I hear her voice screaming
Then crash!! Comes the flying machine
I raise her – all injured and shaken –
I whisper "you're still my heart's queen"
Then just as I kiss, I awaken
To find there's no Dorothy Dean

The song carried a pun. Once she was all serene in Leighton's *serenely wandering in a trance of sober thought* – and then she turned out rather shady, posing in the nude. The undertone of the Chorus made it very clear: Dorothy disappeared to "regions unknown": she was absent from the stage. The moral effect of the song was debated in a Sheffield court, when the Paradise Inn was sued by a Girls' Home directly opposite it, for the loud music and the character of certain popular songs which were sung there. The Matron said that she did not think the words of the Dorothy Dene song were proper ones to be heard by the girls who lived at her institute. The words "'she's turned out rather shady" were thought to be obscene. A witness from the town council defended the pub and claimed that the song was not indecent, since it was a comic parody.

Hetty got her own courtship ditty, though without music, published in *Judy – the London Serio-Comic Journal*:

If thou would'st but my bridelet be
I'd let you skip that horrid vow
Which people in the Daily T.
Are making such a fuss of now.
I'd let you do whate'er you choose,
Nor seek to know the reason why,
I cannot bear the man who show
A searching and suspicious eye;
And, oh, I loath the man who'd say

"I'm master here! You shall obey!"
If thou would'st be my bridelet fair
(Thou could'st not be a bridelet dark)
Thy wish would be my special care
Till life threw up its final spark.
If thou would'st be my bridelet sweet
(Thou could'st not be a bridelet sour),
My lonely life would be replet
With joy until its closing hour!
My hopes – but, no! the thought is rot; –
I'm married, dear. I quite forgot!

Comic songs flattered, but did not pay the rent or lead to offers. For months no role was in sight for Dorothy. Her name appeared on billboards, not advertising her own performances but those of entertainers who sang about her. She became merchandise. The latest was "Dorothy Dene – the lovely lady Dolly," sold at toy-shops. The 18-inch doll – the manufacturer did not make much effort to create a lookalike – could move her arms and legs and open and shut her eyes. She had a wardrobe of 14 fashionable garments. For over twenty years it was a popular Christmas gift both in Britain and the USA.

The American children's writer Mabel A. Clinton turned Dorothy/ Barbie into an educational tool, in her poem, A Decided Contrast:

Dorothy Dene is tall and slender;
Her curling hair is of golden hue;
Her cheeks have the bloom of a rosebud tender,
And her staring eyes are of porcelain blue.
Marjory Mop is short and stumpy
And ugly enough to frighten the crows;
Her figure can only be classed as dumpy,
And gone is the tip of her wooden nose.
Dorothy Dene has a silken sash on;
Around her neck is a string of pearls;
Her frock is made in the latest fashion
And a picturesque hat adorns her curls.

Marjory Mop has a calico bonnet,
Tied down over her tumbled hair.
Her faded frock has no frills upon it
And shows sad traces of wear and tear.
Dorothy Dene is just perfection
From her feathered hat to her silken socks,
But she's far too fine to win affection,
So she spends her days in a cardboard box.
Marjory Mop is a wreck, or nearly;
Countless troubles her life has seen,
But Marjory's owner loves her dearly
And would not exchange her for Dorothy Dene.

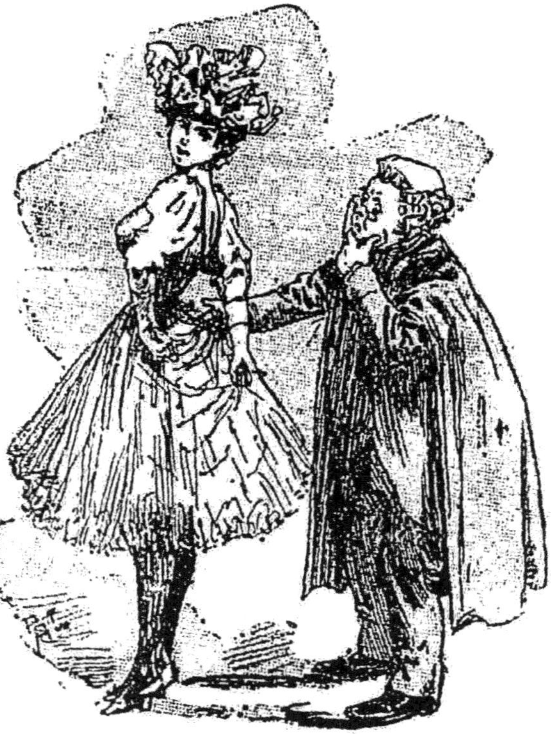

A Judge on Dressmaking, Pick Me Up, May 1891

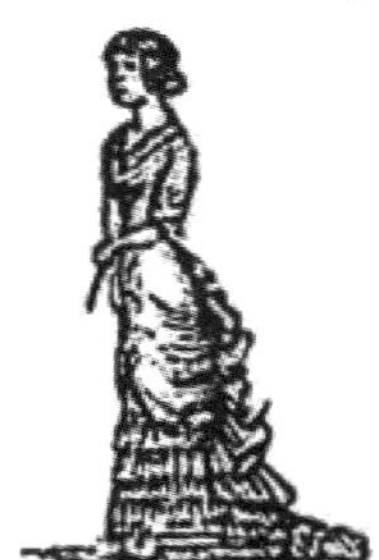

DOROTHY DENE.—The Lovely Lady Dollie, 18 inches high, with clothes to take on and off, fourteen different garments, every one removable, the delight of any child, the most astounding value ever offered, 1s. 6d., carriage free. The Doll's Fairy Wardrobe, real material all properly marked for cutting out and making three complete costumes for any Doll up to 18 inches, 1s. 3d., free; or for five costumes, including Red Riding Hood, 2s. Doll's Hammock, 8d. Jointed doll, opens and shuts eyes, 1s 6d.

Hearth and Home, November 1895

Chapter Twenty-Four

"Everything I owe to you"

At 65, Leighton was still astonishingly prolific. He was working on six paintings for the Royal Academy, two for the Grafton Gallery, four landscape drawings for the Royal Society of British Artists and finishing a large-scale mural. The *Phoenicians Bartering with the Britons* was a group painting for the Royal Exchange, part of a project to celebrate the history of British commerce.

The setting was the Cornish coast where four noble-looking Phoenician traders who had sailed all the way from Tyre and Sidon (now Lebanon) landed to exchange goods with the locals. The three Pettigrew sisters, with Lily in the centre, greedily eyed the colourful fabrics, cheap trinkets and necklaces they were getting in exchange for precious animal furs and Cornish tin. When Lily suffered an attack of nettle rash, which threatened to interrupt the work, Leighton asked his physician, Dr. Arthur Roberts to examine her. The treatment must have been effective, since the physician was subsequently given an oil sketch of Lily's head. After completing the canvas in February 1895 Leighton did not employ the Pettigrews again; there was some kind of fall-out, and Rosie wrote in her memoirs that she "never admired him as an artist".

The star of the summer exhibition was Mary Lloyd, whose dark, dignified beauty could be identified in no less than five paintings. She was the ghost-bride who appeared from the dead in Millais' *Speak! Speak!* Her beloved had been reading their letters through the night, tossing and dreaming of her. "And at dawn, behold, the curtains of his bed are parted, and there before him stands, in spirit or in truth, the lady herself, decked as on her bridal night, and gazing upon him with sad but loving eyes," Millais' son wrote. The young husband sits up, stretches his hands forward, and cries, Speak! Speak! – Hamlet's words as he addressed his father's ghost.

Millais, who was recovering from a severe illness and was in a sombre mood, cast Mary Lloyd in two more macabre scenes: The *Disciple* shows her devout and pure; her face pinched with sorrow, her hands interlocked on her lap, while she looks up and listens piously to an unseen preacher. Mary was also the beautiful, young St. Stephen, the martyr lying on the ground bruised and bloodied. Millais thought that they were the best he had ever done and was delighted by the excellent reviews and the immediate purchase of all three by the Tate. Leighton preferred *Speak! Speak!* and congratulated him on the "beautiful and impressive picture."

There was more work for Mary Lloyd that year: with a wreath on her thick black hair, she was a jubilant Roman maiden in Alma-Tadema's *Coign of Vantage* and in *Silver favourites.* For Herbert Draper, she posed as the watchful goddess Anticlea in the *Youth of Ulysses.* She found time too to squeeze in Frank Dicksee and Leighton. He cast Mary as Lachrymae, the Lady of Tears, weeping for a beloved whose ashes are in a funeral urn at her feet. It was very similar to his earlier painting from 1869, *Electra at the tomb of her father, Agamemnon*; now, grieving his own dominant and forbidding father who had died recently, Leighton recaptured the scene of lamentations.

Mary's return to his studio was made easy especially at times when Dorothy and Hetty had theatrical engagements. In another work, *'Twixt Hope and Fear*, Leighton cast Mary as a stately woman leaning over the back of an antique chair; she was restless and anxious, her face turned over the shoulder, her black eyes challenging and enigmatic.

He also found a role for the unemployed Lena Dene. She featured in *The Maid with the Golden Hair* in a silky amber robe; her blond, wavy hair falls on her shoulders as she reads a romantic novel on her lap. Lena's chaste image stood in sharp contrast to the stark naked Hetty Pettigrew, model and mistress of the painter Theodore Roussel, lounging on a chair and leafing through a magazine as *The Reading Girl.*

Nevertheless, Dorothy always remained Leighton's favourite and most important model. He saw the image of a sleeping woman coiled up upon herself in Michelangelo's statue *Night* at the Medici Chapel in San Lorenzo Church in Florence. Leighton bought a large photograph of the statue and placed it prominently in his studio. Michelangelo developed the pose into the erotic *Leda and the Swan*, a woman copulating with the large bird. Queen Anne of Austria had the scandalous painting burned a century later, but there was a copy in the National Gallery in London.

In public, however, Leighton gave the credit for the pose to Dorothy; he saw her nodding off during a break in one tiring sitting in 1891, as she modelled for the *Garden of the Hesperides*, and quickly sketched her. Two years later, in *Summer Slumber*, he used that pose as a bas-relief decoration on the marble bath that Dorothy was lying on. Feeling that he had not explored its full potential, he decided to enlarge the coiled sleeper into a life-size figure the following year. *The British Medical Journal* analysed the physiology and anatomy of the pose which was, in their expert opinion, impossible for anyone but an acrobat.

Leighton drew passive, exhausted, collapsing women magnificently. Dorothy was vulnerable, and the viewer could gaze at her curves furtively. There was, at the time, a growing interest in states of unconsciousness, and in the use of anaesthesia, opium and cocaine. Experiments were made in hypnosis, and the term "subconscious" first appeared in Sigmund Freud's writings in 1893.

Flaming June invited the viewer to probe into the sleeper's mind and decipher her dreams and desires; they were thought to be erotic and the result of masturbation. Her energy "has apparently been sapped by excessive indulgence in solitary pleasures," wrote Professor Bram Dijkstra in his *Idols of Perversity*. The orthodox view was that masturbation led to perturbation. A contemporary book, *Satan in Society* – by the physician Nicholas Francis Cooke, described the female masturbator as having "a general condition of languor, weakness and loss of flesh; the absence of freshness and beauty, of colour from the complexion, of the vermillion from the lips." Self-abuse also led to "sadness or melancholy, solitude or indifference, an aversion to legitimate pleasures."

The Victorians connected sleep with deathlike states, and art historians draw attention to the oleander in the top right corner of *Flaming June;* it was not just a sensual, beautiful flower, but a poisonous one. The coiled woman may not be asleep, but dead, or deadly. Was she a victim, or was Leighton hinting that a beautiful woman, like the poisonous flower, can be lethal?

It's intriguing to compare the flaming beauty to another portrait of the 35 year-old Dorothy that Leighton made at that time for the Grafton Gallery. It was a sequel to *Serenely wandering* of ten years earlier. He sat Dorothy in profile, wearing her turquoise dress, black coat and broad-brimmed hat. She looked matronly, as she had gained weight and lost her spark. The portrait was in sharp contrast to *Flaming June*: as if there were two Dorothys, that of his studio, sheltered and relaxed, and that of the world, vulnerable, aging and mercilessly exposed. The dream and the reality.

Leighton had found his physical and mental fulfilment in Dorothy and created *Flaming June* to express "his reminiscence of all his experiences with her. Dorothy's dream brings together the past, the present, the future, and the survival of the artist's memory," writes the art historian Alfred Weidinger. It seems that Leighton was trying to hold on to Dorothy's magic before it was too late for both of them.

The art historian Dr Martin Postle suggests, however, that Mary Lloyd, and not Dorothy Dene, was the face of *Flaming June*. But given the many studies which Leighton made, it is evident that he started working on it already in 1891, a year before he ever met Mary Lloyd; Dorothy's face and features are clearly identifiable there and in the later sketches. He re-sketched the pose in the following years, and Dorothy was always the model.

In July 2015, one of the studies was put on sale by Sotheby's of London. It belonged to the Duchess of Roxburghe of West Horsley Place, who inherited it from her grandfather, who had been a friend of Leighton's. When the Duchess died just before she turned a hundred, the drawing was found hanging behind the door of a small antechamber next to her bedroom. This head study – a sleeping woman resting on her arm, is evidently Dorothy, and not Mary Lloyd.

***

"Dorothy Dene, in white, was much noticed," wrote the *Hearth and Home* after the Royal Academy soiree in July 1894, but "Sir Frederick Leighton looked very depressed and fatigued." Already in 1887, the painter George Richmond wrote to Leighton that "many of us have remarked that you draw upon your strength too severely" and pleaded with him to spare himself. "That would not be life to me!" Leighton protested. Two years later, writing from the Italian Alps, he admitted to his father, "if you were to ask me whether I am 'as fit as a fiddle' ... I am not." He complained that while everyone around him climbed the mountains at ease, he has to stop every third yard, "puffy, helpless, effete." Still, he carried on at full steam. On his annual holiday in 1893, he galloped through Germany, devouring 30 towns in 30 days. The next summer, ignoring all warning signs, he attended the Wagner Festival in Bayreuth with his sister Augusta, and then continued alone to Scotland, and later to Italy.

On October 29th, 1894 Leighton attended the Monday Popular Concert at St. James's Hall, sitting next to the Prince and Princess of Wales. Walking back to the Athenaeum Club he had his first attack of angina pectoris. His doctors prescribed a daily Swedish massage, to improve blood circulation: "[it] did my general health immense good. Now I can, by certain movements, stop an incipient attack of my pain," he told Millais. He did not cut down on his commitments, but rather intensified them. Emily Barrington, who saw him almost daily, felt that he kept "much of the pathos of the boy who is known to be doomed, but who plays his game with just as much eager verve." He was struggling with *Flaming June*, passing from the sketching phase to canvas, and Dorothy's continual presence was much needed. Dr. Keren Hammerschlag connects his deteriorating health with painting a woman asleep: it allowed him "to get as close to death as he could without dying."

In March 1895 Leighton got worse; "spasms of pain coming suddenly will make him gasp and cease what he was doing," remembered his physician Dr. Barton. The heart specialist Sir Lauder Brunton was called in and decided not to reveal the full diagnosis to his patient. The gloss-over-reality doctor assured him that there was no organic trouble, and that he just needed a little rest. His worried friends implored Leighton to get a second opinion, and the neurologist Sir William Broadbent agreed that a trip and a change of climate would do him good.

Only when Leighton informed the Royal Academy Council that he was going abroad on medical grounds and would miss the opening of the summer exhibition, did his friends grasp how serious his condition was. He asked Millais to replace him as host of the Royal Academy banquet – "for once only," he emphasized. On April 7th he welcomed his many house-guests on "Show Sunday," proudly presenting his submissions to the forthcoming exhibition. *Flaming Summer*, as it was then called, was the main attraction, contrasting strongly with the appearance of Leighton. He looked tired, suffering, and ill at ease. When the dignitaries were leaving, "dainty figures of girls were still dancing round the fountain in the emptying Arab Hall." Leighton was standing at the outer door, bidding goodbye, and the girls "flew to him, throwing their arms round his neck," remembered Mrs Barrington. "'They are all my god-children', he said, as each, fleet-footed, fled out of the gate."

The New York Times was not impressed with Leighton's work that year, and sneered at the sweetness and simplicity of Dorothy, Lena and Mary Lloyd, calling them "the Leighton girl ... she moans, she sleeps, she muses, she smiles, now with a marble urn at her side, now in a garden, now with the distant sea behind her, always smooth and sleek, and delicately tinted, and always ready to be photogravured and processed for the customers of the print seller." The *Graphic* did buy *Flaming June* and the reproduction copyright for its special Christmas issue. Leighton was usually reluctant to have his works reproduced in colour, since he felt that they would lose considerably in the process, but this time he gave his permission.

In mid-April, a group of friends saw Leighton off at the London Docks, "the spectacle of his handsome form alone on the huge vessel, with no servant to minister to his wants, was a sight to bring tears to the eyes of his comrades." He sailed for Gibraltar, and on to Tangier and Algiers. His sudden departure was worrying. Henry W. Lucy wrote in his column that shortly before his departure they met in Pall Mall: "Sir Frederick is not yet sixty-five as the almanack reckons, but the last twelve months have added as many years to his life." The press published daily health bulletins from abroad, and reported that there was no improvement and that it is highly unlikely that he will be "able to return to Society, and to his artistic career. His position as President of the Royal Academy he will no doubt resign." An angry Leighton immediately cabled from Algiers that he was in good health and had even gone for a long walk. The *British Medical Journal* chipped in by stating that the somewhat pessimistic rumours "are happily much in excess of the fact, the heart affection from which Sir Frederic Leighton is suffering is one which necessitates abstinence from the excitement of public speaking and from all avoidable business, such excitement having proved to bring on distressing attacks. There is, however, good reason to hope that complete repose from all such functions and rest in a favourable climate will largely improve the President's health and general condition." Such hopes did nothing to halt the betting at the Royal Academy on whether Millais or Val Prinsep would succeed him.

To secure his position, Leighton hurried back, and in mid-June was already in London. He immediately resumed all his presidential commitments. At the end of the Royal Academy soiree, attended by 2000 guests, a friend asked him how he was; Leighton dismissed his condition as a matter of nerves: "I have stood here three hours and a quarter and have not had one [attack], --while I was dressing and fearing how I should get through it, I had *three*." If he withdrew from active life, he would become depressed, he feared, which would hardly improve his health. "My care must be to live quietly but not idly." To emphasise he was working as usual, he invited three women columnists, separately, on different days, to his home. He gave each of them an extensive tour, showed the trees he had planted in his garden with his own hands, poured tea and enchanted them with stories from his childhood. Each of the three-, Marion Leslie (*The Young Woman*), Baroness von Zedlitz (*Cassell's Family Magazine*) and Mary Hannah Krout (*Inter-Ocean*) produced a lengthy admiring profile. The American Miss Krout was impressed with his varied topics of conversation and colourful style of dress ("his velvet coat and scarlet neckerchief being strikingly becoming to his picturesque figure"); she was less enthusiastic about his disparaging opinions of women artists and musicians – he was certainly no feminist.

"There was nothing in his appearance or his manner to indicate that he was not in robust health," wrote Miss Krout in her article "Prince of Painters" in September 1895. However, the true situation remained in her notebook and she published it only after his death. "I'm very ill," he admitted in her ears, "I know my own critical condition perfectly ... I shall never recover." Miss Krout was touched by the "perfect calmness and a certain perfect resignation in the manner in which he made this statement, an acceptance of fate."

Though he was occasionally paralyzed with pain, Leighton continued to work on two large-scale paintings and four small ones. In August, Mrs Rylands, widow of the textile magnate, asked whether he would undertake a commission of four life-size panels for her Manchester mansion. Everything played against her: Leighton was unwell and was not pressed for money but pressed with work. He wrote to her that he was "extremely unwilling to accept commissions, as he finds himself entirely unable to work satisfactorily in lines laid down for him by anybody else." But he was not willing to let go and they discussed the subject: he thought that the Four Seasons was "a little threadbare as a motif," and preferred the Four Times of the Day, which called for a "striking treatment." In his drawing room he had four Corot paintings on that subject: morning, noon, evening and night. Mrs Rylands agreed, but had one condition: "that the figures shall be draped." She wanted two panels to be ready by May 1896, but it was too early for him, and he promised to complete them all by spring 1897.

In September, although restless and in pain, Leighton went to Ireland, this time taking a manservant with him. Shortly after returning to London, he started on another trip, visiting his favourite cities: Venice, Naples, Rome, Siena and Florence. He was full of spirits, "keenly alive to artistic enjoyments," and made several drawings, including a study of fruit for *Clytie.* Giovanni Costa remembered Leighton kneeling for his little daughter, "to accede her request that she should have a lock of his hair as a remembrance."

In London there were rumours that taking his doctors' advice, Leighton would winter in Cairo until the spring. But he returned home in early November. He confessed to Emily Barrington that he was no better, rather worse, and that he was having several attacks, sometimes fifteen a day. To cheer him up, Alexandra, the Princess of Wales, sent him her latest creation: an Italian armchair entirely covered with her own needlework.

Dorothy was also back in his studio. When Mrs Rylands first approached Leighton, she confessed that she had chosen him after seeing the *Bracelet* and the *Spirit of the Summit*; Dorothy posed for both, and Leighton took her as the model for the Manchester panels.

***

Throughout that winter Leighton constantly battled with pain, and his friends were often afraid that he was breathing his last. It was believed that he would bequeath his magnificent house to the Royal Academy as a residence for future presidents. The race for his chair resumed, and Edward Burne-Jones wrote in his diary in late November that there is a painter who "goes about saying he is the best man for next President of the Royal Academy": the unnamed campaigner boasted that he had Leighton's all three vital qualifications: he was well-off and a bachelor, but Burne-Jones did not reveal what the third qualification was.

Leighton had always hoped for a seat in the House of Lords, and finally on January 1st, 1896, Queen Victoria announced that he would be raised to the peerage, the first artist ever to receive this honour. To rebuff gossip about the gravity of his illness, and to thank the many who congratulated him on becoming Lord Leighton, he made an effort and attended the Old Masters and Deceased Masters exhibition at Burlington House. On January 19th he kept the tradition of his "at home" Sundays, and the house was full of art lovers. He took small groups around his studio to see the paintings on their easels. He was exhausting himself; "I'm an ailing creature – no better if no worse," he told one of his guests. "My complaint isn't a mortal one. I have no present anxiety concerning it; but it's very troublesome, as you may judge when I tell you that I had no less than twelve attacks yesterday and they come without rhyme or reason. Merely washing my hands brought an attack just now; and yet, I can lift great weights, such as that frame, without any harm".

The next Tuesday Leighton suffered a very bad cough and his doctors insisted he stay in his room. But the next day he was back on his feet, painting Dorothy in the nude. That afternoon he drove in his open carriage to Westminster, getting out and standing in the damp, watching the demolition of some old houses which he wished had been preserved. The following day he was so ill that nurses were called in, but he couldn't bear them to touch him. "Come to see the last of me?" he teased Dr. Barton, the junior of the medical team. It was the first time that Dr. Barton heard Leighton acknowledge his approaching death. As he injected morphine, Leighton said, "I was a dying man, I am a living one now, thanks to your morphine I don't feel like dying, I don't really." What he went on to say reveals how obsessive he was; he told Barton that he only needed three more weeks for his pictures to be finished.

On Friday, January 24th, he assumed the title Lord Leighton of Stretton, but the following day it was clear that he was at death's door. A handful of close friends were allowed to see him. Alexandra, Leighton's sister led Dorothy into his bedroom, to bid farewell. "If I have, or ever will, do anything worth doing, I owe it all to you – everything I owe to you," she whispered. Too weak to reply, Leighton nodded with a smile. If the 20 year-old Fred Mason, or his mother Lily, were brought to see him, it was never disclosed. After an injection of more morphine to his leg, Leighton said, "goodbye. Now I will sleep. Give my love to the Academy and all its members." Dr Barton was quick to jot that down in the corner of his prescription book.

Leighton's coffin was almost hidden by the exquisite flowers and wreaths which were piled up in his studio. Glowing above was "the sun-loving Clytie [who] stretched out her arms, bidding a passionate farewell to her god," remembered Emily Barrington. In the last months of his life, Dorothy had spent more and more time in his studio, as she posed for Clytie. The small figure in the corner of the 1892 work was now enlarged to almost life-size: "I have shown the goddess in adoration before the setting sun, whose last rays are permeating her whole being. With upraised arms she is entreating her beloved one not to forsake her," Leighton said shortly before his death. Clytie was "more powerful than anything I have seen of his for a long time," wrote a friend, who felt that "there is a yearning for the unseen in it, which makes it very fit to be the painter's own 'swan song'." In retrospect, the unfinished painting was seen as the farewell testimonial of a dying man, casting himself as Clytie. It was his attempt to hold on to his life, a "passionate appeal made by a man to whom had come his last moment of waning vitality," said the *Art Journal*.

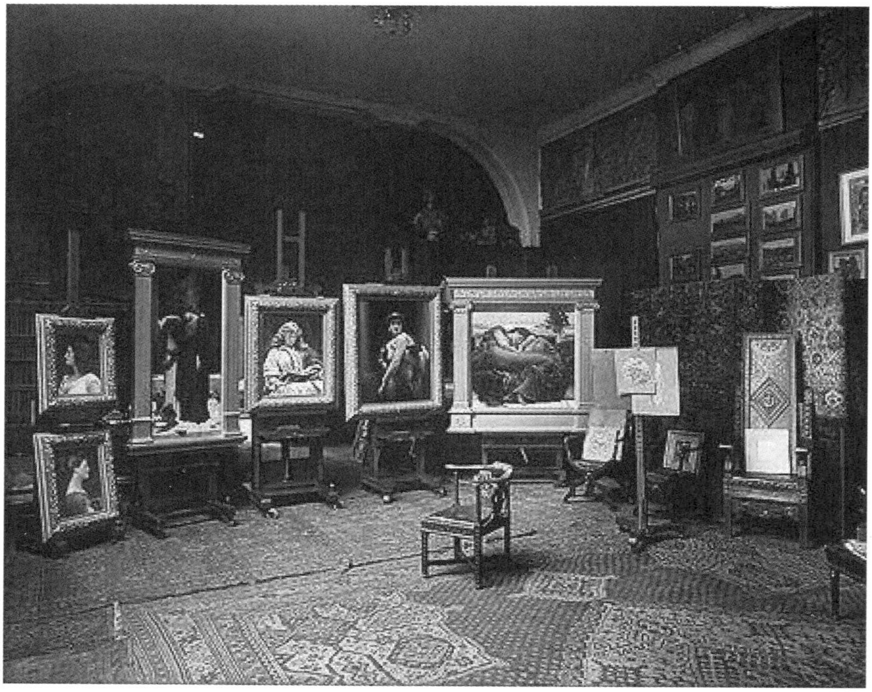

Photographer: A.A. Boucher, 1895
Historic England Archive

Chapter Twenty-Five

A sudden death

Dorothy was among the dignitaries and senior Academicians who filed past the coffin in Leighton's studio and registered their names and condolences in the visitors' book. A week later, the coffin was moved to the Royal Academy. The funeral procession, on February 3rd, to St. Paul's Cathedral, was a national event, as tens of thousands gathered on the streets. "Hundreds of tradesmen closed their premises to honour the memory of a great man, if not of a great artist, showed that England is something more than a mere nation of shopkeepers," wrote Rachel Beer, the editor of the *Sunday Times*. Windows were decorated with reproductions of his work, and a crowd flocked in front of the *Graphic* building on the Strand, which displayed *Flaming June* in its window. The police had to keep them moving.

The British press and Leighton's friends were careful not to mention Dorothy in their obituaries and eulogies. The *Art Magazine*, however, commissioned a full-page illustration of a draped beauty in classical dress, lamenting the dead President. She stood on a balcony, her back to the Royal Academy building, a discarded painter's palette at her feet. Her veiled head bowed, she still looked very much like Dorothy. The caption was a quote from Samuel Johnson: *nullum quod tetigit non ornavit*: "None that he touched did he fail to adorn." The American and Australian press, however, were more direct: they not only mentioned Dorothy but added that shortly before Leighton's death "rumour has woven a romance in his life, in which his model figures. It says he loved her, but that circumstances over which he had no control prevented him from marrying her."

***

Organized as he was, and despite his deteriorating health, Leighton had not made a will. He summoned his lawyers only on his last day. At 2 pm, his breathing was very bad, and his pulse weakening, and Dr. Barton was afraid he might die before the lawyers arrived. He asked his patient whether he had written a will: "there is nothing on paper," Leighton replied, and the doctor offered to write down his last wishes. Leighton dictated briefly: he had just one request – that his sisters would receive all his personal estate. "How his hand shook signing it, but when it was finished, he gave a sigh of relief," recalled the doctor. Augusta and Alexandra were present at his bedside, and the siblings turned to German that the doctor couldn't understand. "They know exactly my wishes," Leighton told him, referring to the verbal orders that he had left with them.

His deathbed statement was to be followed by a cheque of £10,000 to the Royal Academy. £3000 was to be transferred to Giovanni Costa, and Lily Mason and her son Fred were given £1450. Of all his intimate and long-standing friends, Dorothy was the main beneficiary. He left her £5000 outright, and a further £5000 was placed in a trust, "with the greatest secrecy, in order to avoid further scandal."

The details of the inheritance were discovered only 80 years later, when Leonée and Richard Ormond were given access to Leighton's Coutts Bank account. The sum he left Dorothy was colossal, equivalent to over £1,000,000 today, which would secure the future of the entire Dene family for years to come. If money is a measure of emotion, "his wife" the Royal Academy and his Dorothy were of equal importance. It probably came with a price tag of silence; Leighton's letters to Dorothy were handed back to his sisters.

***

All those months, Dorothy continued to place job-seeking ads in the *Era* and the *Stage*. She told the *Boston Daily Advertiser* that she "hopes someday to make a name and fortune not as a professional beauty, but as an actress in some Shakespearean role." Then like manna from heaven, came an offer from the Shakespearean actor and manager Ben Greet for three dream roles: her well-rehearsed Helena of *Midsummer Night's Dream*, and two exciting tragic parts: Juliet and Ophelia, opposite the young Henry B. Irving, son of the famous actor. The program, marking the Shakespeare Anniversary and featuring scenes from his most popular plays, went on from March to May, in London and Birmingham.

George Bernard Shaw, who was late for the key performance of April 23, greatly regretted at first that he missed the 37 year-old actress, but on second thought concluded that "perhaps it is as well that I did not see Miss Dorothy Dene; for it is not conceivable that disuse has matured her powers, or years increased her natural suitability to the part of Juliet," he wrote in the *Saturday Review*. However, the critics were mostly favourable: she did well as Ophelia, and her "Juliet can be accounted a decided success," wrote the *Stage*. "Her reading of the balcony scene was excellent, while the potion scene must be recorded as a very fine effort, enthralling, and in the full tragic vein."

Shaw wondered what had gone wrong in Dorothy's career. "Did she fall into the abyss of opulent matrimony? Did the studio violently reclaim its adored model?" He speculated that it was Leighton's doing, keeping Dorothy almost always for himself. Newspapers blamed Leighton that he "was intensely jealous of her rich beauty and paid her handsomely to keep out of the glare of publicity, and that she willingly made the sacrifice because of her unconfessed love for him ... She always arrived at the door of his studio soon after sunrise, and never departed until twilight." It was assumed that she was his mistress, and that it blighted her chances of marrying. She was the incarnation of Penelope, the faithful wife of Ulysses, who rejected her suitors as she waited for her husband's return.

Leighton did feel some guilt, and once, full of emotion, confided in Mary Watts that "my interest in her has been turned to her disadvantage." Dr. Daniel Robbins, the senior curator, responsible for the Leighton House Museum, offers an interesting, insightful interpretation of Leighton's feelings: "if Leighton is identifying himself with Apollo, it is because he can see how closely the hopelessness of the position into which he has cast Dorothy Dene echoes that of *Clytie*. If anything, this picture is about failure, about the remorse of getting it wrong ... in Clytie/Dorothy's outstretched, imploring gesture, Leighton recognizes that both for himself as an artist and for this woman, the full promise of all that Apollo represents, will remain forever out of reach, inaccessible and beyond their grasp."

By making Dorothy his model and muse, suggests Robbins, Leighton trapped and isolated her in a social dead-end, making her "unable to move beyond the social strictures of the time." However, Leighton also gave Dorothy the chance to transcend the confines of her background, to forge an identity, reach out for her dream and make a name for herself.

***

Nearly a year passed until Dorothy got another worthwhile part: the lead in a romance taking place in the Australian goldfields during the great Gold Rush. She was a young barmaid nicknamed the Duchess of Coolgardie: "the best type of an innocent English girl. A stranger in a strange land. By her mother's death and the loss of her sister, she is driven to obtain her livelihood by honest work of any kind. Proud without being haughty, reticent without being rude." The play was a melodramatic melange of adventure, a lover emerging from the past, a beautiful young sister, murdered by a villain and her orphaned child. The *Duchess of Coolgardie* was a reasonable success: 12 nights at the Islington Grand Theatre and then a tour of the provinces. Dorothy was commended for her "charming personality and bright, intelligent style."

Trying again to take control of her career, Dorothy bought the English rights for *L'Amie Fritz*, a musical comedy which she saw in New York. The hero was a wealthy Alsatian bachelor who scoffs at marriage until he falls in love with a young farmer's daughter. It had the potential to become a hit, but proved to be a bad investment, since Pietro Mascagni had just turned the story into a successful opera. In the rivalry between the two versions, the composer won, and Dorothy could never put hers on stage.

Her sisters were doing better: Lena was seen more and more on stage and was showing great intelligence and promise. Kathleen was also busy, finding her place in Mr and Mrs Kendall's company and touring England, Scotland and Ireland. "Miss Kathleen Dene seemed to us to score the chief success among the minor characters," wrote the

Manchester Guardian. "Her acting had all the charm of 'unconscious' vivacity." She was invited to the Dublin studio of James Stack Lauder, the celebrity photographer better known as James Lafayette. Small and slender, with a large, fluffy white hat in her sister's style, she seemed embarrassed, smiling timidly, looking much younger than her 25 years of age.

Hetty had the most success, playing the lead in the musical comedy *The Gaiety Girl*; it involved singing and dancing in sexy bathing suits, a winning formula, and the play was a hit. Hetty "showed herself the possessor of a sweet and musical voice, while her acting was marked by a quiet charm that showed a true realization on her part of the demands of the part," cheered the Welsh papers. In April 1896 she visited Cardiff again with a new play, the *Wand of Wedlock*, playing the loving young wife of an unfaithful husband. In an interview for the *Evening Express,* she said that comic opera was not to her taste as much as drama, and that her idol was the great French tragedian Sarah Bernhardt. The reporter was impressed by her "remarkably pleasant, refined manner, and at once making you feel at home." She marvelled at Hetty's stage costumes – five in that play – "admirably adapted to set-off her extremely pretty, interesting face on which every emotion she is simulating finds a most real expression".

***

When Leighton died, the London art world wondered who would inherit "the most valuable of his 'properties', Dorothy Dene," wrote the *St. Louis Republic.* "There was no little rivalry between those who could afford to bid for her undivided services." She could have named her own price, but to "the chagrin of many the model refused to pose."

The Royal Academy kept Dorothy on the guest list, and she was still invited to gala nights. She attended other cultural events, mingling with those who could offer her an acting role, but never did. She was slipping into forced retirement. She volunteered for various charity bazaars, usually accompanied by one of her sisters. In the bazaar in aid of the Actors' Orphanage, all four were in charge of the diamonds stall. With each sister having a separate schedule and away on acting tours, the bazaars gave them an opportunity to be together.

There was one modelling project which Dorothy would have loved to do but she was not given the chance. Leighton's tomb in the crypt of St. Paul's Cathedral was marked by a brass ledger carrying his family coat of arms, and the telling motto, *Dread Shame*. A committee of Royal Academicians was set up under the patronage of the Prince of Wales to choose an appropriate memorial in the cathedral's nave. Several artists submitted their proposals, inspired by Michelangelo's tomb in Florence. Lawrence Alma-Tadema suggested a bust of Leighton on a plinth, flanked by three female figures, including one holding a wreath above the dead President's head, and another holding a palette and brushes. George Frampton's idea was quite similar, a bust with two seated female figures. The committee preferred the proposal of W.B. Richmond, who suggested a bas-relief of the President, attached to the wall. He had good relations with the cathedral clergy which, it was assumed, would speed up the work.

Eventually, the winner was Thomas Brock, Leighton's protégé and young friend. He had already made two busts of Leighton, and by June 1897, the sketch was shown and approved by the Prince of Wales and the committee. It was a bronze effigy of Leighton, lying asleep on his casket in his presidential robes. Two women lean on the grey marble sarcophagus: beneath his head sits *Painting*, bare-breasted, holding a brush. Beneath his feet sits *Sculpture*, holding a chisel and a statuette of *Sluggard*, which Leighton made in Brock's studio.

Mary Lloyd was chosen because "her face typified purity", and not long before she was the model for another work, the angels' faces in the St. Paul's mosaics. She modelled for *Sculpture*, "since, it was said, no statue could be a complete tribute to his memory without her." Dorothy, Leighton's acknowledged muse, was overlooked as the inevitable model for *Painting*, probably on the orders of the committee, to stop gossip.

***

Kathleen had taken to acting because of her sisters, but after five years on stage, she was still uptight and uneasy. In October 1897 she appeared in *Sporting Life* as a misunderstood young girl who runs away from home and attempts suicide. The reviews were merciless: while the play itself was well-constructed and well-written, and the actors were "excellent" or at least "pleasing," Kathleen was pilloried as "too lugubrious and lachrymose" and "failed to elicit much sympathy." This was the last straw. She had had enough of the hardships and humiliations of the profession: travelling for hours to small towns, living out of a suitcase, and all of that in order to speak just a few lines and be harshly criticized, or worse, be totally ignored. She missed the gaiety of London too. She moved out of her sisters' nest and rented a room in Notting Hill.

As to Edith: after nine years of marriage to Herbert Schmalz, she had not borne any children, and their best times and rare times were when she modelled for him. Schmalz was preoccupied with his work and Edith was drinking. Since the immense success of *The Return from Calvary* in 1891, he was looking for another crowd puller. "If you start painting sacred subjects," Leighton had advised him, "you must some time paint the most sacred figure of all." But Schmalz distrusted his powers, and when he finally did, it took him two years to complete *Rabboni*.

"I see you have gone in for the conventional Christ!" remarked a friend.

"What would you have me do," asked the indignant Schmalz. "It would be very easy to be original and make a dark, clean-shaven man, but I should not feel it were Christ; besides, I want to paint Christ so that the people who see the picture will know at once who it intended for."

The famous scene from Jerusalem was actually painted in Ventnor, a cheap and cheerful resort on the Isle of Wight. Edith, as Mary Magdalene, posed under a fig tree for hours each day, sometimes at early dawn and again at sunset. On November 26th, 1896, Queen Victoria wrote in her diary, "saw a very fine picture by Schmalz called *Rabboni*." It was the third time that the Queen asked for a Schmalz picture to be brought to Windsor Castle.

Schmalz' next work is puzzling. *Love is Blind* is a semi-classical scene: a young woman down on her knees, her eyes blind-folded, stretching her arm towards a pure, beautiful mask of a Greek god's face. She is unaware that the mask is held by a monster of a man, with leering eyes and an ugly grin, hiding behind a pillar. Schmalz added a caption, "maidenhood, blindfolded by innocence, knows not that behind a God-like mask there lurks the soul of a Satyr." For years, it was used by preachers to illustrate "how often Innocence is lured to ruin through men versed in the world's deceits." The art historian and author Jacky Collis Harvey identifies the Satyr's face as a self-portrait of Schmalz, and the blindfolded girl as Dorothy Dene. She also suggests that Dorothy might have been her brother-in-law's mistress. However, Dorothy stopped modelling entirely after Leighton's death, and at the age of 39, she did not look as young as the girl in the painting. More so, there is not a trace of similarity between Schmalz and this image. If Schmalz was conducting an illicit affair with Dorothy, it is unlikely that he would have flaunted it. As to Dorothy, who was still the mother figure for her siblings, family was of paramount importance, and betraying her sister's trust would be very out of character.

Another portrait by Schmalz, though artistically insignificant, would prove to have immense value to the Dene family. The American millionaire John Morgan Richards who settled in London, befriended Herbert and Edith and introduced them to his 30 year-old daughter. Pearl Craigie had survived a bitter divorce, sought solace in Catholicism and lost all interest in men, raising her young son on her own. She became a best-selling novelist and social activist, using the pseudonym John Oliver Hobbes. Her first play *Journeys end in Lovers Meeting* was staged in London, starring Ellen Terry. For several weeks Pearl came to Schmalz's studio, sitting on an embroidered sofa and looking unsmilingly at the viewer. Edith was proud of her friendship with the famous author, and invited Dorothy to see the portrait when it was exhibited at the New Gallery in May 1897.

***

Two years after Dorothy had last performed in a London theatre, she was still looking for a come-back. In May 1899, *The Stage* reported that she "is hard at work, looking for a suitable play and that when she has found it, she will be in a position to have it produced at a West-End theatre." She said she preferred a strong, refined drama, but failing to find one, would take a comedy. It was more an appeal to theatre managers and playwrights than a reflection of reality. Charles Carson, *The Stage* editor and a friend, was trying to help her.

How did Dorothy compare with other actresses who had studied with her at the School of Dramatic Art?

Nearly all of the students left no mark on the theatre. Among the very few who did was Bessie Hatton. She quit the stage in 1899 after some success, became a playwright and author of romantic novels, and co-founder of the Women's Writers' Suffrage League. Maud Millet also made her mark when she appeared in the original 1895 cast of *An Ideal Husband*, but two years later she married an American military man and quit the stage. Janet Achurch, who took a short course and described herself as one of a "motley crew" that attended the School, became the first English Nora in Ibsen's *Doll House*. She had a good career in England and Australia, but became addicted to morphia, on top of her dependency on alcohol. At 50, exhausted and ill, she retired and died three years later from morphine poisoning. None of the three were ever painted, and none had the gossip-trail and star-dust Dorothy had.

As to Mary Lloyd: the Leighton memorial was to be her last assignment. Her modelling career lasted less than a decade. "I lived for the moment, never dreaming that I should ever be in need. But one by one, the artists died. Each year I grew poorer and poorer," she said. She never married, and a long and serious illness exhausted all her savings. "Now this woman, whose lovely face adorns the walls of palaces, mansions and famous buildings, will darn your socks or sweep your house to earn a few shillings," described the *Sunday Express* reporter who met her in her tiny room in Kensington. Desolate, Mary Lloyd died in 1936.

***

Dorothy's health had never been robust, and she always suffered from anaemia. The pneumonia that she caught in the USA which developed into chronic rheumatic fever weakened her further. "Her complexion at one time looked white and clear, but ill-health brought it to a somewhat muddy colour," remembered T.P. O'Connor. "Then came a painful and chronic form of dyspepsia." In August 1899, overwhelmed by pain, she was taken to bed and quickly got worse. Her sister Hetty was then celebrating her greatest success, as the heroine of the musical comedy *Little Miss Nobody.* She played her love-making scenes "with a touch of genuine art," and her many songs and dances swept the audience into standing ovations. But she cancelled all her engagements at once to attend to Dorothy.

Decades before the discovery of antibiotics, medicine could only offer palliative treatment for Dorothy's severe abdominal pain, vomiting, dehydration and high fever. None of the many doctors who examined Dorothy could make her condition stable. Soon it became critical.

Dorothy was advised to make a will, and on September 18th summoned her lawyer. "This is the last will of me Ada Alice Pullan (generally known as Dorothy Dene) of no. 10 Avonmore Mansions Kensington in the County of London, Spinster." She bequeathed all her estate and effects to Hetty and Lena, asking them to invest a third of it in a trust for the maintenance, support and benefit of Kathleen, and for the education and support of the 22 year-old Samuel "until he shall be reasonably capable of earning his own living."

Charles Carson, the editor of *The Stage* was alerted that Dorothy was mortally ill: "Every attention is being given to her in the way of nursing. But she lies in an unchanged state," he wrote, and continued to publish her job-seeking adverts, as a good omen. *The Era* was blunter: "It is feared that only her youth will enable her to pull through a fearful crisis of uncertainty and anxiety." For a time, she held on.

Dorothy was greatly troubled and displeased by her sisters' stories about Kathleen's misbehaviour. Feeble and agonized as she was, she summoned her lawyer again in late November to amend the will. She added a specific clause: "As long as my sister Kathleen Blanche shall in the opinion of my sisters Henrietta Sarah and Isabel Helena be well behaved, I should like my last named sisters to make such provision for her as in their own absolute discretion."

Dorothy struggled for another month. On Wednesday, December 27th, at 2:30 a.m. she passed away. "Her long illness had been borne with the utmost resignation," wrote *The Stage.* The death certificate was another document which deducted years from her age – it stated it as 33, when in fact, she was three months short of her fortieth birthday.

The causes of her death are rather obscure: Proctitis prolapsed recti, Pelvic peritonitis, Pyaemia dropsy. All pointed to inflammatory bowel and rectal disease, severe inflammation of the abdominal area and, ultimately, to fatal blood poisoning. It could have been the result of traumatic injury to her genitals, an ovarian tumour or of a sexually transmitted disease. The symptoms could also stem from an unsuccessful termination of pregnancy, but it is highly unlikely that she could have survived over four months after a bloody abortion. In the absence of a full medical file, speculation is inevitable.

Some contemporary journalists described Dorothy as a victim of her profession, that "she had contracted the seeds of dread consumption while wrapped in diaphanous draperies in Sir Frederic Leighton's great studio." Others believed that it happened "from playing a death-bed scene in damp sheets, provided by a careless property man"; she contracted "rheumatism which after months of torture reached her heart, and as a soldier who had fallen in battle, so she died on, or for, the stage," wrote the theatre critic Ada Patterson in her article, The Martyrs of the Stage.

Dorothy was buried in the Kensal Green cemetery, and the austere grey tombstone with a tall erect cross, – *In loving memory of our sweet sister Dorothy Dene* – bears only her stage name, but no further sign to her profession or her connection to art. Letters cast in lead paraphrase a quote from the hymn *Lead Kindly Light*:

And with the morn that angel's face will smile
Which we have loved so well and lost a while.

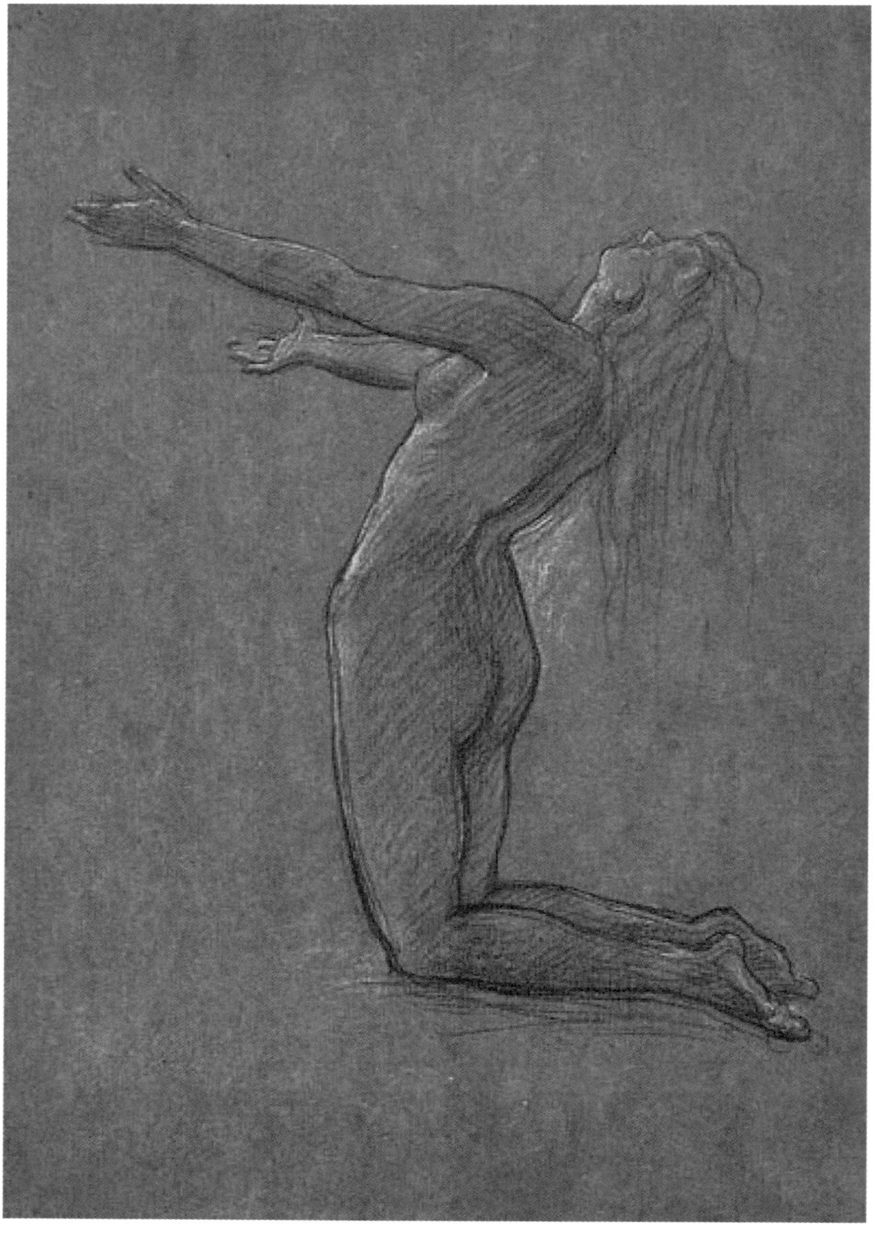

Study for Clytie, c.1895

Epilogue

"The most beautiful model that the world has ever known is dead," lamented newspapers across the globe. "For generations to come, people will rave over the matchless beauty of Dorothy Dene as represented on the canvases of Lord Leighton."

Her beauty overshadowed her acting career, and once again, the eulogists found themselves speechless: "In trying to describe Dorothy Dene one pauses at every feature as if there were no other beyond… Dorothy Dene's needs a language of its own." Tributes highlighted her wit, her good humour, the fact that she was a charming conversationalist, and a fine hostess. She was credited for assisting the President "with the intelligence that may make of a model an inspiration instead of a mannequin." In Seattle, a lengthy article was headed "She has a place in history," and the writer wondered: was it Leighton that made her famous, or was it the other way around? Some obituaries reiterated that there was more to their relationship than to that of an artist and his model: "she had loved Lord Leighton and had hoped to become his wife," wrote the *Weekly Irish Times.* "The beautiful model had not the least desire to turn the heads of men. It was the surest proof that she was in love with only one. Him she sought to please in her every pose, for him she sought to mount higher the ladder of fame," added the *St Paul Globe.*

The poet laureate of Washington, Frank Carlton Teck, wrote a lament:

Dorothy Dene is dead, they say
O beautiful Dorothy Dene!
Leighton's Dorothy laughs, but stay–
Dorothy Dene is dead, they say!
None, I know, could be glad or gay
O'er the classic clay of the queen.
Dorothy Dene is dead, they say–
O beautiful Dorothy Dene!

It was commonly agreed that beauty made and unmade Dorothy as audiences "went to see how she looked and not how she acted," wrote the *Morning Post*, "regret is intensified by the fact that she never quite got, or quite did herself, justice on the stage. Circumstances were strong against her. She started on her career as an actress hampered by a reputation for something else – beauty. Her beauty would have helped her if only it had not been so renowned. Hard working, intelligent and ambitious, she might have done things little short of great. But her celebrity in repose ruined all." T.P. O'Connor gave his final verdict, somewhat paternalistically: "She was a quiet, gentle, somewhat sad girl; much more fitted for the joys of a quiet home than for the garish life and the ferocious struggles of the stage ... Poor Dorothy Dene was not a woman of adventures. She had none of the *joie de vivre* nor lack of principle that would have made such a life agreeable or even tolerable to her, but neither was it her fortune to have that life of the wife and the mother which is the best of all lives for the best of women."

Three days after Dorothy's death, it was startling to read a new short story by the popular novelist Halliwell Sutcliffe. The heroine, Dorothy Dene, was in love with Rex, a painter who was so jealous, that he left her when he thought she was wooed by another. Dorothy, a New Woman determined to earn her own living, disguised herself as a flower-girl, putting on a cockney accent and selling flowers in Piccadilly. All ended well, when she finally married her painter. It was a happy ending that the real-life Dorothy never got with her own Rex, the King of Painters.

***

Less than a year later Dr. Dent, who attended to Dorothy in her last illness, was rushed to the Schmalz residence. The 35 year old Edith was suffering from *Mania a Potu* – insanity from heavy drinking. She became sleepless, restless, and delirious; a nurse was hired to watch her constantly; she was imagining mice and snakes were crawling over her. It was feared that she might jump out of the window to escape. Gradually, her pulse became frequent and feeble, and on November 20th, 1900 she died of a heart failure.

Herbert Schmalz bought the plot behind Dorothy's. The 44 year-old widower remained single and lived on his own in the palatial house in Holland Park. After Edith's death, he became obsessed with the myth of the artist and his model. His *The Awakening of Galatea* (1907) portrayed Pygmalion, in love with his creation, kneeling, hugging the feet of his marvellous Galatea, just at the moment that the nude statue comes to life. In 1915 he changed perspective and painted Galatea on her own, her arms wide open, calling for Pygmalion to appear. In both paintings the model bore a strong resemblance to Edith.

Schmalz's religious work continued to attract crowds on both sides of the Atlantic, but he never achieved his ambition, to become a member of the Royal Academy. He died in 1935, exactly on the same date as Edith and is buried with her. Their shared tombstone is decorated with the Crusaders' Jerusalem Cross.

After Dorothy died, the flat in 10 Avonmore Mansions was too large and too expensive for Hetty, Lena and Samuel. They moved to the elegant Kensington Mansions, less than a mile away, and were well off enough to afford a live-in servant. In the next fifty years they would move flats, but always stay around Holland Park.

Hetty's theatrical career, cut short to be at Dorothy's side, never recovered. She was reduced to repeated shows of the Christmas pantomime *Aladdin*, which she played to raving reviews – "the princess of winsome Miss Hetty Dene is naturalness personified. This clever little lady acts with a daintiness and sings with sweetness that are perfectly irresistible, and somehow we cannot help expressing a regret that she is given so few opportunities," wrote the *Era*.

Kathleen's alcoholic lifestyle distressed and angered her sisters, and they shunned her. In August 1901, she married Charles Warren Marvin, an American working as a potman in the Yorkshire Grey Pub off Oxford Street. He lived on the premises with the owner's family and she joined him there. In their marriage certificate, Kathleen, who was 30 years old, left blank the entry of her profession, while the groom promoted himself to "licensed victualler." None of her sisters and brothers went to the wedding.

Several times during 1904 Kathleen was arrested in the streets, dead-drunk and incapable. Her sisters finally came to her rescue. They alerted Pearl Craigie, who remained a close family friend since sitting for Schmalz. The novelist had herself suffered from a drunk and violent husband. Time and again, Pearl Craigie came to Kathleen's hearings at the Marylebone Police Court. *Authoress and Actress* read the headlines. Though seven years passed since Kathleen took her last bow on stage, her acting career was brought up in court as a point in her favour. The senior magistrate, Mr Curtis Bennett, enjoyed having a celebrity in his courtroom, and talked privately with Pearl Craigie in his chamber. He was persuaded not to imprison Kathleen but to hand her over to the care of her husband, on condition that he would see to her rehabilitation. Kathleen was referred to the Oppenheimer Institute, which ludicrously promised to overcome the craving for alcohol within 48 hours.

The judge was cautious: Kathleen has very kind friends, he said, and they would assist her, but if she gave way to intemperate habits, he would have to commit her to a home for drunkards.

Kathleen was one of the first patients in Britain to try the American Oppenheimer miracle cure. The treatment, endorsed by the World's Women's Christian Temperance Association, was just another expensive scam, offering snake oil for drunks. Two weeks later, in mid-December Kathleen was arrested again. She told the judge Curtis Bennett that she had been to the clinic and undergone the treatment and was warned by the staff "that if she took any intoxicating liquor it would make her very bad; and unfortunately, it did, though she had very little." With tears streaming down her face, "she pleaded pathetically for mercy, and referring to her benefactress, Pearl, said, 'I know that I owe a great deal to that dear lady."

Kathleen had no chance. With the failure of the treatment, and her frequents arrests, the judge's hands were tied. Eighty percent of the drunkards sent to the Inebriate Reformatories, were women. The judicial system considered men to be capable of self-reform and that locking them up in institutions would ruin their families. Women, however, could not control their "hysteria which females develop when under the influence of drink" and needed institutionalized help since they were more prone to drink-related crimes. But the rate of cure was very low.

Kathleen was committed for the maximum term permitted, three years. Her photograph in the Habitual Criminals Register of December

1904 is shocking: a cheap straw hat on unkempt hair, a blank look of resignation. There was no trace of the well-groomed, dainty girl who ten years earlier posed in a fluffy white lace dress for her first and only fan photo. While she was away at the reformatory, her husband died of hepatic cirrhosis, the result of his own heavy drinking. Kathleen never overcame her addiction. When she was discharged from the institution, she was not taken into her sisters' home and moved from one shabby room to another. She tried to eke out a living as a charwoman in a hotel.

On October 22nd, 1908, Kathleen collapsed in the street and was rushed to the Strand Union Infirmary, where she was pronounced dead. A coroner was called in to rule out a violent death. The post mortem showed that she died of natural causes, from cirrhosis of the liver. "A debilitated condition, habitual," wrote the coroner. From a piece of paper found on her, the police figured out the hotel she was working in and her name, but she had "no fixed abode known." It took a while to locate Hetty, who at least took care of the burial. Kathleen Blanche Marvin was interred in Kensal Green, inside Dorothy's grave.

Earlier that year, their father, Abraham Pullan, who had been hospitalized in the Greenwich Infirmary for several years as a result of diabetes, was struck with cerebral haemorrhage. Their older brother Thomas took him in for his final months. It was some sort of late reconciliation. Thomas was widowed and bereaved; his young wife had died tragically in 1891 soon after child-birth, together with their one-year-old baby boy. Left with the new-born Kathleen, the three-year-old Thomas-William and the four-year-old Margery, Thomas was unable to cope. His sisters were too busy with their theatrical careers to be of any help. He placed his toddlers with a childless widow who ran a pub in Hampshire, paying for their keep from his job as an engineer. Thomas Pullan and his children were reunited only much later. He died in 1927, aged 70. His great-grandchildren are the only Pullan descendants.

After fifteen years on the road, the Dene sisters were too tired of the vagaries of the stage. Hetty was in her late 30s, Lena had just turned 30, and with over £7000 of Leighton's money that Dorothy had left them, they could manage comfortably. They were also among the beneficiaries of his sisters' wills: Alexandra Sutherland Orr had died in 1903 and left them £500, and Augusta Matthews died in 1919 and left each of them £600. Their brother Samuel qualified as a mining engineer, and his expertise took him away for long periods of work in the Far East, Canada, Siberia, Costa Rica and Mozambique. There was always a room kept for him at his sisters' flat. From Dorothy, they inherited a collection of drawings, sketches and engravings, given to her by Leighton and other artists. The sisters sold them one by one, but as the years passed by, and the art world turned its back on Victorian artefacts, their value plummeted. In 1946, Hetty negotiated a sale to the British Museum but failing to get anything for them, donated 16 engravings of Leighton's.

These three siblings never married, and they all carried Dorothy's theatrical surname. Samuel died in October 1944, Hetty in May 1951. Lena, the last of the Dene sisters, was found dead in her small flat in June 1955, aged 81.

***

With the discovery of *Flaming June* in the 1960s, Dorothy Dene resurfaced like Venus from the waves. Most artists' models are anonymous, objects for the artists to exercise their talents on. But not Dorothy Dene. She is inseparable from Lord Leighton, acknowledged as the most influential figure in his last 16 years, when he made his most celebrated paintings. A blue plaque was recently attached to her home in The Chase, Clapham, celebrating the "artist's model and stage actress."

At her death, T.P. O'Connor was more generous than he had often been and anticipated that "perhaps, a century hence some young lover, looking at one of Leighton's pictures, where love appears in all its intoxicated joy, will hardly believe that the original of that beautiful creature, with the throat like a column of white marble, was a quiet, poor little Clapham girl, who suffered much and died young."

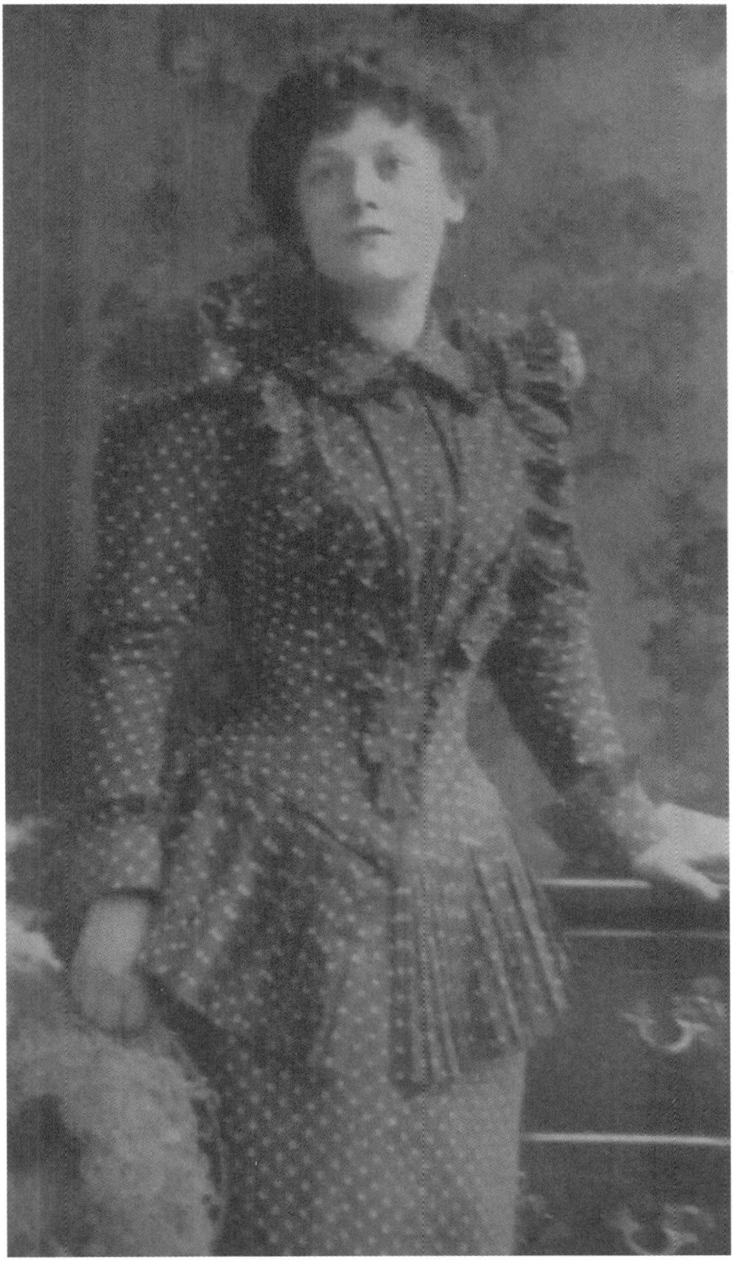

Last picture of Dorothy Dene, *The Sketch*, 3 January 1900

Selected Bibliography

Books

Agresti, Olivia Rossetti, *Giovanni Costa, his Life, Work and Times*, Grant Richards, London, 1904

Ash, Russell, *Lord Leighton,* Pavilion Books, London, 1995

Ash, Russell, *Victorian Masters and their art*, Pavilion Books, London 1999

Archer, William, *Masks or Faces? the Psychology of Acting*, Longman's, London and New York, 1888

Barkan, Elazar & Ronald Bush (eds.), *Prehistories of the future: the primitivist project and the culture of modernism*, Stanford and Cambridge University Press, 1995

Barringer, T. & Prettejohn, E., eds. *Frederic Leighton: Antiquity, Renaissance, Modernity*, Yale University Press, New Haven, 1999

Barrington, Russell, Mrs, *The Life, Letters and Work of Frederic Leighton*, vols. 1 and 2, G. Allen, London, 1906

Barrington, Russell, Mrs, *G. F. Watts, Reminiscences.* G. Allen, London, 1905

Barrington, Russell, Mrs, *Lena's Picture – A Story of Love*, Volume 1 and 2, D. Douglas, London, 1892

Barrington, Russell, Mrs, *A Retrospect, and other articles*, Osgood, London, 1896

Barton, Edwin Alfred, *A Doctor Remembers*, Seeley, Service & Co, London, 1941

Bendiner, Kenneth, *An introduction to Victorian painting*, Yale University Press, New Haven and London, 1985

Berk, Jimenez, Jill & Joanna Banham, (eds.) *Dictionary of Artist's Models*, Fitzroy Dearborn, London, 2001

Bills, Mark and Barbara Bryant, *G. F. Watts: Victorian visionary*, Yale University Press, New Haven, London, 2008

Blakemore, Trevor, *The Art of Herbert Schmalz*, G. Allen, London, 1911

Blainey, Ann, *Fanny and Adelaide: the lives of the remarkable Kemble sisters*, I.R. Dee, Chicago, 2001

Booth, Michael, *Theatre in the Victorian Age*, Cambridge University Press, Cambridge, 1991

Borzello, Frances, *The Artist's Model*, Junction, London, 1982

Brandlhuber, Margot, ed. *Frederic Lord Leighton,1830-1896 : painter and sculptor of the Victorian, age,* Prestel, Munich, 2009

Cardoso, Rafael and Colin Trodd. (eds.) *Art and the Academy in the nineteenth century*, Manchester University Press, Manchester, 2000

Cooper, Emmanuel, *The Sexual Perspective: homosexuality and art in the last 100 years in the west*, Routledge, London and New York, 1994

Corkran, Alice, *Frederic Leighton*, Methuen, London, 1904

Corkran, Henriette, *Celebrities and I,* Hutchinson & Co, London, 1902

Crane, Walter, *An Artist's Reminiscences*, Methuen & Co, London, 1907

Dakers, Caroline, *The Holland Park Circle: artists and Victorian Society*, Yale University Press, New Haven and London, 1999

Davis, Tracy, *Actresses as Working Women*, Routledge, London, 1991

Dijkstra, Bram, *Idols of Perversity*, Oxford University Press, New York, 1986

Frith, William Powell, *My Autobiography and Reminiscences*, Bentley & Son, London, 1889

Furniss, Harry, *Some Victorian Women, good, bad, and indifferent,* John Lane, London, 1923

Gaunt, William, *Victorian Olympus*, Cape, London, 1975

Gere, Charlotte, *Artistic Circles : design & decoration in the aesthetic movement*, V&A, London, 2010

Grein, Jacob Thomas, *Dramatic Criticism*, J. Long, London and Amsterdam, 1899

Hammerschlag, Keren Rosa, *Frederic Leighton: Death, Mortality, Resurrection*, Routledge, London, 2016

Hawthorne, Julian, *Shapes That Pass,* John Murray, London, 1928

James, Henry, *The Private Life and other stories*, Harper, New York, 1893

Jenkyns, Richard. *Dignity and Decadence/ Victorian art and the classical inheritance*, HarperCollins, London, 1991
Jopling, Louise, *Twenty Years of My Life,* John Lane, London and New York, 1925
Kestner, Joseph, *Mythology and Misogyny*, University of Wisconsin, 1989
Lamb, Joseph Frank, *Lions in their dens: Lord Leighton and late Victorian studio life*. Ann Arbor, Mi. University Microfilms International, 1988
Lang, Leonora, *Sir Frederic Leighton: His Life and Work*, London, 1884
Leighton, Frederic: Drawings and other studies of Lord Leighton in pencil, chalk and other mediums, The Fine Art Society, London 1898
Leslie, George Dunlop, *The Inner Life of the Royal Academy*, John Murray, London, 1914
Maas, Jeremy, *Victorian Painters*, The Cresset Press, London 1969
Martin Philippa & al., *A Victorian Master: Drawings by Frederic, Lord Leighton*, Royal Borough of Kensington, London, 2006
Morse, Belinda, *John Hanson Walker, the life and times of a Victorian artist*, A. Sutton Publishing, Gloucester, 1987
Newall, Christopher, *The Art of Lord Leighton*, Phaidon, Oxford, 1990
Newall, Christopher & al, *Frederic Lord Leighton 1830-1896: Painter and Sculptor of the Victorian Age*, Villa Stuck, Prestel, Munich, 2009
Ormond, Leonee & Richard, *Lord Leighton*, Yale University Press, New Haven and London, 1975
Postle, Martin, *The Artist's Model: from Etty to Spencer*, Merrell Holberton, London, 1999
Postle, Martin, Jane Desmarais and William Vaughn (eds.) *Model and supermodel : the artist's model in British art and culture*, Manchester University Press, Manchester, 2006
Powell, Kerry, *Women and Victorian theatre*, Cambridge University Press, Cambridge, 1997
Prettejohn, Elizabeth, *Art for Art's sake: Aestheticism in Victorian painting,* Yale University Press, New Haven-London, 2007
Price, Julius Mendes, *My Bohemian Days in London*, T. W. Laurie, London, 1914

Redesdale, Lord, *Memories*, Hutchinson and Co, 1915

Rhys, Ernest, *Frederic Lord Leighton: An Illustrated Record of His Life and Work*, George Bell, London, 1895

Robbins, Daniel, ed: *Closer to Home, The Restoration of Leighton House and Catalogue of the Reopening Displays,* The Royal Borough of Kensington and Chelsea, 2010

Robbins, Daniel: *Leighton House Museum*, The Royal Borough of Kensington and Chelsea, 2011

Schmidt, Arnika, *Nino Costa (1826-1903) Transnational Exchange in European Landscape Painting*, Silvana Editoriale, 2016

Shuttleworth, H. C, *The Diary Of An Actress: Or Realities Of Stage Life* London, 1885

Smith, Alison, *The Victorian Nude: Sexuality, Morality and Art,* Manchester University Press, Manchester, 1996

Staley, Edgcumbe, *Lord Leighton of Stretton, PRA*, London, 1906

Trodd, Colin and Stephanie Brown, *Representations of G. F. Watts: art making in Victorian culture*, Ashgate, Aldershot, 2004

Tromans, Nicholas, *Hope: the life and times of a Victorian icon*, Watts Gallery, Compton, 2011

Tynan, Katharine, *Twenty -Five Years: Reminiscences,* London, 1913

Warner, Malcolm, *Friendship and Loss in the Victorian Portrait*, Kimble Art Museum and Yale University Press, 2009

Watts, M. S. *George Frederic Watts*. Macmillan & Co., London, 1912

Wearing J. P, *The London Stage 1890-1899: a calendar of plays and players*, Metuchen: Scarecrow Press, 1976

Weidinger, Alfred et all, *Sleeping Beauty: Masterpieces of Victorian Painting from Museo de Arte de Ponce*, Belvedere, Vienna, 2010

Wilton, Andrew and Robert Upstone, eds. *The age of Rossetti, Burne-Jones & Watts*. Tate Gallery Publishing, London, 1997

Wood, Christopher, *Olympian Dreamers: Victorian Classical Painters, 1860-1914,* Constable, London, 1983

Exhibition Catalogues:

Leighton House: a collection of essays on Lord Leighton and his works, with illustrated catalogue of the contents of Leighton House, 1900

Frederic, Lord Leighton: Eminent Victorian Artist, Jones et al., Royal Academy of Arts, London, 1996

Exposed: the Victorian Nude, ed. Alison Smith, Tate Britain, Tate Publishing, London, 2001

A Victorian obsession: the Pérez Simón collection at Leighton House Museum. Véronique Gerard-Powell and Daniel Robbins, Royal Borough of Kensington and Chelsea, London, 2014

Leighton's Flaming June, by Susan Grace Galassi and Pablo Perez D'Ors, The Frick Collection, New York, 2015

Flaming June – the making of an icon, ed. Catherine Blake, Leighton House Museum, London, 2016

Articles:

Bailey, Kate, '*Leighton – Public and Private* Lives: Celebrity and the Gentleman Artist', *Apollo Magazine*, February, 1996

Barlow, Paul, 'Transparent Bodies, Opaque Identities', In *Frederic Leighton: Antiquity, Renaissance, Modernity*

Barrow, Rosemary, 'Desiring Women: Myth, Love and Leighton's Clytie'. Lecture given at Leighton House in 2012, full text on *the Victorian Web*

Bryant, Brabara, 'G.F. Watts and the Symbolist Vision', In *The Age of Rossetti, Burne-Jones and Watts*

Dakers, Caroline: 'Leighton: The Truth? Frederic Leighton and his Relationship with Lily and Fred Mason', *Apollo Magazine*, December 1996

Hammerschlag, Keren,'The Deathly Sleep of Frederic Leighton's Painted Women', *Women: a cultural review*. Vol 23; n. 2, Taylor & Francis, 2012

Martin, Philippa, 'The Tragic Muse', *Apollo Magazine*, November 2014

Mayer, David, 'The Actress as Photographic Icon', in *The Cambridge*

Companion to the Actress, ed. Gale, Maggie and John Stokes, Cambridge University Press, 2007
Myrone, Martin, 'Prudery, Pornography and the Victorian Nude'. In *Exposed*
Ormond, Richard and Leonee, 'Frederick Leighton', in *Victorian High Renaissance*, City Art Gallery, Manchester, 1978
Perkin, David, 'Ada Alice Pullan (Dorothy Dene)', a talk given at the Clapham Society's meeting in 2001. On the website of *The Clapham Society Local History Series*
Postle, Martin, 'Naked Civil Servant: the professional life model in British art and society', in *Model and Supermodel*
Postle, Martin, *'Leighton's Lost Model*: The Rediscovery of Mary Lloyd', *Apollo Magazine* 143, February 1996
Postle, Martin: 'Behind the Screen: the studio model', in *The Artist's Model*
Prettejohn, Elizabeth, 'Leighton: the aesthete as academic', In *Art and the Academy in the nineteenth century*
Prettejohn, Elizabeth, 'Painting indoors: Leighton and his studio', *Apollo Magazine*, 143, February 1996
Prettejohn, Elizabeth, 'Morality versus Aesthetics in critical interpretations of Frederic Leighton', *Burlington Magazine*, February 1996
Robbins, Daniel, 'Between Life and Death: Leighton and Clytie'. A talk given at Leighton House in 2012, on the Leighton House Museum website
Simon, Robin, ed.: 'Lord Leighton and Leighton House: a Centenary Celebration', *Apollo Magazine*, 143, February 1996
Smith, Alison, 'Nature Transformed: Leighton, the nude and the model', In *Frederic Leighton, Antiquity, Renaissance, Modernity*
Smith, Alison, 'The British "Matron" and the bad beautiful: the nude debate of 1885', In *After the Pre-Raphaelites*: ed. Prettejohn, Elizabeth
Spielmann, M.H., 'The Late Lord Leighton', *Magazine of Art*, 1896
Stephenson, Andrew, 'Leighton and the shifting repertoires of masculine artistic identity', in *Frederic Leighton: Antiquity, Renaissance, Modernity*
Vaughan, William: 'Models and Muses', in *The Artist's Model*
Vaughan, William, 'The Naked and the Nude', in *The Artist's Model*

Notes

Chapter One: The discovery

On Flaming June:
Leighton's Flaming June, by Susan Grace Galassi and Pablo Perez D'Ors, the Frick Collection, New York, 2015
Flaming June, the Making of an Icon, curator – Dr. Daniel Robbins, Leighton House Museum, London 2016
'The breath of the sleeping girl': Staley, Edgcumbe, Lord Leighton of Stretton, PRA, London, 1906
Mr Fincke was not thrilled: e-mail exchange with his son Ben Fincke, April 2014
Bernard Nevill, a young lecturer: 'From Outcast to Icon', by Jeremy Maas, in *Royal Academy Magazine*, winter 1995
'Probably the most wonderful painting in existence': Samuel Courtauld's collection of French 19th century paintings and drawings, Courtauld Institute of Art, London, Arts Council of Great Britain, 1976
Frederic Leighton gave credit to his model: Staley, Leighton
'Picture impossible to pass over': The Country Gentleman, 4 May 1895
'Reform bills, strikes, socialism': 'Lord Leighton's Art', by Greenough White, *The Sewanee Review*, vol. 7, number 4, October 1899, John Hopkins University Press

Chapter Two: On becoming Eliza Doolittle

GB Shaw – preface to Pygmalion, in *Pygmalion,* Penguin Books, London, New York 2003
On the Pullan family: we thank Colin Craven, their descendent, for the Pullan family tree.
Abraham Pullan's first patents: *The London Gazette*, 13 July 1860, 8 April 1862, 10 April 1863. Also, *The Practical Mechanic's Journal*, 1861. Last patent – an attachment to typewriters – United States Patent office, 18 November 1888.
'The product of a serious family': The Dramatic peerage, 1892
Father "a well-known civil engineer", mother "intensely intellectual": Interview to *Lloyds Weekly*, 4 August 1895
Reciting Shakespeare: The Dramatic peerage, 1892
Soliciting 'young girls': *Evening Post,* 17 January 1880
An actress was 'a frivolous': H.C. Shuttleworth, *The Diary of an Actress*, London, 1885
Save Ellen Terry 'from the temptations': 'G.F. Watts and Ellen Terry', by David Loshak, *Burlington Magazine*, 105 (1963)

The opposition served only to incite her: *The Dramatic Year Book*, 1891
'I don't see how you can rock the cradle': Edward Gordon Craig, *Ellen Terry and Her Secret Self*, Dutton, 1932

Chapter Three: The new Galatea

'Happy is she with the flashing eye and the pretty head': 'On Models', by Joseph Howard Jr, in America, a Journal of Today, 3 January 1889
'between employer and employed': 'Models', the Star, 22 May 1883
A model is 'anyone who has lost her self-respect': *Harry Furniss at Home*, G. Bell, London 1904
'I felt this was indeed a delightful opportunity': Mrs Russell Barrington, *G. F. Watts, Reminiscences*, G. Allen, London, 1905
Barrington 'a rumpled, scrumpled little brown paper woman': *Selected Letters of Vernon Lee*, edited by Amanda Gagel, Routledge, London, 2016
'young girl, with a lovely white face': Barrington, Leighton op cit
'a good advertisement': Henriette Corkran, *Celebrities and I*
'when the model is sulky or a dolt': Stephens in Rhys, Ernest, F*rederic Lord Leighton*, George Bell, London, 1895
'I thought, giving me a dinner at eight o'clock': Valvona's memoirs, unpublished, courtesy of Mr. Ian Valvona
'the paragon of manners in the highest society of the mind': Alice Corkran, Leighton, Methuen, London, 1904
'To find a handsomer specimen of manhood': Julius M. Price, *My Bohemian days in London*, T.W. Laurie, London, 1914
'I pray God I may die before I am seventy': Alice Corkran, Leighton op cit
His art 'exists to create beautiful images': *Scribner's Magazine*, Volume 19, Charles Scribners Sons, 1896
'for their hands and feet': Alison Smith, *The Victorian Nude: Sexuality, Morality, and Art*, Manchester University Press, Manchester, 1996
'what can be more beautiful than an English girl': Henriette Corkran, *Celebrities and I*, Hutchinson & Co, London, 1902
Criticism of Leighton: the Graphic, 11 May 1878; *Leeds Mercury*, 3 May 1879; *Sheffield Independent*, 8 May 1879; *Birmingham Daily*, 3 May 1879
'he at last felt free fully to express through his canvases': Jones, Newall, Ormond et al, *Frederic Leighton: 1830-1896*, Royal Academy of Arts, London, 1996
'His manners were courteous': Mrs. E.M. Wards's *Reminiscences*, Pitman & Sons, London, 1911
Ada face, 'a clouded pallor': Barrington, Leighton op cit
'her form and features': *San Francisco Chronicle*, Dec 30, 1899
'with a glory of curls': *The St. Paul Globe*, Minnesota, 28 January 1900
'brilliant and light blue of the Scandinavian': T.O. O'Connor, Mainly About People, 6 January 1900

'Preserved even rarely in our statues': *The St. Paul Globe*, Minnesota, 28 January 1900
Mary Anderson – 'Beautiful women', *Waikato Times*, 13 April, 1889 (also in the New York World,)

Chapter Four: A nymph was born

Connie Gilchrist: 'she is losing her beauty': *Lewis Carroll's diaries,* Lewis Carroll Society, 2003
'Years later, the story goes': Julius M. Price, *My Bohemian Days*, op cit
Leighton 'instantly dropt on one knee': George Dunlop Leslie, *The inner life of the Royal Academy*, John Murray, London 1914
'He loved little things': Barrington, Leighton op cit
On Sisters kiss: *The Diaries of Lewis Carroll*, vol 2, Cassell and Co 1953 – entry for 4 July 1879 – description of Sisters kiss that he saw in Leighto's studio
Eleven-year-old model, Ada Smith: *Lewis Carroll and His Illustrators: Collaborations & Correspondence,* 1865-1898, edited by Morton N. Cohen & Edward Wakeling. London: Macmillan, 2003
'the artistic nude implicated a general spread of vice': Alison Smith, *The Victorian Nude: Sexuality, Morality, and Art*, op cit
Also – Nature Transformed – Leighton, *The Nude and the Model*, by Alison Smith, in Frederic Leighton – Antiquity, Renaissance, Modernity, ed. Tim Barringer and Elizabeth Prettejohn, 1999 Yale Center for British Art
'well-covered limbs, and paint no more Venuses': Barrington, op cit
'She is a creature who can never age': Barrington, op cit

Chapter Five: Roses and Thorns

On Leighton's personality and methods of work, throughout the book: interviews with Dr. Daniel Robbins, Senior Curator at Royal Borough of Kensington and Chelsea
'a nice innocent damsel or two': Fiona MacCarthy, *The Last Pre-Raphaelite: Edward Burne-Jones and the Victorian Imaginaion*, Harvard University Press, Cambridge, MA, 2012
'What Is Burne-Jones like?' Dorothy Dene interview, The Press, New York, 27 November 1892
'left a letter unanswered': Julius M. Price, My Bohemian Days in London op cit
'I never give my whole attention': Leighton Interview with Harry How, the *Strand Magazine*, August 1892
'you will in places be able to trace the forms beneath': The Pall Mall Budget 1886, The President's Pictures
'I can paint a figure in three days, but it may take me thirty to drape it': Staley, Leighton op cit
'draped they are English': Sizeranne in Review of Reviews, vol 13, 1896

'You must think as little as possible while sitting', *Pearson's Magazine*, vol 8, 1899
On Louisa Starr-Canziani: Estella Canziani, Round about 3 Palace Green, Methuen & Co, London 1939
'There's another there': Gaetano Valvona, from his unpublished memoirs.
'on which he received visits, those of work': Giovanni Costa in *The Cornhill Magazine*, March 1897
'bodily, as well as mental feebleness': *The Medical Press and Circular*, 14 April 1880
'I confess that I regret very much indeed': Leighton's letter in the *Graphic*, 24 December 1881
'a vision of that divine loveliness': Laura Beatty, *Lillie Langtry: Manners, Masks and Morals*, Vintage Digital, London 2012
'the delicate porcelain whiteness of her unblemished skin': Leighton House Museum website

Chapter Six: "Impossible! with that voice!"

Payments to the Pullan siblings: records of Frederic Leighton's account at Coutt's Bank, Royal Borough of Kensington Archive.
The poems of Catullus, translated by Theodore Martin, Parker, Son & Bourn, London, 1861
'beyond the desire of recording for posterity the aesthetic craze': William Powell Frith, *Further Reminiscences*, Volume 2, R. Bentley, 1887
'Leaving mamma so soon?': Richard Ellmann, *Oscar Wilde*, Penguin, London, 1988
'all the world is at their feet': Alice Corkran, Frederic Leighton op cit
'I find a poetry in that man's work': Barrington, Leighton op cit
'fine female head and bust': *The Art Journal*, 1882
'My father was at first, averse to the idea': 'A chat with Frederic Leighton', Cassell's *Family Magazine* 1895
'What can he hope for, if I let him': Barrington, op cit
'There is no question that at the present moment': School of Dramatic Art, the Era, 20 May 1882
'No one can make you an actress': *Lloyd's Weekly Newspaper*, 4 August 1895
'the fundamental stone': chat with Frederic Leighton, Cassell's *Family Magazine*, July 1895
'The training, if any, is a mere chapter of accidents': the *Era*, 20 May 1882
'Leighton made the sittings enchanting': Alice Corkran, Leighton op cit.
'here is an example of the best kind of drawing': Art and Artists, *Otago Witness*, 23 April 1896
Condescending from the majesties of Olympus – *The Works of John Ruskin*, J. Wiley, 1889

Chapter Seven: "The sensitive and prickly Tragic Muse"

'I want you to help me in a little conspiracy': Barrington, op cit
Dorothy sat for Costa: Arnika Schmidt, *Nino Costa (1826-1903) Transnational Exchange in European Landscape Painting*, Silvana Editoriale, 2016
Leighton 'will remain with us for thirty-six hours, sixteen minutes': Costa to George Howard, the Archives of Castle Howard, J22/35/68
'fair as an angel': Staley, Leighton op cit
'drawing from the model': Mary S. Watts, *Watts, The annals of an artist's life*, Macmillan & Co., London, 1912

Chapter Eight: A very promising debut

'She wishes to be a worker': *Lloyds Weekly*, 4 August 1895
'Miss Pullan wants to get in the Lyceum': May Hartley to Bram Stoker, 8 August 1884, Leeds University Library – special collections, ref BC MS 19c Stoker ref 7961
'I certainly did not mean to seem churlish': Barrington, op cit
'was fair as the moon': Hugh Conway, *Called Back*, J.W. Arrowsmith, Bristol, 1898
'Don't be frightened': Dorothy's letter to Leighton, in Barrington op cit
'I've heard so much of Miss Dene's genius': letter, 9 October 1884, in *The Letters of Oscar Wilde*, edited by Rupert Hart-Davis. Butler & Tanner, London, 1962
'the mushroom': Barrington, Leighton op cit

Chapter Nine: "Too good to be true"

Teasingly called her 'the mushroom': Barrington, op cit
'Nymph of the downward smile': *The poems of John Keats*, edited by Jack Stillinger, Heinemann Educational, London 1978
the greeting between the President and the professional beauty: *The Northern Whig*, 23 November 1904.
'Dorothy Dene is the prettiest of them all': Mary Anderson on Dorothy – 'Beautiful women', *New York World*, 28 February 1889, also *Waikato Times*, 13 April; 1889
'accentuates her subtle expression': on Phebe, in Art Renewal Center website
'promises to become a rival to Mary Anderson': *Saturday Evening Mail*, Vigo County, Indiana, 18 July 1885
'single purpose of corrupting the morals of youth': *Morning Post*, 26 June 1857
'that you should lay down a cornerstone': Barrington, Leighton, letter written in February 1881.
'always the poorest, the weakest': *Seeking and Saving*, a monthly journal of home mission and penitentiary work, January 1885
'a strong mark along the crimson leather': *Dundee Evening Telegraph*, 22 May 1885
'the poor and struggling students': *Saturday Review*, 12 December 1885

A letter to Sir Frederick Leighton from Frederick George Lee, in *Immodesty in art: an expostulation and suggestion*, George Redway, London 1887
'to abolish the model': interview with Watts, the *Pall Mall Gazette*, 9 October 1885
Professor Graf's trial, *The Times*, 9 October 1885
'one of the happiest things Leighton has ever put together': Alma-Tadema to Marquand, 26 February 1886, Marquand Papers, Princeton
'Sir Frederic has never done anything more charming': *The Art Journal*, November 1886
'more luscious than sugar, more fragile than Dresden china': *London Evening Standard*, 1 May 1886
'an abominably bad example to students': Fun, 12 May 1886
'showing the beauty of tender, undeveloped forms': M. H. Spielmann, *British Sculpture and Sculptors of Today*, Cassell & Co, London 1901

Chapter Ten: "Because of her personal worth"

On Hope:
G.F. Watts and the Symbolist Vision, by Barbara Bryant, in *The Age of Rossetti, Burne-Jones and Watts*, ed. Andrew Wilton and Robert Upstone, Tate 1997
Representations of G.F Watts, Art making in Victorian Culture, Colin Trodd, Stephanie Brown 2004
'above any particular model': Mary Seton Watts, G.F. Watts op cit
'A beautiful friend of mine': Barrington, Watts
'we found her very intelligent': Barrington, Leighton
'all the strings of her instrument': Mary Seton Watts, G.F. Watts op cit
'as one of the sources for his late masterpiece': Nicholas Tromans, *Hope: the Life and Times of a Victorian Icon*, Watts Gallery, Compton, 2011
'a rebellious reaction against an unhealthy orthodoxy': Debbie Challis, *The Archaeology of Race*, Bloomsbury Academic, London, 2013
'nobody noticed her looks': Public Opinion, April-October 1886
'I write to ask your sanction for an alteration': Walter Crane, *An Artist's reminiscences*, Methuen & Co, London, 1907
'not only on account of her abilities': 15 May 1886. All quotes from correspondence between Leighton and Browning are from letters kept at the Armstrong Browning Library of Baylor University, Waco, Texas
The delighted audience: 'the schoolmaster abroad', in *Punch*, 29 May 1886
'everybody was astonished at her great beauty': Public Opinion, 1886
'To listen to Miss Dene's blank verse': *Wells Journal*, 4 January 1900
Browning was 'a great flirt and proud of his conquests': Mr Browning and his lady friends, *Pall Mall Gazette*, 19 June 1889
'for I believe such friendships': *Lloyd's Weekly*, 4 August 1895

Chapter Eleven: London went mad over her

Poem on Dorothy Dene – *Globe*, 18 May 1886
'Her gown was of blue satin': *Whitby Gazette,* 14 May 1887
'Miss Dorothy Dene in one of the big hats': *South Australian Weekly Chronicle*, 10 September 1887
'a lovely Norwegian silver chatelaine': *The South Australian Advertiser*, 18 July 1887
'Leighton glance with a look of recognition': *Derby Daily Telegraph*, 3 June 1887
'Aesthetic, saucer-eyed, powdery-faced': Letter from London, the *Auckland Evening Star*, 9 March 1889
'with some or other Society friend': *Stage*, 13 July 1893
'the most be-photographed person in England': A Lady's letter from London, in the *Auckland Star*, 10 July 1886
Dorothy received royalties: *The Photographic News*, 31 August 1888
'will attract crowds who would fail': *Glasgow Herald*, 3 April 1882
Dorothy a hot-house lily: *Cosmopolitan*, January 1890
Actresses' waists: *Daily Gazette* for Middleborough, 12 March 1889
'the most beautiful of any woman in Europe': *Cincinnati Enquirer*, 6 March 1898
She said that she never uses cosmetics: interview with actress Mary Anderson, the *New York World*, 28 February 1889
'with a novel in her hand': *The Daily Times*, Davonport, Iowa, 21 July 1890
'he positively worships': *The New Zealand Herald*, 15 October 1887
'came to gaze at the fair face': *The Sporting Times*, 19 June 1886
'she hit the right note': *Illustrated London News*, 10 July 1886
"still more firmly on her pedestal in England": *Chicago Tribune*, 11 June 1887
'perhaps the day will come': *Sheffield Independent*, 24 December 1886
She told William Archer: *Masks or faces? A study in the psychology of acting*, Longman's, London and New York, 1888
Dorothy Dene's questionnaire, in the V&A archive, THM/368/4/3/17
'I left him chatting and smiling': *Staffordshire Sentinel*, 19 January 1889
Pictures were known not as Helen or Andromache': *Pall Mall Gazette*, 19 June 1889

Chapter Twelve: "Those well-formed maidens"

Alfred Edward Matthews was sent to fetch her: *Matty: an autobiography*, by Alfred Edward Matthews, Hutchinson, 1952
'though as a neck nothing can be said against it': Funny Folks, 10 July 1886
'entirely to the kindness of that very gifted young actress': correspondence in the Ryland Library, University of Manchester, Eng Ms 1226,25
'perhaps widening wisdom': *Bernard Shaw on the London Art Scene*, ed. Stanley Weintraub, Pennsylvania State University Press, 1989
'parleying with endless persons of importance': *Pall Mall Gazette*, 30 April 1887
'Yellow and pale as ripened corn': Rhys, Leighton

'sending me such a beautiful epigram': Letter from Leighton to Browning, 5 April 1887, Armstrong-Browning Library, L2-376
'the canvas is full of prettiness': *The Era*, 3 March 1888
'should hide her silver face behind a cloud': Elizabeth O'Connor, *I Myself*, Methuen, London 1910
'she is adding, as she deserves': Barrington, op cit
'each dew drop being turned': *Glasgow Herald*, 20 July 1888
'threatened by premature adiposity': *Illustrated Sporting and Dramatic News*, 15 January 1887
'has none of the weird faith': *Pall Mall Gazette*, 30 April 1887
'more than one member of the Academy': 'Glimpses of Artist life – the Artist's model', by M.H. Spielmann, *Magazine of Art*, vol 10, 1887

Chapter Thirteen: Matchmaking

On Leighton-Dene marriage rumours:
Sheffield Evening Telegraph, 7 April 1888
Dundee Evening Telegraph, 11 April 1888
Sidney Morning Herald, 11 May 1888, dispatched from London 6 April
Australian Town and County Journal, 19 May 1888
York Herald, 5 June 1888
Yorkshire Gazette, 9 June 1898
'Why doesn't Leighton marry?': Henriette Corkran, *Celebrities and I*, Hutchinson & co, London 1902
'will probably retire into private life': *Australian Town and Country Journal*, 19 May 1888
'I should, by marrying again': Louise Jopling, *Twenty Years of My Life*, John Lane, London, New York, 1925
'gave out she was engaged to Leighton': Estella Cazianni, *Round About Three Palace Green*, Methuen & Co, London, 1939
'Let me know if, and when, I may congratulate': Louise Jopling, *Twenty Years of My Life Life*, op cit
'tell all my fellow members there's nothing in it': Leighton to Fred Eaton, secretary of the Royal Academy, in Estella Canziani, *Round About Three Palace Green*, op cit
'Not only was he glorious to look upon': Sir James Rennell Rodd, *Social and Diplomatic Memories*, Edward Arnold & Co, London, 1922
'A hero of romance in aspect and bearing': Julian Hawthorne, *Shapes that Pass: memories of old days*, John Murray, London, 1928
'Yes, replied Whistler. 'And he paints, too, sometimes': Staley, Leighton op cit
'very good looking, suggestive of the young Raphael': *Harriet Hosmer, Letters and Memories*. Ed. Cornelia Carr, John Lane, London, 1913
'lionised Isabel all over Rome': Barrington, Leighton op cit

On relationship with Sartoris:
Friendship and loss in the Victorian Portrait, by Malcolm Warner, Yale University Press 2008
Fanny and Adelaide, by Ann Blainey, Ivan R. Dee publishing, Chicago 2001
'A Week in a French Country-House', by Adelaide Sartoris, illustrated by Leighton, 1867, *Cornhill Magazine*
'Representations of the Victorian Art world in Disraeli's Lothair', by Simon Poe (1870). In *British Art Journal*, V 5, n 2, Autumn 2004

Chapter Fourteen: "Half-hidden from himself"

'Somewhat lacking in a capacity for love': *Portraits by Sir Joshua Reynolds*. Introduction and notes by Frederick W. Hilles. Yale University, William Heinemann, London, 1952
'lived and died free from the thraldom of Hymen': *Sheffield Evening Telegraph,* 22 September 1893
'Should artists marry': 'London bachelors and their mode of living', in The Leisure Hour, April 1886
'Art should be the artist's only bride': *Glasgow Evening Post,* 20 May 1889
'The unmarried or childless men': Francis Bacon, 'Of Marriage and Single Life,' in *The Essays or Counsels Civil and Moral of Francis Bacon,* Clarendon Press, Oxford, 1890
Leighton was unfathomable even to his closest friends: interviews with Dr. Daniel Robbins.
'known him from a boy': 'The Late Lord Leighton', by M.H. Spielmann, in the *Graphic*, 1 February 1896
'as he passed them hurriedly, as if afraid to linger': Frances Elliot, *Roman Gossip*, J. Murray, London, 1896
'his fits of depression, the psychosomatic disorders': Ormond, Lord Leighton
'was temperamentally averse to intimate human relationships': Stephen Jones in *Frederic Leighton*, Royal Academy of Arts, London 1996
'but it was with his art': Lord Redesdale, *Memories*, Hutchinson 1915
'put too much of himself into it': Christopher Newall, *The Art of Lord Leighton*, Phaidon, 1990
'a possible result of it may be to increase': *Saturday Review*, 19 May 1866
'Whatever noble fire is in our hearts': Rhys, *Frederic Lord Leighton: An Illustrated Record of His Life and Work*, George Bell, London, 1895
On Leighton's alleged homosexuality:
The Sexual Perspective: Homosexuality and art in the last 100 years in the west. Emmanuel Cooper, London; New York: Routledge, 1994
Mythology and Misogyny, by Joseph A Kestner, University of Wisconsin Press, 1989
Alfred Gilbert's aestheticism, by Jason Edwards, Ashgate, 2006

Henry Greville's letters to Leighton are quoted in Barrington, op cit
'I am *very* glad you are trying to help yourself': Ann Blainey, *Fanny and Adelaide: the lives of the remarkable Kemble sisters*, I.R. Dee, Chicago, 2001
'resistance to or escape from homoerotic desire': Christopher Reed, *Art and homosexuality: a history of ideas*, Oxford University Press, 2011
'How is it that my pleasure is not unalloyed?': Barrington, Leighton op cit
'I cannot help thinking that an imaginative': Barrington, Leighton op cit
Caroline Dakers has discovered: 'Leighton, the Truth? Frederick, Lord Leighton and his Relationship with Lily and Fred Mason', *Apollo* CXLIV. 418, December 1996

Chapter Fifteen: His wife

'The feminine part of the male artist': 'The role of the artist's muse' by Germaine Greer, the *Guardian*, 2 June 2008
A notable Hetaira: Alison Smith, *The Victorian Nude* op cit
'She brought a new degree of warmth': Christopher Wood, *Olympian Dreamers*, Constable, London, 1983
'and they will propose right and left': *Weekly Irish Times*, 6 January 1900
'I don't know whether you would like him': *The Young George du Maurier, A selection of his letters*, Edited by Daphne du Maurier, Peter Davies, London, 1951
'Dorothy Dene is a type of the wild flower': *Cosmopolitan*, January, 1890
In the circles that Leighton moved in: interview with Philippa Martin, 2012
'For an artist to marry his model'; Oscar Wilde, 'on London Models', in *Essays and Lectures*, Putnam's, New York, 1894
'I think I should play Juliet better': Archer, *Masks or Faces* op cit – and Dorothy Dene's questionnaire
'broken off by his parents': Ormond, Leighton and an interview with Professor Leonée Ormond, London, 2012
Recently discovered correspondence: Philippa Martin, 'The tragic muse', Apollo, Nov. 2014; On the Trail of Dorothy Dene: talk by Philippa Martin, Leighton House, September 2012
the mysterious "wife": interviews of Philippa Martin with the authors, London 2012-13
'In the morning, lunch with the Dorotheas': Agresti, Giovanni Costa
'and you will have your usual one upstairs': Ibid.
'in a paternal and a proprietary manner': *Lancashire Evening Post*, 9 June 1888
'With all her beauty, she had none of the charm': Mainly about people, January 1900
'Although Sir Frederic is over 60 years old': *Madison County Times*, February 7 1896
Lena's Picture, a story of love: By Emilie Isabel Barrington, D. Douglas, London, 1892

Chapter Sixteen: Faithful unto Death

'pleasant and effective speaking voice': *The Era*, 30 March 1889
'sadly-serious, though not unlovable girl': *The Stage*, 13 April 1888
twenty-five years' thought: *Dundee Evening Telegraph*, 15 December 1888; *Liverpool Mercury*, 19 December 1888The embarrassing details of the price-haggling: *Daily News*, 14 December 1888; *Liverpool Mercury*, 19 December 1888.
'As a Christian': *Art Journal*, March 1893
'which includes a similar scene': Alison Smith, *Exposed – the Victorian Nude* op cit

Chapter Seventeen: Nocturnal Visits

'with a far-away look': *Northampton Mercury*, 4 May 1889
'If he lived with Phidias and Praxiteles': E.E. Minton in *Manchester Quarterly*, A Journal of literature and art, VOL. XXX, 1911
'idealized and magnified edition': *The Advertiser* (Adelaide, Australia), 17 July 1889
'ruddily handsome face and grizzling beard': Katharine Tynan, *Twenty-Five years: reminiscences*, Smith, Elder & Co, London, 1913
'not complimentary to his bride': the *Illustrated London News*, 18 May 1889
'somewhat the effect of a cameo': *Mansfield Reporter*, 17 April 1891
The celebrity interviewer Helen C. Black: *Lloyds Weekly Newspaper*, 4 August 1895
'too frequent habit of turning': *London Daily News*, 15 October 1888
Leighton commissioned a young sculptor: *Pall Mall Gazette*, 29 March 1889
'twenty-five years' thought and of two years hard work': *London Evening Standard*, 14 December 1888
When Mary Watts: Watts Papers, at the Watts Gallery, Compton

Chapter Eighteen: "Not fit for public inspection"

On scandals of nudity – 'Prudery, Pornography and the Victorian nude', by Martin Myrone, in *Exposed: the Victorian Nude*, ed
Alison Smith, Tate Publishing, 2001
'what sort of subject do you expect me to paint on this?' *Strand Magazine*, December 1902
'No man could have filled the panel better': Staley, Leighton op cit
'the great test in looking at nude': 'Artists at Home', *Pall Mall Gazette*, 2 July 1890
'even Mr Horsley and the British Matron': *Nottingham Evening Post*, 3 May 1890
'what would be thought of those ladies': *Liverpool Mercury*, 25 September 1890
'would any of the ardent supporters': *Liverpool Mercury*, 26 September 1890
'the flesh is frail': *Liverpool Mercury*, 24 September 1890
Watts asked for a copy: Leighton's letter to Mary Watts, Leighton House archive, LH/1/6/092

'Is Sir Frederick Leighton to be prosecuted': *Bradford Daily Telegraph*, 5 December 1891
'not fit for public inspection': *St James's Gazette*, 17 April 1894
'Time alone, and the increasing influence': Leighton's letter, published in the *Lancashire Evening Post*, 23 April 1894
the police raided a Dublin gallery: *Freemen's Journal*, 17 May 1899
In Richmond, Virginia: *The Washington Post*, 5 March 1905.
'displays her charms for the admiration of mankind': James Harlaw, *The Charm of Leighton*, E.C. Jack, London 1913
'seen to be a little faded': *The Newcastle Weekly Courant*, 17 May 1890
'her place was admirably filled': *The Era*, 2 November 1889
'had to struggle against obvious hoarseness': *The Era*, 30 November 1889
'young as she is she is not a novice': letter from Leighton to Pooley, Ryland Library, University of Manchester, Eng.ms 1226,22

Chapter Nineteen: "To fit or not to fit"

'the awful event': 'A Painter's Pilgrimage', by Herbert Schmalz, Art Journal 1893
Leighton strongly recommended a trip: *The art of Herbert Schmalz*, by Trevor Blakemore, G. Allen, London 1911. Also 'The Art of Mr. Herbert Schmalz', by Austin Chester, in *Windsor Magazine*, 1906
'as fascinating a lady as ever lived out of Fairyland': Estelle Blyth, *When we lived in Jerusalem,* Murray, London, 1927
Magdalene with 'luxuriant golden hair': the *Graphic*, 21 November 1891
'the picture being apparently all they needed': *Eastern Daily Press*, 4 November 1896
'faithfulness with which the features': *Belfast News*, 10 November 1891
'Although of the requisite type': *Western Daily Press*, 31 March 1892
'in the very shadow of death': *Pall Mall Gazette*, 19 March 1891
'lovely, and fresh as a blush-rose': *Birmingham Daily Post*, 1 May 1891
'Why are you always so Greek': *Pall Mall Gazette*, 2 July 1890
'of beauty rescued from the ugliness': Malcolm Warner, *The Victorians: British painting 1837-1901,* National Gallery of Art, Washington, 1996
'pale and grave and wistful in the unfamiliar': John Bull, 7 March 1891
'Every effort had been made to suit them': *St James's Gazette*, 10 April 1891
'utterly spoiled them': *London Evening Standard*, 24 April 1891
'women did not wear such great flowers': *Sheffield Evening Telegraph*, 16 July 1908
'I am standing as I always do': *Globe*, 23 April 1891
'could not understand that it was impossible to wear': *Mansfield Reporter*, 17 April 1891
'were viewed with a double interest by many': *Dundee Evening Telegraph*, 2 May 1891
'past gastronomic delights': *Newcastle Courant*, 14 May 1892

Chapter Twenty: The Misses Dene

'the handsomest host in London': *Pall Mall Gazette*, 27 June 1889
'profoundly pompous': *Dundee Evening Telegraph*, 25 November 1892
'how many of those who appeared': *The Theatre*: A Monthly Review and Magazine, Volume 27 1891
'so strong feeling for character': *The Theatre*, vol 21-22, 1893
'The tendency seems to be to keep the actor': *NY Dramatic Mirror*, 12 November 1892
'I read your little play': Dorothy Dene's letter 12 January 1891, in the Harry Ransom Center, the University of Texas at Austin
'at a respectful distance in point of beauty': *New York Times*, 21 February 1892
'surprised even her previous admirers': *Birmingham Daily Post*, 26 February 1892
'considerable tragic power': *Sheffield Daily Telegraph*, 27 February 1892
'If I were you': Jacob Thomas Grein, *Dramatic Criticism*, J. Long, 1899
She still hoped to play Juliet: *New York Tribune*, 20 October 1892

Chapter Twenty-One: America

'looking unusually handsome in a long cloak': *Hearth and Home*, 7 April 1892
'I have myself a weakness for this picture': Leighton letter to Pooley, in the Fitzwilliam Paintings catalogue, 1977
'Sunlight can never be accessory': Leighton's notebook XV, Royal Academy archives, quoted in Ormond, Leighton
Theatres were going bankrupt: *Glasgow Herald*, 17 June 1892; *Yorkshire Evening Post*, 18 June 1892
'some misunderstanding': *New York Tribune*, 20 October 1892
'Why! The actresses that are ladies': *The Press*, 27 November 1892
'to take a look around at American life and manners': *New York Times*, 18 October 1892
'Her Face is Her Fortune': *Pittsburgh Dispatch*, 6 November 1892
'sat up till two the last night in Dorothy Dene's apartments': Frederic Jessup Stimson, *My United States*. Scribner's Sons, New York, London, 1931.

Chapter Twenty-Two: The queen was not dethroned

'a tall, graceful girl of the well-known Leightonian': *Evening Herald*, 29 March 1893
'permits her fair form to be traced': *Graphic*, 13 May 1893
On Mary Lloyd: Leighton's Lost Model, by Martin Postle, *Apollo Magazine*, February 1996
She told the *Sunday Express*: 22 October 1933
'not so much on account of the excellence of her verse': *Pall Mall Gazette*, 14 March 1893

Hetty, Lily and Rosie Pettigrew: 'The Beautiful Miss Pettigrew', by Neil Pettigrew, *The British Art Journal*, vol XV, number 1, 2014
'It is a gruesome scene': *Aberdeen Press and Journal*, 29 April 1893
'her head thrown back': *Birmingham Daily Post* – 5 May 1894
'The Spirit of my Painting', Robert de La Sizeranne, *English Contemporary Art*, A. Constable, 1898
'not one in a hundred English painters': *Dover Express*, 18 May 1894
'conscious of his inability': *St Louise Republic*, 18 February 1900
Leighton amused the seven-year-old Estella: Estella Canziani, *Round About Three Palace Green* op cit
'the girl's light draperies veil': *Glasgow Herald*, 20 March 1894
George Moore's poem: George Moore, *Confessions of a young man*, Heinemann, London, 1928
'resemblance to the originals being noted': *The Era*, 30 June 1894

Chapter Twenty-Three: "The art of pushing"

'greatly pleased the audience': *Globe*, 6 October 1894
'played with care and finish': *The Era*, 1 December 1894
'even the pleasure of seeing Miss Hetty Dene': *The Theatrical World of 1894*
Edith 'exceedingly intense and cultured': *Evening Post*, New Zealand, 4 April 1896
Beethoven's prayer: O God, give me strength to be victorious over myself, for nothing may chain me to this life. O guide my spirit. O raise me from these dark depths, that my soul, transported through Your wisdom, may fearlessly struggle upward in fiery flight. For You alone understand and can inspire me. Amen. Translation The Westminster Collection of Christian Prayers, edited by Dorothy M. Stewart:
'talking, but they did not seem to be on particularly good terms': *Morning Post*, 11 December 1894
where he died fifty years later: Kate Summerscale, *The Wicked Boy*, Bloomsbury, London, 2016
'so that it might not be a harbour': *The Times*, 11 December 1894
She told the *Sporting Times*: 25 May 1895
'I hardly give anybody a letter of introduction': Letter to George Du Maurier, 27 July 1895, quoted in *The Tragic Muse*, by Philippa Martin.
'She had not the robustness nor the push': Mainly About People, January 6, 1900
'Her speech showed unusual signs of artistic cultivation': George Bernard Shaw, *Our theatres in the nineties*, Constable, London, 1934
Annie Oppenheim – Dorothy Dene's character analysis: *Le Follet*, March 1, 1895
The man on his flying machine: *Sheffield Weekly Telegraph*, 12 January 1895
The song was debated in a Sheffield court: *Sheffield Evening Telegraph*, 20 September 1895
The lovely lady Dolly: *Hearth and Home*, 14 November 1895

'Dorothy Dene is tall and slender': A Decided Contrast, by Mabel A. Clinton, in *Exchange*, Saskaton Phoenix, 27 February 1903
Hetty got her own courtship ditty: Judy, 10 October 1894

Chapter Twenty-Four: "Everything I owe to you"

Rosie wrote in her memoirs: Rosie Pettigrew's memoirs, held at the department of Art History, Glasgow University, MS MacColl P64
'And at dawn, behold': John Guille Millais, *The Life and Letters of Sir John Everett Millais*, Methuen & Co, London, 1899
On Flaming June:
Athenaeum, 2 March 1895; *Athenaeum*, 4 May 1895;
The Art Journal, 1895; *The Magazine of Art*, 1895; *The Graphic*, 29 June 1895;
A Victorian Master: Drawings by Frederic, Lord Leighton. Leighton House Museum 2006
An Introduction to Victorian Painting, by Kenneth Bendiner, Yale University Press, New Haven, Conn. 1985
Flaming June – impossible position: *The British Medical Journal*, 4 May 1895
'his reminiscence of all his experiences': Alfred Weidinger, 'Magnificent Extravagance', in *Sleeping Beauty, Masterpieces of Victorian Painting*
On Leighton's illness:
A Doctor Remembers by Edwin Alfred Barton, London, Seeley, Service & Co, 1941.
Royal Academy, Documents describing Lord Leighton's death and funeral, LEI/48
Leighton looked depressed and fatigued: *Hearth and Home*, 12 July 1894
'many of us have remarked': Barrington, op cit
'as fit as a fiddle': Barrington, op cit
'to get as close to death as he could without dying': 'The Deathly Sleep of Frederic Leighton's Painted Women', by Keren Hammerschlag, in Women: a cultural review. Vol 23, issue 2, 2012
'the spectacle of his handsome form alone': *St James's Gazette*, 27 January 1896
'Sir Frederick is not yet sixty-five': *Leicester Chronicle*, 4 May 1895
His position as President: *Hull Daily Mail*, 2 May 1895
On the condition of his heart: *British Medical Journal*, 11 May 1895
'I have stood here three hours': Barrington, op cit
she published it only after his death: Mary H. Krout, *A Looker-on in London,* B.F. Stevens, London, 1899
In August, Mrs Rylands: Leighton's letters to Mrs Rylands, in the John Rylands University Library, En Ms 380/1235
'keenly alive to artistic enjoyments': Agresti, Giovanni Costa
'I'm an ailing creature': St James's Budget, 31 January 1896
Edward Burne-Jones wrote: Burne-Jones talking, ed. Mary Lago, John Murray, London, 1982

'If I have, or ever will, do something worth doing': Barrington, op cit
'I have shown the goddess in adoration': Rhys, Leighton
'more powerful than anything': Letter from Anne Dundas to Harriet Hosmer, February 1896, in *Harriet Hosmer, letters and memories*, edited by Cornelia Carr, John Lane, London 1913

Chapter Twenty-Five: A sudden death

'rumour has woven a romance in his life': The Independent from Hutchinson, Kansas, 25 March 1896
'with the greatest secrecy': Leonee and Richard Ormond, Lord Leighton
hopes someday to make a name': *Boston Daily Advertiser*, 7 February 1896
'perhaps it is as well that I did not see': George Bernard Shaw, *Saturday Review*, 2 May 1896, also in *Dramatic opinions and essays*, Brentano's, New York, 1928
'was intensely jealous': *Weekly Irish Times*, 31 March 1900
'my interest in her has been turned to her disadvantage': Mary Watts' catalogue, Watts' Gallery, Compton
Dr. Daniel Robbins, Senior Curator of the Royal Borough of Kensington and Chelsea: 'Between life and death – Leighton and Clytie'. Talk given at Leighton House in October 2012. On Leighton House Museum website.
'the best type of an innocent English girl': Euston Leigh and Cyril Clare, *The Duchess of Coolgardie*, Henry Drane, London, 1896
'charming personality and bright': *The Era*, 13 March 1897
'the most valuable of his 'properties': *The St. Louis Republic*, 18 February 1900
"her face typified purity": Mary Lloyd to the *Sunday Express*, 22 October 1933
'If you start painting sacred subjects': Trevor Blakemore, *The Art of Herbert Schmalz*, G. Allen, London, 1911
'I see you have gone in for the conventional Christ!': 'The Apostle of the Brush', a chat with Mr. Herbert Schmalz, in *Good Words 46*, December 1905
victim of her profession: *The St. Paul's Globe*, 28 January 1900
The Martyrs of the Stage, by Ada Patterson, in *The Theatre Magazine*, vol 10, 1909

Epilogue

Dorothy's obituaries:
The Era, 30 December 1899
T.P. O'Connor: *Mainly About People*, January 6, 1900
The Dramatic News of 1900
The Saint Paul Globe, Minnesota, January 28, 1900
The *Seattle Post-Intelligencer*, February 18, 1900
The *St. Louis Republic*, February 18, 1900
The San Juan County index, May 04, 1900
The poet laureate wrote a lament: *Seattle Daily Times*, 5 May 1900

Three days after Dorothy's death: 'My Rival of the Pavement', by Halliwell Sutcliffe, in the *Newcastle Courant*, 30 December 1899
Kathleen's trial:
Daily Mail, 3 December 1904; *London Daily News*, 3 December 1904;
Daily Mirror, 16 December 1904; *Daily Telegraph*, 16 December 1904
On habitual drunkenness:
'Alleged Inhuman Treatment': *Yorkshire Evening Post*, 25 February 1903;
'The Detention of Inebriates': 28 November 1904, *Yorkshire Post*
Oppenheimer Treatment:
'if you must have a drink': ad in *London Daily News*, 6 December 1904;
'Personal statements of drunkards cured': ad in *London Daily News*, 2 January 1905;
Can drunkenness be cured? *The Review of Reviews*, February 1904